Politics in Hunger-Regime:
Essays on the Right to Food in West Bengal

Edited by

Sibaji Pratim Basu and Geetisha Dasgupta

frontpage

frontpage
www.frontpagepublications.com

First published 2011

Frontpage Publications Limited
5 Percy Street, London W1T 1DG, United Kingdom

Frontpage
Level 6, Constantia, 11 Dr U N Brahmachari Sarani, Kolkata 700017, India

ISBN 978 93 810430 1 1

Printed in India
By Sadhana Press Private Limited
76 B B Ganguly Street, Kolkata 700012, India

Typeset by Compuset International
85 Park Street, Kolkata 700016, India

Politics in Hunger-Regime:

Essays on the Right to Food in West Bengal

Contents

Bio-sketch

GEETISHA DASGUPTA is a Research Associate at Calcutta Research Group, Kolkata.

KUMAR RANA is a Senior Research Associate with the Pratichi Trust, Kolkata and Santiniketan, India.

MANISHA BANERJEE, a social activist, is involved in the ongoing struggles for rights of the minorities and the other oppressed castes in the state of West Bengal.

PRADEEP BHARGAVA is Professor and Director, Govind Ballabh Pant Social Science Institute, Allahabad, India. Engaged in policy dialogue with the governments, Bhargava also interacts with the civil society. He is presently Advisor to the Commissioners of the Supreme Court of India in the PUCL Case on Right to Food.

RUCHIRA GOSWAMI, an MA in Human Rights, is a Lecturer, Department of Sociology, West Bengal National University of Juridical Sciences, Kolkata, India.

SIBAJI PRATIM BASU is Associate Professor of Political Science at Sree Chaitanya College, West Bengal, India. A regular contributor to academic journals and popular dailies, periodicals and news channels, he specialises in modern Indian political thought and politics and socialist thought having interest in forced migration in contemporary South Asia and people's "sustainable rights" in India.

Acronyms

AAY	Antyodaya Anna Yojana
APL	Above Poverty Line
BPL	Below Poverty Line
BLF	Bought Leaf Factories
CEDAW	Convention on the Elimination of All Forms of Discrimination against Women
CPI(M)	Communist Party of India (Marxist)
CRC	Convention on the Rights of the Child
FAO	Food and Agricultural Organisation
FCI	Food Corporation of India
FPS	Fair Price Shops
GP	Gram Panchayat
ICDS	Integrated Child Development Scheme
ICESCR	International Covenant on Economic, Social and Cultural Rights
JSY	Janani Suraksha Yojana
MASUM	Manabadhikar Suraksha Mancha
MDMS	Mid-Day Meal Scheme
MRP	Mixed Reference Period
NAC	National Advisory Council
NFBS	National Family Benefit Scheme
NFFWP	National Food for Work Programme
NFHS	National Family Health Survey
NGOs	Non-Governmental Organisations
NHRC	National Human Rights Commission
NMBS	National Maternity Benefit Scheme

NREGA	National Rural Employment Guarantee Act
NSSO	National Sample Survey Organisation
PDS	Public Distribution System
PHE	Public Health Engineering
PIL	Public Interest Litigation
PLB	Poverty Line Basket
PUCL	People's Union for Civil Liberties
RTI	Right to Information Act
SC	Scheduled Caste
SHG	Self-help group
SGRY	Sampoorna Gramin Rozgar Yojana
ST	Scheduled Tribes
TPDS	Targeted Public Distribution System
UIDAI	Unique Identification Authority of India
UPA	United Progressive Alliance

Foreword

Hunger and Politics of Life

RANABIR SAMADDAR

I should begin with a caution to the readers. Even though the essays in this volume deal with a particularly damning aspect of our political life today, they are not covered in the standard accounts of political science that one learns in colleges and universities in West Bengal or for that matter India. They are also not the standard lessons in rural sociology dealing with villages. Nobody speaks of hunger and makes it the subject matter of educational instruction. We discuss and learn elections, democracy, party system, local self-government, planning, theories of development, history of nationalism, kinship, marriage systems, caste and politics, and other respectable themes. The underlying consensus is that, and this may be true for quite some number of individuals and groups, that hunger is over, life is assured, and now we must get on with big themes of life. This book, on the contrary, takes us back to the basic question of life, and asks what hunger is, how large parts of West Bengal remain hungry year after year, and what it means for politics when it concerns the basic issue of living, that is food. Even though we are living under a democracy, which concerns freedom and promises us improved life conditions, this book nonetheless asks: does democracy do away with basic challenges of living? Is the savage condition of biological existence met satisfactorily so that political life can now engage with higher requirements of civic life and participation? At least one answer clearly comes out of the book – the answer is in form of the fact that in a democracy, under conditions of political equality, there is durable inequality, differential access of groups to food and food market.

It was in the late 18th and 19th centuries when the idea of democracy was overwhelming the European continent that reports of famines started rocking the political establishments across the continent – famines in the colonies and reports of hunger in the metropolitan countries themselves. The reports on Irish Famine (1845-1852) tell us of deaths of approximately one million people and emigration of another million. Ireland's population in that time fell between 20% and 25%. The Famine was a watershed in the history of Ireland, so much so that modern historians regard it as a dividing line in the Irish historical narrative. Considering the food riots and near famine conditions in colonies and several European countries in the 19th century, we should not be surprised that in that period democracy was not the only idea available to people; socialism emerged as a competing idea, and today's belief in an all-curing capacity of democracy was not so overwhelming then. People, it seems, were wiser and more literate then. Soon breadlines appeared in the United States – the new *el dorado* of prosperity. Those breadlines continue till date. They are as one journalist Sasha Abramsky puts the "hidden scandal of American hunger" (*Breadline USA*, 2009). Charles Tilly's accounts of collective actions in seventeenth and eighteenth century Britain and France show how food riots were occasions for the development of various tools of collective protest – night vigil, torchlight processions, burning, looting grain stores, sit-ins, slogan-shouting, barricading, formation of committees and vigilante groups, drawing up and submissions of memoranda, charters, and manifestos, setting up popular councils, etc. In short, democracy never did away with differential access to resources. Inequality proved durable. Hunger accompanied the onward march of democracy. Hunger provoked collective protests and violence.

Interesting to note is the role of the fledgling public media at that time. Before the social anthropologists, reporters and correspondents started covering incidents of famine and chronic hunger conditions. Reporters were sent from metropolitan countries to cover such incidents in India, China, Egypt and other colonies and semi-colonies, and the resultant published reports made the audience at "home" aware of the phenomenon of hunger at home itself. Initially, the political class attempted to dismiss the reports from colonies on famines as evidence of the idle nature of the "natives"; hence hunger was treated as their fate. But soon these reports impacted on unemployed workers in the "home" countries, their family members, particularly housewives, some sections of church, and the new trade unions in the metropolitan countries. Hunger appeared as a question mark for democracy. In this respect, our own history in Bengal and India seems to be following the social history of Britain in late 19th and most of the 20th centuries – certainly up to 1950, when we are told breadlines disappeared in Britain.

Exactly as then, we can now find in our own country different categories of hungry people – categories created by government policies, such as BPL and APL. Thus with the governing principle of creating a hierarchy of eligibility for food provision and assistance, the situation is like what it was after the New Poor Law of 1834, enacted in Great Britain. Exactly as then, journalists now have brought to attention here news of hunger and hunger deaths. Exactly as then, new social policies are now being discussed and implemented in order to tackle hunger in the wake of the humanitarian discovery of hunger. The discovery of hunger, as these essays testify, has led to a discovery of the "social", on the basis of which new social legislations such as the NREGA have been founded. The government can now address the social only by addressing hunger. The social discovery of hunger possible due to investigative journalism led also to the use of hunger in order to oppose government policies. Thus began the tradition of hunger strike (in India and Ireland for instance), the message being, *it is better to die in starvation than to accept a wrong government.* And as in Britain, in India too, in the wake of protests over scarcity of food, a new form of social government emerged with the welfare of the hungry as its aim.

This has required expertise in form of science and calculation of hunger so that government can devise policies and measures to assuage hunger. James Vernon tells us in his *Hunger: A Modern History* (2007) how nutritionists became important in this form of social governance. In India in the 1980s and 1990s of the last century, nutritionists debated the quantum of calories required to assuage hunger, and specialists argued as to who could be called full hungry and who partially. On this depended quantum of assistance, the kind and form of assistance, the mode of supply, the budgetary requirements, and identification of most needy areas, and along with all these emerged entire panoply of graded vulnerabilities. Science facilitated administration of food provisions. The discovery of vitamins and a bio-chemical explanation of nutrition meant that social governance of hunger has become possible and a reality. Yet precisely because of this social governance, a picture of which the readers will find in these pages, hunger has become politically relevant, forcing all sections of the political class in the country to join the "hungry India" debate. Exactly the same thing has happened in West Bengal. The public interest litigation on universal access to food, the debate on the role of panchayats in mitigating hunger, legislation of NREGA and its efficacy, administrative inefficiency in the state, judicial activism on this, quarrel over the exact cause of a hunger-death – starvation, or illness, or suicide – all these are dimensions of this social governance. This is what Vernon calls "the government of hunger". Readers will remember, soon after Patu Mura, an old hungry woman died in Purulia. Debate arose: did she die of hunger, or of physical weakness, of unavailability of food, or availability of food but absence of access to food, or of disease? If some said that her death signified lack of development in the district, the secretary of the ruling party in the state famously said that this death was not an indication of lack of development. Patu Mura had died, but Purulia was developing. When farmers or tea garden workers or members of urban poor have died, the government has to decide the exact cause of death, because policies have been prepared to quell hunger. Science must tell us precisely, what is hunger and what is hungre death? Studies of famines are like nutrition studies. They form the scientific background in which we can locate the government of hunger.

These essays on hunger and the state of the Right to Food teach us a number of other lessons as well. They tell us that even though we can at will speak of the *Right to Food*, social governance of food access cannot but be disciplinarian, and be at best welfarist, and therefore cannot accept access to food as *right*. Moreover, market mechanisms dictate the nature of institutional efficacy in this matter, and welfare will be dictated by market considerations. The rights bearing institutions, such as judiciary, trade unions, farmers' organisations, civil rights groups, state bodies such as the National Human Rights Commission or the State Commissions, meant to guarantee the Right to Food, become adjuncts of this disciplinarian welfare regime, which cannot allow any illegal claim making process.

What these essays tell us if not always loudly is the fact of durable inequality and continuance of the colonial pattern in making inequality durable. There is one essay in this volume, written by Kumar Rana, which shows how all through the Left Front regime, while hunger disappeared as a public theme of politics after the declared success of land reforms, rural employment generation schemes, rural decentralisation and growth of public distribution system, differential access remained. The middle classes gained food security, while dalits and indigenous population groups had less access to the so-called food security West Bengal had supposedly achieved. The early signs in stagnation in agricultural productivity were ignored. Droughts were thought of as not important. Stagnation in acreage under small irrigation was again ignored. Middlemen prospered. Industrial closures resulting in thousands of workers being retrenched with nowhere to go were again put under the carpet. The bureaucracy as a whole became complicit in the elite propaganda game of "prosperous West Bengal", so much so that common sense deserted, governmental attempts commenced to take away agricultural land for dubious programmes of industrialisation. We have scores of eulogising articles and scientific essays on the success of rural Bengal, but very few on the impending disaster. Hence when food crisis started soon to be followed by deaths of labourers in tea gardens, ration revolt in the countryside, violent protests in the dry areas of South West Bengal, the political class was taken aback. Continuing price rise, shrinking plate, endemic poverty, chronic hunger, successive disasters like long spells of dry weather, droughts, suicides in the countryside and in urban slums, drop out of several segments of population from the food market in large swathes of West Bengal, and the mutiny in the countryside – all these should remind us of what had happened in our land in the colonial era in 1860-1885.

Then too dry weather had continued. There was, of course, no public food distribution system then; the government ignored the early signs of stagnation in agriculture, neglected the condition of the dalits and indigenous population groups, and thought that with some welfare schemes and opening of relief camps and gruel kitchens in areas where people would be interned and restricted in their movement so that they could be fed easily, the disaster could be tackled. The marginal small holders and the bulk of the rural poor consisting of landless labour too were then neglected. Then farmers' suicides became too many in number to be ignored. Mike Davis has termed that era of hunger and famine as one of "Late Victorian Holocausts" (*Late Victorian Holocausts: El Nino Famines and the Making of the Third World*, 2001).

I shall request the readers to keep this background in mind when they read this book. What is particular in this volume is the focus on the state of the right to food in India, and the condition of the rights bearing institutions, their relative inefficacy in preventing hunger or enabling the disadvantaged in accessing food right. It may, of course, be argued that after all this is not late 19th century, that there is an awareness of rights, and that there is awareness of something called food security. Hence, many do not die; otherwise they would have died. But this is small mercy. In fact, the essays of this book tell us that unless there is collective action, direct distribution of foodgrains, involvement of peasants and the landless in accessing food, we do not have escape from the evil consequences of the governmentalisation of the right to food. Is it possible to take out foodgrains from the market dynamics? This is a challenge to any governance of our time claiming to have public purpose. As David Arnold showed 22 years ago in *Famine: Social Crisis and Historical Change* (1988), calamities like famines appear as engines of historical transformation. We are again witnessing in India a renewed phase of primitive accumulation, in which another round of destruction of peasantry and small holders seems imminent. In this there will be another round of forcible destruction of the means of livelihood. The watchword has become *survival* as the other of *development*.

Politics in such time becomes irrevocably biological – exactly the opposite of civil politics. How to survive, how to get food, how to distribute food, how to demand food, how to tackle hunger protests, how to die, and how to explain away deaths – all these suddenly take the centre stage of politics. This is what I have termed as "hunger and the politics of life". It speaks of politics in such biological condition when inequalities increase, the old liberal framework of rights fail, justice becomes the cry of survival, but more importantly bio-crisis appears as the core of social crisis. This book is a minimal reflection of that crisis.

Lastly, the book can be approached from another angle. It can be asked: Why when farmers have still worked, peasants have toiled, workers have run the mills, the government has supposedly done its work, civil rights groups have performed tasks in their agenda, and the social conscience of the collective is on guard, the hunger regime persists? We must think on the immanent singularity of hunger, on the closed nature of this world where labour in the form of wage labour becomes unfruitful in bringing to us food. Labour process is said to have freed us from the biological process of sheer survival. Nothing is more distant from this fabricated story. Marx had told us long back, at one level, labour process is the process of biological survival. Our social sense has to be woven around the politics of biological survival, *the politics of life itself.*

Acknowledgments

This book is a result of collective labour. We are indebted to a number of persons, besides contributors, especially those, who participated in various seminars and workshops on Right to Food, organised by the Calcutta Research Group for the past two years, and influenced directly or indirectly the present endeavour with their comments and suggestions. Our thanks are of course to the contributors who were the mainstay in this research endeavour. Special thanks are to the colleagues of G B Pant Institute of Social Sciences, Allahabad, who extended graciously their help by offering us suggestions towards improvement and revision of these chapters.

Professor Pradeep Bhargava, Director of the Pant Institute, allowed us to include one of his essays in this volume as its epilogue.

The reports which form the basis of these essays were sent to the National Human Rights Commission (NHRC) for their attention, given the fact that the NHRC attaches great importance to the notion of Right to Food in its rights ensuring agenda. Though we did not receive any acknowledgement from the NHRC, we hope that the NHRC will take the reports in consideration when framing its policies and responses. We similarly hope that this book will be of some value to human rights organisations and colleagues working on the Right to Food and attracting judicial attention towards guaranteeing this right.

The small amount of resources needed to carry this research came partly from a small grant from the Asia Pacific Forum of National Human Rights Institutions and partly from the Ford Foundation programme on governance. We acknowledge our indebtedness to them. We are also happy that Abhijit Mazumder of Frontpage supported the idea of publishing these essays in the form of a volume.

Finally, big thanks are due to all our colleagues in CRG.

Sibaji Pratim Basu
Geetisha Dasgupta

November 2010

Introduction

Hunger rules. Even after six decades of independence and planned economy, even after initiating so many "pro-poor" assistance programmes by the Centre and the states, the hunger regime has consolidated its empire in many parts of India. Parts of West Bengal also belong to it. This book is about the population living under the shadow of hunger, especially in West Bengal. In the following pages, the reader will find the true narratives of sufferings and struggle of these people, and also sincere attempts as in-depth analyses of the problem. The Right to Food – as a constitutional/legal and also as a social/human right – becomes meaningful only in the context of history, geography, economics and politics of the prevalent hunger regime in this part of the globe. And, since this volume mainly focuses on the situation in West Bengal, let us begin with this state.

West Bengal: The Story of Hunger and Struggle

For the last 33 years, West Bengal is being governed by a left alliance, called Left Front – a conglomeration of many left/democratic parties with predominance of the Communist Party of India (Marxist) (hereafter the "CPI(M)"), which came into being in 1964 after a faction split from the Communist Party of India (hereafter the "CPI"). Since late 1940s, just before the Independence and Partition of India, the CPI had launched a serious land reform movement – *Tebhaga* (giving two-thirds of the share to tillers) – in many districts of Bengal Province. The movement affected both sides of the border even after the Partition. The main aim of the movement was to give the landless peasantry and the rural poor a minimum food security above everything, and to ensure freedom from the yoke of exploitation under the *zamindars/jotedars* (landlords/big landowners) and *mahajans* (moneylenders). The *Tebhaga* movement assumes a greater significance if we remember that it was launched just three years after the Bengal Famine of 1943, which claimed the lives of around 3 million people who died of starvation and malnutrition.

This apocalyptic disaster has been immortalised by Chittaprosad Bhattarcharya (1915-78), an artist and communist activist who would always be remembered for his visual documentation of the Bengal Famine of 1943.[1] The mood of this hungry time found its most popular expression in the lines of a prodigy poet, Sukanta Bhattcharya (1926-47): '*. . . Kobita tomay dilam ajke chhuti/Khudar rajye prithibi godyomoy/Purnima-chand jeno jhalsano ruti!*'[2] [Poetry, I give you a break today/In the regime of hunger, the earth belongs to prose/The full moon now reminds us of toasted bread.][3]

After Independence, the left incessantly launched movements for food justice to the poor in West Bengal. Among other things, the demand for the proper functioning of the Public Distribution System (hereafter the "PDS") – especially the availability of sufficient quantity of foodgrains through ration shops at a subsidised price for the poor – ranked the highest. This was coupled with another long-standing demand for radical pro-tiller land reforms. The food crisis in the state became more pronounced owing to tremendous population pressure (of "refugees" – most of whom were unemployed) after the Partition, the virtual continuation of the *zamindari* system through *benami* (keeping property under anonymous/non-existing persons) landholdings under the old system of sharing (one-half to the landlord and the other half to the tiller), whimsical/calculative non-cultivation in a large part of the land by the landlords to put their *bargadars* (share-croppers) under continuous pressure and making them ever dependent on landlords, hording of foodgrains by *mahajans* and food merchants along with a corrupt, and an inefficient PDS. All these thrived under the ruling Congress government.

The situation worsened further in the late 1950s. As hunger assumed famine-like proportions, the people organised themselves into a Committee to Combat Famine under the leadership of the CPI and other left parties. From the second half of the 1950s, between 1956 and 1958, food movements became an annual occurrence. But the Food Movement of

1959 was a turning point in the history of West Bengal. Food insecurity, by this time, had reached frightening proportions in the rural and urban areas and the marginal and landless peasantry, the workers and lower middle classes were in a state of acute distress. On 31 August, a huge mass demonstration was organised in Kolkata where thousands of them arrived from villages, under the leadership of the Kisan Sabha, a CPI-led peasants' organisation. Primarily a mass protest by peasants, rural women with babies walked alongside high school students, and office workers merged with the columns of manual workers. The entire central Kolkata (then Calcutta) turned into a sea of 300,000 people demanding an end to destitution and hunger.[4]

At the end of the meeting, a procession began and started making its way towards Writers' Building. By then, evening had descended. First, the demonstrators were cordoned off by the police. Then, unexpectedly, without any warning, violent "action" began. Contemporary observers have noted the way the police attacked directionless, panic-stricken people blinded by teargas. Eighty people died in the carnage that day. Most of them were starving peasants who had survived the devastating man-made Bengal Famine of 1943. Not a single bullet was fired. The police used sticks to beat people to death. 1,000 people went missing and 3,000 were injured.

The Food Movement continued through the first half of 1960s. In February 1966, a student agitation was launched by the left demanding food, kerosene oil and exercise books. But the police opened fire on the students. A school student, Nurul Islam, was killed. A huge students' movement now roared across West Bengal, followed by a still larger mass movement. Several districts such as Nadia, Hooghly, Bardhaman, and 24 Parganas including Kolkata became the volcanoes of protests. In March, a one-day strike against police oppression in Bengal evoked two-day or even three-day strikes in some of these districts.

THE LEFT RULE

The effect of the Food Movement in West Bengal was so intense that it changed the political complexion of the state. The massive discontent among the common people created a negative atmosphere for the ruling Congress party which split into two. Ajoy Mukherjee and a number of other leaders left the Congress to form the Bangla Congress. And after the State Legislative Assembly elections in 1967, a United Front (hereafter the "UF") Government – formed by an alliance of left parties and Bangla Congress – came to power. Radical peasants' and students' movements broke out throughout the state, which led to dismissal of the UF government by the Centre on the pretext of "breakdown of constitutional machinery". In 1969, the UF came to power again. But this time serious differences broke out among the partners of the UF, especially between the Bangla Congress and the CPI(M). Again, during this time, a radical (revolutionary) section of the CPI(M) formed CPI(ML) advocating peasants' revolution and cultural revolution in the line of Mao Ze Dong. The second UF government was again dismissed shortly in the wake of widespread anarchy and utter confusion.

The leftists once again came back to power in 1977 – this time in a new avatar called Left Front (hereafter the "LF"). In its initial years, the LF took the question of food security very seriously and implemented various legal as well as social policies from a radical land reforms (Operation Barga, which allowed three-fourths share to share-croppers) and establishment of three-tire Panchayat (rural local government) to effective functioning of PDS and successful running of many Central government-sponsored programmes. However, these efforts and initiatives started fading after a few years. The process of land reforms was only partially completed. In most cases, it was not further radicalised by programmes like cooperative farming, which were necessary for increasing productivity. Generally speaking, the official left seemed to be self-complacent about its twin policies of Operation Barga and the three-tire panchayat system.

Despite these pitfalls, it should be acknowledged that in many southern districts of the state, the general food situation had improved "substantially" compared with the 1950s and 1960s. But this cannot be claimed about many parts of the arid lands of south-western districts, especially of a large jungle-infested area popularly known as Jungle Mahal. Even after three decades of the LF rule, these remained (and still remain) a region of scarcity in terms of basic amenities such as education, health, drinking water, roads and, of course, in terms of food. There are few jobs in non-agricultural (industrial/service sector) fields and agriculture could only partially accommodate their needs. Also the "modern" law does not allow them to use the forest resources for subsistence.

The northern districts of West Bengal are also generally considered as less developed in comparison with the prosperous southern districts. And to make things even worse, there is a sharp decline in the once-affluent tea industry. For reasons more than one, many tea gardens have become or have been made "sick". As a result, a large number of tea labourers mostly constituted by descendents of the tribal population of central India, who were settled in the tea gardens by the planters in the 19th and 20th centuries – face extreme difficulties in their mere existence. Slowly, but surely, a section of them is inching towards death. Others are just living on the verge of ruin.

The response of the state government to this increasing challenge has been, on the whole reactive, rather than proactive. It is difficult to find any long-term vision or policy with respect to these areas of scarcity and hunger. In the extreme cases of hunger deaths, the usual reaction of the government and the ruling regime, especially of the CPI(M), is primarily of denial.[5]

It is not easy to prove that a particular death has been caused only by hunger. In other cases, they try to blame "others", pointing out the non-cooperation/resistance on the part of the opposition or the Centre. Simply put, they never own responsibility in this regard. Rather, they repeatedly (and self-complacently) take pride in implementing Operation Barga, establishing the three-tire rural self-government and claiming the top rank in India in terms of agricultural products.

Probably, this mindset of the regime gives us a hint about the launching of the much hyped slogan by CPI(M) – *Krishi amader bhitti/Shilpa amader bhabishyat* [Agriculture is our foundation/Industrialisation is our future] before the Assembly elections of 2006. Clearly, it indicated a policy shift of the LF: from an agriculture-centric development policy to an industry-directed (also industry/industrialists "friendly") development policy. Then, in 2007, a mass outrage over the malfunctioning of PDS burst out in many districts of the state. Popularly known as ration riots, this apparently anomic movement in three southern and one northern districts only indicates the gap between the claims of the ruling regime and the reality. All these events compel everybody, who cares for peoples' sustainable rights, to look deeper into the issue of food in the left-ruled West Bengal and simultaneously understand the importance and problems of a new evolving right – the Right to Food.

Evolution of the Right to Food: From Inside the Courtroom to the Theatre of People's Participation

This account of the consolidated effort at ensuring Right to Food by the government, the civil society organisations, the individuals and all the rights – bearing and – rights exercising bodies aims at analysing how far the right was established as a political right over the last decade such that the right did not remain only on paper but also became substantive, and on that, the basis claim making for food would be possible and entertained. We all know that a specific juridical discourse on this is developing around a case in the Supreme Court. A perusal of this case helps us to form an idea of the evolution of the case within the paradigms of law and policy. But a far more interesting trajectory is offered by the evolution of the case outside the Court, which, in turn, affected the opinions of the highest court in a number of ways.

All through, what has been most interesting was that with the twists and turns of the way in which the people were to access this specific right – the Right to Food. Thousands of activists with the help of the Supreme Court Commissioners, acting as agents of the people and the Court, kept the Court informed about all developments. Through this mutual overlap of interests, the discourse over the governmental responsibility to ensure food for all developed. While a survey of how the case developed is necessary, we have to devote attention to the dynamics and the mechanisms by which public pressure was intended to bear upon the government in the interest of transparency and improving policy performance. In the same breath, one may say, it will not be sufficient to see only the food component; the understanding must be holistic, accommodating all other rights that complement the Right to Food, like the Right to Work and the Right to Information. In fact, the latter two have developed hand in hand with the Right to Food.

The debate over access to food has evolved in the last decade into a phase where one can talk of access to food as a public right and not just something that the government distributes out of welfare consideration. The shift from the welfare syndrome is more or less apparent and people do demand food from the government; they also interrogate the latter for food unavailability. The Right to Food constitutes a critical component in the overall scheme of the Right to

Life with Dignity. It is also a matter, which cannot be left unattended and given less than full attention – since the need for food of a starving individual is most immediate and, therefore, deserves attention without any delay. Therefore, a huge part of the question of ensuring the Right to Food perhaps lies in the access to situational measures without delay. Lack of implementation, corruption and lack of accountability have long been identified as the impediments for making food available to all, while, at the same time and perhaps not strangely, the crisis continued unabated.

BRIEF STORY OF THE CASE INSIDE THE COURT

The Introduction to the second edition of *Right to Food* by the Human Rights Law Network (hereafter HRLN) states that India cannot deliver a viable answer when one asks why so many people in this country starve while the government granaries overflow with grains and plans to dispose the "excess" grains into the sea. "Hunger spreads not because the State lacks the funds to act but it chooses to use its money elsewhere . . ." and ". . . a litigant would have to move the highest court merely for a direction to the Government to implement its own schemes". The Supreme Court Orders understood in consonance with the Commissioners' Report offers a story of its own and has a logic that unfolds as the case proceeds at the Court and helps in understanding the Right to Food in India.

As early as in 1988, when starvation deaths were brought to the notice of the apex Court, the latter accepted the assurances of the Government of Orissa that the situation would be looked into and hoped that starvation deaths would cease to occur. Starvation was brought to light afresh after a long time and analysed afresh subsequent to the case of Pradeep Kishen. Starvation as a phenomenon was common enough in this country, but it was not admitted in the administrative parlance. Ten years after the Pradeep Kishen case, another petition was filed, detailing several hundred deaths due to starvation. "In December 2000, the Union Minister for Consumer Affairs and Public Distribution wrote to the Chief Ministers admitting that five crore people are victims of starvation." This was perhaps the first time when the state machinery in India had, in principle, accepted that people under its protection were actually less protected; they suffered from hunger or lack of food and even died from it. But "lack of food" was not always the real case. In fact, a few days later, the Chief Minister of Rajasthan in a letter to the Union Minister for Consumer Affairs and Public Distribution, wrote that lakhs of tonnes of foodgrains lay undistributed in FCI warehouses and there was a proposal of dumping it in the seas, to create storage space for the new crop.

This was the point from where the Peoples' Union for Civil Liberties (hereafter the PUCL), Rajasthan, took up the case and Kavita Srivastava, on behalf of the former, filed the Writ Petition (Civil) 196 of 2001 (with the Supreme Court of India). It was also about the same time that Manoj Parida, Senior Regional Manager of the FCI was interviewed on the Star TV news channel where he commented that he could only give the grain to the states if the Central government allocated it. Thus, the fact that there was a policy deadlock responsible for the idle and rotting grains yet not reaching anyone came to be admitted inadvertently. The PUCL case was in itself path-breaking because it took up a long-existing socio-economic reality of India and opposed it. It also came to be acknowledged that though there was no dearth of production following the "green revolution" and the introduction of the high-yield method, the produce hardly trickled down. The Supreme Court of India issued several interim orders attached to the Writ Petition (Civil) 196/ 2001. These interim orders were instrumental in keeping a watch continuously on the government as far as the implementation of the food schemes or the availability of employment opportunities were concerned. They also sensitised the media as well as the civil society organisations which, in turn, made the campaign and the Court better informed. This was largely possible owing to the work of the Supreme Court Commissioners for the Right to Food.

This dateline story of the case aspires to analyse a few significant Court orders or interim orders and trace the development of the Right to Food case. In doing so, it keeps in mind that food is not an integral case in itself. It is linked to two other rights – the Right to Work and the Right to Information – and is anchored in the fundamental Right to Life with Dignity guaranteed in Article 21 of the Indian Constitution.

The Third Report of the Commissioners for Right to Food[6] summarises the Writ Petition (Civil) 196 of 2001 aptly. It says, "The Petition essentially demands the country's gigantic food stocks should be used without delay to prevent starvation and hunger. In the petition and subsequent deliberations, the petitioner has argued that the best means of preventing hunger is a combination of (a) employment guarantee for the able-bodied, and (b) social security arrangements for the destitute".

THE FAMINE CODE OF 1833

The colonial Famine Code (1833) was more or less the model on which all the currently available schemes for providing food were constructed. The Famine Code guaranteed that anyone needing food in a famine-struck area would only have to turn up at a worksite to get work. The person in question would be paid one-half of the wage in terms of grain. Records elaborate that this was one of the most significant ways of mitigating food scarcity. Furthermore, for those unable to work, there was a dole of fifty paise per day. Therefore, while there was a working underpinning thought behind the management of food scarcity, the people who turned up to seek refuge in the scheme were perhaps not numerous. Otherwise, a continuous monitoring would have been necessary on the part of the colonial administration, and famine mitigation would not have been easy.

But everyday hunger is different from famine. A famine by virtue of its recognition by the administrative mechanism as an abnormal state of affairs has the benefit of schemes pouring in to mitigate it. But hunger in its unitary or group nature was so commonplace and an accepted syndrome that it was extraordinary to challenge the state in the Court to show that the state could not protect its people enough. "In case of famine, there may be shortage of food, but hunger is a situation, where among plenty, there is scarcity. Plenty of food is available, but distribution of the same amongst the very poor and the destitute is a scare and almost non-existent activity, leading to systematic malnutrition, starvation and other related problems."[7] However, a very interesting point to note about the famine code is that, the colonial government kept it as a provision of convenience: being unaccountable to its subjects, the British Government dispensed with the Code whenever it thought the former would be unsustainable.[8] Thus, there remained the difference between assistance and guarantee as rights and as welfare measure.

NEW SCHEMES

The Famine Code was also the precedent to the Food for Work schemes available now, like the Sampoorna Grameen Rozgar Yojna (hereafter the SGRY) that vowed to provide work to everyone in any village for at least 10 days a year or the National Rural Employment Guarantee Scheme (hereafter the NREGS) which has been implemented in 2005 and promises to make 100 days of work available to all at the village level. Between the first levels of Food for Work schemes to the NREG, there has been much evolution. Almost all food schemes had flaws, if not in their conceptualisation, at least in their implementation patterns that created impediments for proper channelisation of foodgrains. However, the flaws could be recognised only after the schemes were put into action and the latter sharpened accordingly. The PUCL case has been instrumental not only in bringing into public and Court attention the non-availability of food to all, but also in shaping the way towards inclusive policies by informing the Court continuously. Additionally, there was the Right to Food movement, whose activists maintained total contact with the case. The research, therefore, was three-fold: the Supreme Court, the petitioners and the activists for the movement – all were involved in it. Along with this, the Supreme Court appointed Commissioners for Right to Food, who would look after the implementation of Court orders and would note the lapses in the latter. Flaws were recognised in almost all the food schemes like the Public Distribution System (hereafter the PDS) – improved as the Targeted Public Distribution System (hereafter the TPDS) in 1997 – segregating the population as Below Poverty Line (hereafter the BPL) and Above Poverty Line (hereafter the APL), the Mid-Day Meal Scheme (hereafter the MDMS) initiated in 1995, the Antyodaya Anna Yojna (hereafter the AAY), etc.

Briefing the Government of India after the beginning of the case, the Supreme Court, among many other decisions, ruled that the Government should consider distributing grain for free among the poor. To begin with, the Apex Court directed that the TPDS should be fully implemented by January 2002. This implied that BPL families were to be identified, ration cards were to be issues and at least 25 kilograms of grain per month per family were to be distributed by that timeline. This was a huge project for a government, which had a rusted PDS, an incomplete and much contested enumeration of BPL and APL families, and a historical background of considering hungry people as acceptable constituents of the society. Almost simultaneously, the Court started handing out verdicts on various other schemes too, for example, the AAY. Many new schemes were also drafted and introduced during this period. Among them – resuscitated and rehashed – were the Integrated Child Development Services (hereafter the ICDS) and the TPDS.

A significant feature of the Right to Food campaign and the case has been the initiation of creative use of the available policies. Removing the hindrances to the creative use of policies at the grassroots level of implementation reinforces the idea that these schemes, whichever segment of the society they target, are part of one integral effort to ensure food for the maximum number of people. This would also ensure the involvement of the people in seeing that the schemes designed for them work. For example, under the SGRY – later drafted into the NREGS – the job seekers in a particular village can suggest to the panchayat what needs to be done in the locality for which they could sell their labour and, in turn, get paid. On the other hand, while the Mid-Day Meal Scheme is actually targeted at the primary schoolchildren, it does not turn away from feeding a destitute family that the Panchayat might assign unto it perceiving an emergent situation.

Another very important aspect of the campaign and the case was that of bringing the TPDS once more into the public debate. Questions have been raised throughout about why the TPDS was increasingly rendered the status of not being an alternative while it needed to be freshly evaluated and was a much needed institution because it was the only set-up through which coarse grain could be ensured to reach the people at a much subsidised rate. There are certain Supreme Court orders, which can be classified together as the "umbrella orders".[9] These are orders, which apply in an overarching manner, for the implementation of Right to Food in general, whatever be the particularity of the scheme in question. In a Supreme Court hearing dated 28 November 2001, cited below, the former took stock of the schemes like the TPDS, the AAY, ICDS, NMBS (National Maternity Benefit Scheme) and the NFBS (National Family Benefit Scheme) and issued orders for empowering these schemes in a way that would enable these to address the cause of hunger at all levels. The Court also directed, "... the Doordarshan and the AIR [All India Radio] to adequately publicise various schemes ..."[10]

This ruling also directed that the Chief Secretaries of each state and union territory would be responsible for ensuring compliance of the powers with this Supreme Court order. To ensure the attention of the Chief Secretaries, the Court ruled that they must report compliance by filing affidavits in the Supreme Court within eight weeks from the date of the issue of the order. However, the Court Order states that the Chief Secretaries would be responsible in case of "confirmed" news of starvation deaths.[11] This matter of confirmation is often open to interpretation and often starvation deaths are bracketed off by calling them "cardio-respiratory failure". For example, in tea gardens of the Dooars, only one case of starvation death was ever recognised as a result of acute malnutrition while hundreds of similar other cases were written off as cardio-respiratory failures.

Importance of Commissioners

By the Order of 29 October 2002, the Apex Court also established the post of Nodal Officers who would provide the Commissioners with full access to relevant records and information. Whenever the states/union territories have a meeting with respect to food scarcity, the Commissioners and, in their absence, the Assistants or the Nodal Officers would be present in the meeting.[12] The Supreme Court allowed much ground to the Commissioners for flexible use of their power by saying that ". . . Commissioners shall be at liberty to take the assistance of individuals and reliable organisations in the State and Union Territories".[13] The Court Order of 28 November 2001 is very important as it details the measures required to be taken regarding the individual food access schemes. The Third Report of the Commissioners summarises this Order as: "First, the order effectively converts the benefits of eight food-related schemes into legal entitlements. Second, the order directs all state governments to introduce cooked mid-day meals in all government and government-assisted primary schools within six months. Third, the order includes further direction to ensure the wide dissemination of information relating to the schemes in question."[14]

In the following hearing (8 May 2002), further detailed and individualised directives were given by the Supreme Court with respect to the implementation of various schemes mentioned above. In the same breath, the Supreme Court appointed Commissioners who would look into various grievances among the people with respect to hunger and non-implementation of the measures designed, once the grievance resolution procedure laid out by the Court Order is exhausted. The first two Commissioners were Dr N C Saxena and Mr S R Sankaran. They would take up any problem pertaining to the Right to Food which could not be resolved by the Chief Secretary or the Collector.[15] The Commissioners would present reports from time to time based on reports from the policy recipients, the civil society organisations and the campaigners about the functioning of the food schemes and other related policies and provide counsel to the Court in form of the report. The First Report of the Commissioners[16] written by Dr N C Saxena and published in October 2002 was proactive in spirit. It identified Bihar, Jharkhand, Uttar Pradesh, Andhra Pradesh, Karnataka, West Bengal, Chattisgarh and Gujarat as non-compliant with the Supreme Court orders on the Right to Food. The first report also suggested to the Court that instead of keeping the Commissioners' action limited to the case when no state mechanism succeeds in addressing the problem of access to food, the Court should allow the Commissioners to monitor the work under the scope of Right to Food. In this way, the Commissioners would be able to work on grievances that they anticipate.

A System of Checks and Balances

This was a novel policy drafted by the Court to form a system of checks and balances whereby the failure of the Right to Food initiative could be minimised. As the Court Order below enumerates, in order to have access to further money entitlement, utilisation certificates of funds provided under different schemes need to be submitted to the Government of India by the state governments. For utilising the money allocated to the panchayats, the latter would frame employment generation proposals in accordance with the SGRY principles and would focus on creating more employment scope for the agricultural wage earners, non-agricultural unskilled wage earners, marginal farmers and persons belonging to Scheduled Caste (SC) and Scheduled Tribe (ST) communities. Since there were several cases of administrative lack of will, the Court formulated a structure of work where there was scope of social audit. This social audit would be carried out by civil society organisations, activists and individuals as well. Each unit would, therefore, be a micro-system to enable maximum utilisation of the rights available vis-à-vis food. Social audit would be, in the first place, carried out by the respective Gram Sabhas, because it is implied that Gram Sabhas should have maximum and immediate access to relevant local information. For transparency, the Court ruled that ration shops should maintain a board with respect to the status of availability of grains and other ration goods outside the ration shop, which would remain open throughout the month for fixed hours. The hours should also be displayed on the board.

The Court Order of 8 May 2002 is significant because it lays out the structure of answerability of the government to the Court and the people of India in implementing and the failure to implement the Right to Food provisions. Apart from the above, the umbrella orders also stipulate that the schemes put into action by the Court or any of the schemes in action, which pertain to the Right to Food should not be discontinued or stopped.[17] The state governments were also directed to lift their total quota of grains available to them under various food schemes and arrange for complete distribution of the same under the specific schemes.[18] In a landmark judgment, the Supreme Court mitigated the existing dilemma in High Courts when matters of Right to Food came to their counsel, as the matter was already subjudice at the Supreme Court. The Apex Court ruled that High Courts would be able to entertain petitions under the scope of the Right to Food and deal with them appropriately.[19] This meant that from now on, the common man could come to High Court and seek the latter's opinion on any grievance regarding the Right to Food. The common man, in this case, has been the Right to Food activist, the citizens in unitary capacities, the citizens concerned with redress of denial of Right to Food to fellow citizens and even the people who were adversely affected by the Supreme Court orders, namely the contractors and the ration shop owners.

From Right to Food to Right to Work

At the same time, attempts were being made to extend the realm of the legal tools for the Right to Food. For example, the Supreme Court ordered to develop the SGRY into a more effective policy so that people could be made self-reliant in terms of earning their bread. An evolution was set rolling, the culmination of which would be the NREGS. In an order dated 2 May 2003, the Supreme Court held, "... we direct that on pro rata basis, the recommendation that present SGRY scheme should be expanded at least doubled be implemented, both in regard to allocation of foodgrain as also cash, for the months of May, June and July. The State Government shall lift those allocations and ensure that the same reach those for whom it is meant".[20]

The Third Report of the Supreme Court Commissioners observes that in addition to the implementation of the different food schemes to reach food to everyone, the Government of India cannot afford to forget that the principal aim should be to empower people by giving them employment opportunity. Thus, a special stress was given to SGRY in the order of 2 May 2003. Creating employment opportunity should be considered as a much bolder intervention in the aim of eradicating endemic hunger. The food schemes could always develop loopholes and people would be adversely affected if they depend solely on the schemes. Keeping this in mind, the original petition of PUCL had made a case for the initiation of an all-India Employment Guarantee Scheme that would make people self-reliant in terms of food. Thus, Right to Work would ensure the Right to Food.

The Commissioners note that there have been wide disparities with respect to the implementation of SGRY among different states as well as among different districts of the same state simply because the SGRY does not automatically give way to the Right to Work. Work is provided on the basis of necessity and availability and is not compulsory. Even if funds are lying unutilised, the potential workers cannot force the powers to give them work. The SGRY happens to be a policy, which is supply-driven and not demand-driven. The employment guarantee scheme which the PUCL petitioned for would be demand-driven. This enables to match resources with needs. For example, if the people living under a particular Panchayat come up with the demand for social forestry, the panchayat would have to make arrangements for employing the maximum number of people for meeting the demand. Moreover, employment guarantee scheme would make it mandatory for the panchayat to provide wage work to anyone under its jurisdiction who comes up and says that he/she needs work.

May, June and July (the drought months of the previous year) were mentioned in the Court Order of 2 May 2003 and doubling the SGRY provisions for work was also recommended. The drought almost came to an end by August. When the Fourth Report of the Commissioners was ready, the drought was already over. Even then, the order for doubling the SGRY was not repealed because it anticipated that the next crop would be ready only by October or November. In the meantime, drought relief measures would be discontinued. Employment opportunities in the private sector would also not be much. Earlier, demographic evidences had always shown that there were a large number of starvation deaths when monsoon set in after a drought. In order to prevent this, the Government of India should continue to keep the SGRY provisions double.[21]

The Supreme Court further held: "In this Petition, . . . various issues have been framed many of which may have a direct and important relevance to the very existence of poor people; their right to life and the right to food of those who can ill-afford to provide to their families two meals a day. Their misfortune becomes further grave during times of famines and drought."[22] The PUCL petitioned for implementation of Famine Code[23] (not the colonial Famine Code[24]) during the relatively dry months seeking immediate release of surplus foodgrains for the drought-affected areas. However, the Court also stipulated that if the schemes available under the banner of Right to Food are found to be better equipped to deal with the drought situation, then those schemes should be employed instead of the Famine Code.[25] In order to deal with problems of the BPL people, this order says that it will deal with the problem of an inclusive BPL category subsequently but immediately wants to create alternative measures by which the eligible people left outside the BPL lists may have a guaranteed access to food. PUCL reported that approximately 1.5 crore people are eligible to get the Antyodaya Anna Yojna cards. The Court directed the Government of India to place the following groups of people in the AAY category:

1. Aged, infirm, disabled, destitute men and women, pregnant and lactating destitute women.
2. Widows and other single women with no regular support.
3. Old persons (aged 60 or above) with no regular support and no assured means of subsistence.
4. Households with a disabled adult and no assured means of subsistence.
5. Households where due to old age, lack of physical or mental fitness, social customs, need to care for a disabled, or other

reasons, no adult member is available to engage in gainful employment outside the house, and

6. Primitive tribes.

Moreover, in the same order, the Court said that the Government of India must take initiative to include all poor families within the BPL bracket. Licences of ration shop dealers were to be cancelled if they (i) did not open on time, (ii) overcharged customers, (iii) retained ration cards, (iv) made false entries in BPL cards, or (v) engaged in black marketing. Additionally, the BPL cardholders should be allowed to buy grain in instalments.[26]

FURTHER REPORTS

By the next significant date of hearing (19 August 2003), the Fourth Report of the Supreme Court Commissioners was submitted. The Court directed the petitioners to meet relevant authorities of the Government of India to discuss possible interventions to upgrade the food right situation in India. The Fourth Report stressed food schemes like Mid-Day Meal, ICDS, AAY, Social Security Pensions, PDS, Annapurna Anna Yojna, National Social Assistance Programme, urban destitution, employment guarantee and restraint on exports of foodgrains to other countries while food scarcity continued in India. It also magnified the importance of transparency and monitoring for the fruitful implementation of the Right to Food. Transparency came to be recognised by this time as an important component as the Right to Information Act was being campaigned for. All papers pertaining to the schemes and works under the umbrella of Right to Food should be considered as public papers now on.

A Special Report of the Commissioners[27] followed shortly. This report was the result of the several meetings that took place between the petitioners and the Government of India after the Fourth Report, as the Supreme Court had ordered. Some agreements like the discontinuation of the use of machines at relief work sites and the discontinuation of grain exports were reached. However, the Commissioners still found the union and state governments non-compliant in several aspects like the mid-day meal, AAY, ICDS, employment programmes, etc. The Commissioners also found the government action in making Right to Information accessible completely inadequate.

A number of Court hearings followed the Special Report. The Court orders dated 20 April 2004, 27 April 2004, 29 April 2004 and 7 October 2004[28] were all directed at the governments of the state and the Union to see that the latter implement the food schemes appropriately and do not violate anyone's Right to Food. The Court reckoned that this violation could be direct as well as indirect. The significance of the orders of 29 April and 7 October 2004 was that they dealt with the ICDS and urged the government to immediately increase the number of Anganwadi Centres to 14 lakhs from 6 lakhs. The Court expressed anxiety at the government's failure to bring all children below six years under the umbrella of the ICDS and directed the government to prepare a plan of action to bring all children under the ICDS by July 2004. The ICDS was again taken up in a much later hearing dated 13 December 2006. Meanwhile, the Fifth Report of the Commissioners came out in November 2004. The Fifth Report notes the following:

(a) Though the schemes covered by Court orders provide an excellent opportunity to assist the destitute through successive stages of their life, problems with implementation erode all possibility of the same.
(b) The repeated mention of particular states, including Madhya Pradesh, Uttar Pradesh, Bihar, West Bengal, Assam and Jharkhand, where problems of non-implementation of court orders, non-utilisation of funds (often wilful, as in the case of Jharkhand for ICDS), poor allocations, irregularities in the implementation and corruption are endemic across issues and schemes.
(c) While the Central authority had not been explicitly blamed for non-compliance in any earlier report, this report illustrated that the performance of the Government of India could, at least, have been improved in several cases.

The Fifth Report also analyses the flaws within the methodology of enumerating the BPL people and criticises the concept of BPL ceiling as well. By the time of the Seventh Report, the NREGS had already been implemented in October 2005, thus completing the exercise of developing the SGRY, and introducing the much-awaited assurance for the Right to Work and Food for Work.

SOCIAL AUDIT: THE CASE OUTSIDE THE COURT

Apart from the legal proceedings of the case inside the Supreme Court, a lot was happening outside. The debate over social cross-checking has been going on for quite some time. A social audit envisages community control over the functioning of the programmes adopted, by the government from time to time. Assigning the responsibility or part thereof, adds effectiveness to the programme in general because the former would best know what is suitable for itself and what is not.

Food-related problems are contextual; they vary a lot depending on the particularities of the problems. Solutions, therefore, often have to be tailor-made. Let us take an example of Patina Gram Panchayat located in Nayagram block in Paschim Medinipur District. When Bimal Bhogta's family of Singdhui village faces destitution and cannot gather or buy food from the ration shop close by, the panchayat decides that the family will be supplied with cooked meals from the mid-day meal kitchen of the village primary school. Here, the panchayat has made a good use of power vested in it. This leads to the popular expectation that the same institution would also try to create appropriate job opportunity for a family member so that the unit can sustain itself on a longer run. Often, the measure adopted to deal with a particular situation is a mix and match of several provisions under different schemes directed ultimately towards providing food. What appears is the relative importance of the end before the means and, thereby, the will of the distributing authority has a decisive role to play.

It is the absence of such competent grievance redress mechanism that largely limits the Right to Food in India. Almost all the food and food-related schemes have very weak tools to cope substantively with complaints. It has even failed, in many cases, to register the complaints with the competent authority. People do not have sufficient information about the entitlements and the specific aspects of the right. The lack of information impedes them from asking questions and the breach of right is the result of the absence of thought. Over the years, the question has been how to equip the government as well as the people to ensure that no one starves. Here lies the significance of the concept of social audit which has been introduced as the most important tool to review the actions of the state. In order to facilitate the implementation of the Right to Food, the Right to Information is also seen as an effective and complimentary weapon of the former. In fact, the enactment of the Right to Information has majorly encouraged people to strive for Right to Food in an effective manner because the former has penal provisions in case of violation and this comes to use while conducting social audits.

But the question regarding the effectiveness of the social audits remains. In this regard, the Comptroller and Auditor General of India, Vinod Rai, emphasised the need for partnership between the civil society organisations and the Government of India to promote social audit of the employment guarantee scheme. Admitting the lack of human resources on behalf of his office, Rai acknowledged that the 50,000-odd employees working under him and a few lakhs working for the offices of state accountant generals were "inadequate for the huge volume of public funds expenditure auditing that had to be done. So civil society organisations had to step in to assist them . . .".[29] There has been clearly a lackadaisical attitude towards social audit at every level of governing schemes like the National Rural Employment Guarantee or the Mid-Day Meal and Integrated Child Development Services. While in some cases, *jan sunwai* has happened, it has been very difficult to bring about changes because the verdict of the peoples' Court is not binding. This is what largely discourages the activists. This has been also corroborated by several reports over the last few years.

A case in point was the souring of relations between the activist groups and the state government in Rajasthan, where repeated interventions by civil society organisations were rendered fruitless because of the non-abiding nature of the public hearing directives on the authorities. ". . . There are visible manifestations of the growing unease among the activist groups – whose activities, even though by default, once formed the mainstay of the Congress campaign against the BJP leadership in Rajasthan – over the government's 'soft' approach towards those who have ganged up on the process of social audits."[30] This reaction of the activist groups grew from the Rajasthan government's decision to call off *jan sunwais* in several panchayats in the 16 districts of the state. Some recent studies also strengthen the belief that the *jan sunwai* method is not always effective in making the programmes work in favour of the people. At least in these cases, social audit has failed to curb corruption and increase accountability of the officials, who siphon away resources from public programmes.[31] But it does not mean that we can write off a means like social audit. In some cases, it really has had some restricted effect upon food channelisation schemes like the NREGS.

NREGS, RIGHT TO INFORMATION AND SOCIAL AUDIT

Designed to provide food by way of ensuring work, where every rural household can demand 100 days of work in a financial year (within 15 days of applying for it), this scheme has very high potential for reaching food to all and creating community assets which, in turn, would help in ensuring further access to food. A research by the Centre for Study of Environment in 2007 shows that much of the funds, allocated to the programme, is appropriated by unintended beneficiaries. Only about 15% of the funds allocated to such public programmes generally would reach the targeted people.[32] And, such misallocation is likely to assume quite high proportion since the expenditure of the resources in the NREGS is basically demand-driven.

Tables 1 and 2 present an idea about the status of NREGS' work in West Bengal over 2008-09 till date. The tables show that the performance of NREGS in West Bengal has been of a low to moderate level, when compared with very poor performance states like Sikkim or states belonging to India's northeast. Group 1 consists of 24 Parganas (South), Bankura, Birbhum, Dinajpur (Dakshin), Dinajpur (Uttar), Jalpaiguri, Maldah, Murshidabad, Paschim Medinipur and Purulia districts. Group 2 consists of 24 Parganas (North), Bardhaman, Coochbehar, Hooghly, Nadia, Purba Medinipur and Siliguri Mahakuma Parisad. Group 3 consists of the Darjeeling Gorkha Hill Council and Howrah.

Both over 2008-09 and 2009-10, the figures for performance of work under NREGS have been advertised by the Ministry of Rural Development. But, interestingly enough, pages for social audit have been left blank making data unavailable to the people! This betrays the basic purpose of social audit as one of the hallmarks of the food schemes now in operation (and also the NREGS) is said to be transparency, which is to be ensured by the application of right to information. In fact, much cheering has been there after the Right to Information was made available because it promised the biggest infrastructure for *jan sunwai* at all levels of administrative reach. However, there are two very big holes in the net,

TABLE 1: Status of NREGS Work (Availability and Utilisation of Funds) in West Bengal over 2008-09

Cumulative No. of HH issued Job	Cumulative No. of HH demanded cards	Cumulative Labour estimation of employment	Cumulative No. of HH provided employment provided	No. of HH working NREGS employment	Cumulative Labour estimation of persondays	Cumulative Persondays generate (in Lakhs)	Cumulative No. of HH completed 100 days
GROUP 1							
Phase I							
5714710	1590935	2849219	1590935	444890	1065.96	418.62	9569
GROUP 2							
Phase II							
3669736	1399217	1785726	1399217	610274	628.52	364.84	13481
GROUP 3							
Phase III							
171621	35702	0	35702	12531	0	3.16	0

Source: Ministry of Rural Development, Government of India[33]

TABLE 2: Status of NREGS Work (Availability and Utilisation of Funds) in West Bengal over 2009-10

Cumulative No. of HH issued Job	Cumulative No. of HH demanded cards	Cumulative Labour estimation of employment	Cumulative No. of HH provided employment provided	No. of HH working NREGS employment	Cumulative Labour estimation of persondays	Cumulative Persondays generate (in Lakhs)	Cumulative No. of HH completed 100 days
GROUP 1							
Phase I							
5894585	1783176	2359549	1778568	654321	1030.78	558.31	8561
GROUP 2							
Phase II							
3888819	1216497	1674129	1216497	511014	723.07	318.73	4883
GROUP 3							
Phase III							
288513	67936	96451	65443	26203	38.58	9.96	104

Source: Ministry of Rural Development, Government of India[33]

which allow the government to get away with its failures. The Right to Information presupposes a minimum average literacy level among the ordinary unassisted citizen who seeks to know facts and figures under or not under suspicion of fraud.

On one hand, the citizen must access data which is digitalised and, therefore, they will have to wade through the cobweb of computerised data sheets. Internet data may excite transparency of "busybodies",[35] but it causes unnecessary delay in an issue of immediacy like food, when internet data is the sole source of knowing figures about the schemes in operation. Regarding NREGS, the Gram Sabha is the institution which is responsible for seeing that the funds available in an intended way are utilised to the maximum. The panchayat is responsible for receiving the job applications, distributing the job cards and making work available in due time prescribed in the rules. The panchayat is also supposed to maintain a shelf for keeping the projects, data and keeping them accessible to the people.[36]

A typical page for social audit published by the Ministry of Rural Development for NREGS in West Bengal fails to offer any data. The page for record of grievances for the Patina Panchayat in Nayagram Bloc of Paschim Medinipur District of West Bengal reads "no grievances"! This is the second jeopardy which may result from the fact that the government, at all its levels, may just choose not to advertise the data gathered from social audit or, worse, social audit may just be another farce and never have had happened for the particular block or panchayat. Of course, it needs a mind of a sceptic to discern a flaw in everything, but this is definitely a huge loophole in the system, which indicates a total failure. Social audit, when at it its maximum, is a tool which can ensure immediate implementation of policy; action emanates right from the audit table. *Jan sunwai* should also ensure the people's right to be heard. It is a cyclical process where the failure of one compartment will break the entire loop.

The primer on Right to Food prepared by the Right to Food Campaign Secretariat says, experience shows that *interim orders* can be a useful tool for action. First and foremost, this is an opportunity to hold the state accountable. For instance, if starvation deaths are reported in a particular area, or if there is no food in the ration shops, or if the state government fails to provide cooked mid-day meals in primary schools, the Supreme

Court orders can be used to demand prompt action from the authorities concerned.[37] The interim orders were issued in a serial manner consequent to a review of the ground situation, fieldwork and research and social audit reports. And, therefore, they came in a stream which, in turn, sensitised the people associated like the petitioners, the government and the beneficiaries. It also created a sense of "entitlement", which again fostered the confidence to ask questions regarding the non-fulfilment and demand compliance with Court orders.

Here begins the domain of the political process. Reaching the audit table is a big bargain for the ordinary citizens. There is a mountain that needs to be crossed before one actually stands before the *jan sunwai*. The ordinary citizen needs administrative and political assistance to reach the audit table, which, in itself, can be a rider. The political will of the collective people assumes significance here. The audit table itself has a huge role to play. It is supposedly an impartial body, which hears the case from citizens, interprets it to the citizens' maximum benefit and recommends and oversees immediate remedy. Thus follows a process of collective action in which the civil society actively involves itself to ensure a just implementation of people's Right to Food. All the way, the process ultimately empowers the citizen. Otherwise, food will fail to be a right.

ABOUT THE BOOK

The present book is a sincere attempt at a comprehensive understanding of the difficulties and prospects of Right to Food in West Bengal. This has been a collection of multi-dimensional individual researches, in which, despite diversities, the common thread is a concern for the food situations and food rights in the state, especially in the areas of scarcity.

In the first chapter, Kumar Rana takes an account of how inequality in access to food became categorical and durable in West Bengal. Based on his findings as a researcher of Partichi Trust, Rana locates the reappearance of hunger in various districts of the state. He also narrates the political story of the Right to Food in West Bengal over the last 50 years beginning with the food movements of the 1950s and 1960s in West Bengal and culminating into the present-day struggles over the PDS.

The second chapter, by Geetisha Dasgupta, investigates the Right to Food situation in the tea gardens of northern West Bengal. This essay aims at understanding the *Right to Food among the tea garden workers* against the backdrop of several starvation deaths in plantations of the Dooars region during the last decade, when many gardens started closing down and the tea economy faced severe economic backlash.

Manisha Banerjee, on the other hand, deals with a popular movement in West Bengal in 2007-08 in the third chapter. This movement, popularly called "ration riots", rose against the unavailability of food in the Public Distribution System. This movement considerably influenced the results of the panchayat elections that took place soon after the agitation. The analysis is based on a study of a panchayat region of Burwan district in West Bengal.

In the fourth chapter, Geetisha Dasgupta takes stock of the right to food situation in South Bengal, especially in Paschim Medinipur. This is the region where starvation and hunger deaths have been reported repeatedly. The chapter aims to understand if any advances have been made at all in augmenting the subsistence agricultural production in the region over the last 50 years to make the people self-reliant in terms of food.

The fifth chapter, written by Ruchira Goswami, focuses on the legal development of the Right to Food as a concrete right and analyses the problem of the Right to Food as a complicated case of "adequate" laws formulated by the courts and an inadequate will on part of the administration and optimistic campaigns by the ground-level activists. It seeks to capture the tension and reciprocity within the triangle of these participatory elements: courts, administration and activists.

In the last chapter, Sibaji Pratim Basu attempts to look at the Right to Food through the lens of Right to Information. He focuses on the weak interlink between these two rights in West Bengal compared with other parts of India, especially Rajasthan. This essay also questions the future status of sustainable rights, including the Right to Food, under the omnipotent UIDAI – the new information regime, which seeks to ensure the automatic functioning of power.

SIBAJI PRATIM BASU
GEETISHA DASGUPTA

NOTES

1. Bhattarcharya Chittaprosad, *Hungry Bengal: A Tour through Midnapore District, 1943*, People's Publishing House, Bombay, 1946.
2. *Sukanta Samagra*, [Complete Works of Sukanta Bhattacharya] Saraswat, Kolkata, (1380 BS/1973 AD).
3. Translated by Rini Bhattacharya Mehta. (http://www.facebook.com/Sukanta.Bhattacharya – accessed on 21 June 2010).
4. Das Suranjan and Premansu Bandyopadhyay (eds), *Food Movement of 1959: Documenting a Turning Point in the History of West Bengal*, K P Bagchi, Kolkata, 2004.
5. The Sunday Times, *Times of India*, Kolkata Edition, 22 January 2006, p.4. The following is an excerpt from a report of the above edition: "'Rat, ant-eggs are delicacies': Biman/ 'I've eaten a roast rat. Believe me, it tastes good. Since we came to power, no one has starved': BIMAN BOSE WB LEFT FRONT CHAIRMAN/ By Pinak Priya Bhattacharya/TNN Falakata: People of Amlasole, Bandwan and tea gardens in north Bengal consume rats and ant-eggs, because they are delicacies for them, said Left Front chairman Biman Base at a public meeting organised by the All India Krishak Sabha in Falakata, Jalpaiguri, on Saturday. There is no sign of starvation anywhere in the state', claimed the CPM Politburo member with an air of nonchalance".
6. Third Report of the Commissioners on Right to Food available at: http://www.sccommissioners.org/pdfs/comreports/3rdreport.pdf.
7. 'Supreme Court of India: Record of Proceedings; Writ Petition (Civil) No. 196/ 2001' published in "Right to Food", Third Edition (p.44) by Human Rights Law Network, January 2008.
8. Chopra, Surabhi, 2009, 'Holding the State Accountable for Hunger' in *Economic and Political Weekly*, 15 August 2009, Vol.XLIV, No.33, pp.8-12.
9. Name from http://www.righttofoodindia.org/data/scordersprimeratoolforaction.pdf, accessed on 12 August 2010.
10. Supreme Court Order dated 29 October 2002.
11. Third Report of the Commissioners on Right to Food available at: http://www.sccommissioners.org/pdfs/comreports/3rdreport.pdf.
12. 'Supreme Court of India: Record of Proceedings; Writ Petition (Civil) No. 196/ 2001' published in "Right to Food", Third Edition (p.40) by Human Rights Law Network, January 2008.
13. *Ibid.,* p.36.
14. Third Report of the Commissioners on Right to Food available at: http://www.sccommissioners.org/pdfs/comreports/3rdreport.pdf.
15. In the Supreme Court Order dated 29 October 2002, the highest responsibility for compliance at the State level has been vested in the Chief Secretary and the Collector. For any persistent default with compliance to orders, they would be held responsible. This has also been described in the order of 8 May 2002, and clarified by the Court in a detailed enumeration of accountability published by

the Right to Food Campaign as Supreme Court Orders on the Right to Food: A Tool for Action (available at http://www.righttofoodindia.org/data/scordersprimeratoolforaction.pdf) as the 'Lines of Accountability: The 8 May 2002 order.

16. First Report of the Supreme Court Commissioners on Right to Food available at: http://www.sccommissioners.org/pdfs/comreports/1streport.pdf.
17. Supreme Court Order dated 27 April 2004.
18. Supreme Court Order dated 17 September 2001.
19. Supreme Court Order dated 1 May 2006.
20. Source: http://www.righttofoodindia.org/orders/sum_may203.html.
21. Fourth Report of the Supreme Court Commissioners on Right to Food available at: http://www.sccommissioners.org/pdfs/comreports/4threport.pdf.
22. Supreme Court of India: Record of Proceedings; Writ Petition (Civil) No. 196/2001' published in "Right to Food", Third Edition (p.42) by Human Rights Law Network, January 2008.
23. *Ibid.,* p.4.
24. This Famine Code was different from the colonial Famine Code. This was designed and implemented by the Government of Rajasthan drawing from Article 21 and Article 47 of the Indian Constitution. Similar Codes have been formulated by other States also. The first three chapters of the Rajasthan Government's Famine Code deal with the steps to be taken as preventive measure before the famine and drought sets in while the rest of the chapters deal with declaration of distress and commencement of relief, setting out in detail the relief measures and the officers responsible thereof.
25. Supreme Court of India: Record of Proceedings; Writ Petition (Civil) No. 196/2001' published in "Right to Food", Third Edition (p.45) by Human Rights Law Network, January 2008.
26. *Ibid.*, p.47.
27. Special report of the Supreme Court Commissioners on Right to Food available at:http://www.sccommissioners.org/pdfs/comreports/specialreport november2003.pdf.
28. Source: http://www.righttofoodindia.org/orders/interimorders.html#box12, accessed on 26 June 2010.
29. Shukla, Saurav. 2010. 'Social audit of development schemes necessary', in http://www.topnews.in/law/social-audit-development-schemes-necessary-26663, accessed on 6 June 2010.
30. Sebastian, Sunny. 17 December 2009. 'We will not sit quiet on social audit issue in NREGS, Aruna Roy tells Gehlot government'; in http://www.thehindu.com/2009/12/17/stories/2009121761471000.htm, accessed on 21 December 2009.
31. Afridi, Farzana, 'Can Community Monitoring Improve the Accountability of Public Officials?' in *Economic and Political Weekly*, Vol.43, No.42, 18-24 October 2008, p.35.
32. *Ibid.*, p.36.

33. http://nrega.nic.in/netnrega/homestciti.aspx?state_code=32&state_name =WEST%20BENGAL, accessed on 3 March 2010.
34. *Ibid.*, accessed on 10 January 2010.
35. Gopal, K S, 2009, 'NREGA Social Audit: Myths and Reality' in *Economic and Political Weekly*, Vol.44, No.3, 17-23 January 2009.
36. Afridi, Farzana. *Op. Cit*, p.36.
37. Supreme Court orders on the Right to Food: A Tool for Action available at: http://www.righttofoodindia.org/data/scordersprimeratoolforaction.pdf.

CHAPTER 1

Food Crisis, Right to Food and Popular Politics in West Bengal

KUMAR RANA

FOOD-SCARCITY AND LEFT POLITICS

"There is no other way. Hence the struggle!" – Such were the words in *Swadhinata,* the organ of the West Bengal unit of the undivided Communist Party of India, and then followed these lines, on 9 July 1959:

> There is no dearth of food in our state, but still the people of towns and villages have been compelled to buy rice at Rs.30-33 per maund. In the rural area the supply of ration is almost stopped. There is no food in the deficit and distressed areas and no provision for test relief work for the poor landless labourers and unemployed. In the distressed areas people are dying of starvation. The agriculture is in severe crisis. The peasants are without any work or money. People in the towns and villages, peasants, workers, middle and lower middle class, all strata of the society have been shattered because of the food crisis.[1]

The passage above took me back to my childhood. These lines had appeared three years before my birth. But, the distress of the people had continued. So had the struggle. Just seven years after the 1959 Food Movement, a landmark in West Bengal's post-independence political history, the state witnessed another vigorous food movement, both larger and stronger, in 1966. In its ferocity, this was to surpass all previous food movements. I was yet to be enrolled in primary school, but I vividly remember a song from a local *jatrapala* (Bengal's popular open-stage play) that classified the society into two distinct parts: one that eats and the other that starves.

> *Duniyata bhai ajab karkhana*
> *Kei ba khaye khiri khechiri, kahar pete uda kana*
>
> [What a crazy theatre this world is! Some enjoys delicious food while others starve wrapping a wet rag around the belly (to minimise the pain of hunger)].

Hunger was widespread, but it did not really affect "all strata of the society". There was a small section that still enjoyed lavish varieties of food. The *mahajan* in our area – from Gopibalbhpur (earlier situated in the undivided Medinipur district, now, since 2001, it is in the new Paschim Medinipur district) – belonged to this solvent group. Immediately after the harvest, in winter (only kharif crop was grown; boro was yet to come to occupy the field and economy), the *mahajan* came with his bullock carts and apart from his "due" collections – that ruined the peasant households – he exacted from each of the households a bowl of rice, a bowl of ghee, one cock or hen and a bottle of *mahua*[2] liquor as "gift". And these were not only from the borrowers; the free households too had to pay this tribute: after all, who can anticipate "when we would need the support of the *mahajan*?" He went on feasting everyday during his stay in the village. His departure from the village signalled the beginning of starvation: he took with him the major portion of the harvest.

The agricultural wage rate in the area was far too low. When I took part in a movement for wage enhancement in 1977, the existing daily wage rate was 1.5 kg of unhusked rice; women got even less. In the first phase of the movement, we demanded increasing this to 3 kg and later to 5 and then 8 kg – for both men and women. Survival was a tough battle: people used to eat various sorts of wild roots, vegetables, coarse cereals and so on. The public distribution shops sold rice and wheat at a cheaper rate, but people could hardly afford even buying from these shops. The ration dealer sold their stock in the open market to make a substantial profit.

Those days, the condition all over West Bengal was more or less similar to what the *Swadhinata* had described. The Communist Party of India had formed an alliance with other left and democratic parties in order to launch a movement against the faulty "Congress Government and its food policy", which "are fully responsible for their [the peoples'] destitute condition". The *Swadhinata* asked, "How will the people survive if the Government is not forced to do something to ease the problem?" And, "hence the struggle and its preparation".

Nevertheless, despite the prevalence of widespread hunger across the state, the 1959 Food Movement did not have universal spread and momentum; it remained confined to areas of influence of the Communist Party and its allies. In our area, there was no such influence and, hence, it did not participate in the 1966 movement. However, the anger and sense of deprivation which had built up among the people in our area never died down, and West Bengal witnessed its outburst in 1969, through the harvest movement.[3] Also, despite the vehemence of the struggle, the actions taken by the successive governments were less effective than required. As we know, after a brief hibernation, the crisis reappeared in 1966. And once again reappeared the alliance, now led by the Communist Party of India (Marxist). The CPI was split into two in 1964; despite the CPI retaining the original name, the newly formed CPI(M) emerged as a much bigger force. Prafulla Chandra Sen, the Minister-in-Charge of Food and Supply in Bidhan Chandra Roy's government during the 1959 Food Movement, now became the Chief Minister of the state. Sen was particularly infamous for his insensitive remarks. "Eat green bananas instead of rice" was one of his most (in)famous quotes. Both Roy and Sen adopted brutality as the most effective method for handling the situation and Sen perhaps surpassed his predecessor in applying state violence on the masses. When thousands died of hunger, numerous protesters were gunned down by the police.

However, state violence failed to silence the mass fury; rather, this precipitated the end of Congress rule in the state. The CPI(M) played a crucial role in guiding the public outrage over high prices and scarcity of food not only in building a strong support base for its own but also for strengthening the unity of the left parties. As Das and Bandopaddhaya comment:

> The emerging Left political unity in electoral politics in West Bengal reached a turning point in the 1967 general election, which resulted in the formation of the first non-Congress United Front Government in West Bengal. This regime, however, had a short life. But the social and political consciousness in West Bengal had become so deeply motivated and shaped by organised Left politics that the decade-long post-1967 political turmoil could not stem the surging tide of a political process that culminated in 1977 with the formation of a CPI(M)-led Left Front government . . . The Food Movement of 1959 can thus be justifiably considered as a significant landmark that set the ball rolling for a new political alignment in West Bengal.[4]

Food not only became a central issue, it became the strongest tool for the left politics in West Bengal that "shaped" the political future of the state. One may say that the food crisis in itself did not generate a movement; the movement had to be organised. There were many areas marked by food scarcity; yet, not all areas were marked by protests now remembered as the great Food Movement. The map of the Food Movements of 1959 and 1966 is very similar to the geographical reach of the left movement in West Bengal: the movements started and took massive form in areas where the left, more precisely, the communists had some organisational strength, and in Kolkata (then Calcutta), which became the epicentre of the movement. In other words, it was politics, guided particularly by the leadership, which shaped the movement for food. Of course, the crisis of food created a situation where politics could garner popular support. In the absence of such a situation, it would not have been possible for the left parties, particularly the CPI and later the CPI(M) to build a solid organisation that would transform the party into a ruling power in due course. The ruling Left Front was, therefore, fully aware that food was seminal in West Bengal popular politics. In its initial years (1977-82), the government perhaps took this issue much more seriously than it has taken in the latest phase (2006 onward), when it was more busy fulfilling its much-heralded agenda of industrialisation. Amidst poor records of the delivery of other basic services, the successful implementation of the centrally sponsored Food for Work (FFW) programme in West Bengal in the initial years of the Left Front rule is testimony to this.

The success of the FFW programme was largely due to the informed activism on the part of the left parties. The memory of the 1959 and 1966 Food Movements was yet to fade away – many stalwarts of those movements now headed the government. They depended more on societal activism than following bureaucratic ways. Therefore, the Left party workers were given a greater role in ensuring that the FFW is implemented. However, before long, the enthusiasm dried up: programme implementation became a routine governmental work than an issue of politically motivated activism. Several factors might have influenced the situation. Exclusive dependence on the success of land reform in isolation of other empowering measures is perhaps a key factor for such a shift. This definitely led to other programmes such as the functioning of the public distribution system, programmes concerning enhancement of wages and increase in the purchasing power of the agricultural wage labourers, maintenance of food security, etc. being neglected. As a result, people were forced more to depend on free market rather than government's own programmes and initiatives.

Apparently, the food crisis of the 1960s and 1970s came to an end. The free market saw an abundance of food. The degree of hunger reduced possibly also among the lower-income groups in the society. This was perhaps the reason for food not becoming a crucial issue during the middle phase of the Left Front rule. Dreze and Sen noted, "regimes where the political power is particularly concentrated in the hands of the rich have a tendency to favour development models which give greater prominence to economic growth – whether as an element of a strategy of growth mediated security, or in the form of un-aimed opulence (or indeed in the form of opulence aimed at the privileged classes)".[5] Perhaps the Left Front government was quickly turning into such a regime.

Hunger Reappears?

But, did hunger go away? If so, what makes it reappear to the embarrassment of the government and the West Bengal society as a whole? In fact, it did not go away. It did exist among sections of the population, however invisible these groups may be. The Pratichi Trust's report on primary education[6] provided evidences of acute hunger among the adivasis of Purulia and Birbhum. The NSSO reports found that a large number of people did not have access to sufficient food. There were many other evidences of persistent hunger, one of the major evidences being the wide acceptance of the Mid-Day Meal Scheme in the primary school launched in 2004. Also, the acceptance of the supplementary nutrition through the Integrated Child Development Scheme (ICDS), notwithstanding its abysmally poor quality, among the marginal sections of the society was another indication. Surprisingly, despite these evidences, hunger continued to kill hundreds of people in Dreze and Sen's words "in a 'legal' and 'orderly' way".[7] It became an issue only after the media reports on the cases of hunger death in Amlashole, an adivasi village in Paschim Medinipur district, "shocked" the middle classes. News of hunger deaths also came in from North Bengal tea gardens. Yet, the government and the Left Front leader CPI(M) appeared unconcerned: while the Chief Minister admitted casually the existence of hunger – not just in Amlashole, but also in Kolkata – the Minister in Charge of Backward Classes Welfare Department echoed the Left Front Chairman's claim that the deaths were caused by ailments, not by hunger.[8] There were some declarations of relief measures, but it was doubtful whether the promises would be transformed to action. And, regrettably, the issue of food as a human right quickly disappeared from the public domain.

Despite persistent hunger among sections of population, there was not much political activism either of the "socially and politically conscious" Left or of the opposition parties. It was the so-called civil society – in the beginning, a few NGOs – which tried to bring the issue of hunger into the public domain. But, their activism on Right to Food copied the all-India pattern of ensuring this right primarily through legal activism. Given the socio-political fabric of West Bengal, where public policies are guided more by organised politics than through legal and other administrative manoeuvres, the issue of Right to Food in this phase never took the form of a movement. The civil society through its reports succeeded in influencing the Supreme Court to pass orders directing the government to ensure the availability of food to the hungry.[9] However, the government did not care much and even the compliance with the Supreme Court Orders was partial.

We can take the example of the Mid-Day Meal Scheme. The Supreme Court had directed that all primary schoolchildren should be brought within the fold of this scheme by 2002;[10] yet, even today, large chunks of the urban primary schoolchildren are not provided with meals under the scheme. The coverage of the children of upper primary schools under this scheme, despite the Court Order, is still about 25%.[11] However, the implementation of the Mid-Day Meal Scheme is more successful than many other programmes, and this is closely linked with the acuteness of hunger prevailing in the society. Despite severe opposition from bureaucracy, media and the reluctance of the political leadership to mobilise in support of the scheme, the programme was welcomed by the village population, and the implementation of the scheme became a political demand. Similar is the case of the ICDS; the implementation is still partial,[12] and while the Supreme Court Order has influence in enforcing the partial implementation, this too was connected with a political demand among the working population in cities and towns. The difference in the strength of the response concerning the ICDS from that concerning the Mid-day Meal has much to do with the "beneficiaries" of the two schemes. The primary schools are attended by all sections of the children, including the affluent in the rural areas. In fact the affluent families grumble against its poor implementation. But the ICDS centres are yet to have universal attendance. Generally, only children from poor families attend the centres, and the marginalised condition of the parents whose children avail of the ICDS is reflected in the lacklustre nature of the delivery of the programme.

But the question remains: What made the central leadership of the West Bengal Left Front shut its eyes towards the issue of hunger? Before attempting to answer this question, let us examine the extent and pattern of hunger prevailing in the state.

SHIFT IN THE TARGET OF HUNGER

In July 2001 we visited, in connection with the Pratichi Trust's study on primary education, Khuditand village of Puncha block in Purulia. The inhabitants, members of kheriya sabar community, told us that that they ate only once a day. To assuage hunger, they took tea added with salt (they could seldom buy sugar). The area was drought-prone; rain-fed agriculture could not ensure either food security or wage employment. Moreover, the kheriya sabar community was a new entrant in agricultural practices (either as cultivator or as labourers). And, when we reported this in the Pratichi report,[13] we were told by the authorities and also by some academics that this was a sporadic occurrence and could not be generalised for the entire state.

In 2004, I spent a week in my village, which is much different from Khuditand. Agriculture was diversified; with locally developed irrigation system, most of the land was brought under multi-cropping system. Though 75% of the village population consists of the Adivasis, these groups (santals and mundas), with a rich history of settled agriculture, differed much from the sabars. Yet, the village had some similarity with that of Khuditand.

In November 2006, I visited a village in Jalpaiguri district. The kharif paddy had already been half harvested. Yet, when I asked an agricultural labourer household about their usual menu those days, the old man who was the head the family asked me if I intended to accompany him to see with my eyes what they ate. I followed him. We walked about a kilometre inside the forest. He dug out a wild yam, no less than 10 kg in weight. He took enough care to protect his skin from the sap of the yam the contact of which would cause severe harm. Bringing it home, he cut it into round pieces and laid them on the wall so as to drain out the sap. Then he would leave the pieces in salt water overnight. After drying the pieces properly, they would be boiled. This used to be the staple food for them – at least for a substantial part of the year. And, the diet was not out of choice but was a forced one ("*keu sakhe khayna go, garta bharate gilte hoy*").

The above incidents are only a few of many that one can come across in the villages in West Bengal. But, what was most surprising was the prevalence of hunger in some villages in Bardhaman – the "rice bowl of West Bengal". Nevertheless, personal experiences have their own limitations, and it is difficult to generalise them. But, when they are corroborated by further studies, the concern on the issue cannot but deepen. As Chakraborty and Mukherjee observe on the basis of the National Sample Survey Organisation (NSSO) reports:

> It is generally well known that household food insecurity may very well coexist with adequate availability of food at the national or sub-

national level. Yet, the fact that the percentage of people in West Bengal who reportedly do not get two square meals a day at least some days in a year is the highest among all the major states would definitely surprise all, given the state's remarkable achievement in agricultural production. The state has been holding on to this dubious distinction for more than a decade now, as revealed by NSS reports on 'reported adequacy of food intake'.[14]

The NSSO reports categorise two kinds food inadequacy: (a) households reporting "not getting" two square meals a day in some months of the year, and (b) households reporting not getting the same throughout the year. From the NSSO reports, it is found that the reported inadequacies of both kinds were not only higher in rural West Bengal as opposed to the All India average but also that the inadequacies have remained for over a decade (See Table 1).

TABLE 1: Reported inadequacy of food intake in West Bengal

	Percentage of households whose members do not get two square meals a day					
	Throughout the year			Some months of the year		
	1999-00	1993-94	2004-05	1999-00	1993-94	2004-05
West Bengal						
Rural	2.3	3.0	1.3	8.1	11.1	10.6
Urban	1.1	1.5	0.7	0.9	2.0	0.6
India						
Rural	0.7	0.9	0.4	2.6	4.2	2.0
Urban	0.6	0.5	0.4	0.3	1.1	0.1

Source: NSS Report nos. 415, 466, 512[15]

The acuteness of hunger, particularly in rural West Bengal, was reported by the NSSO (2004-05) to be much higher than the all India average. While reported food inadequacy for one to three months in the year was reported by 9.1% of rural households in West Bengal, the all India figure appeared to be 1.7%. Round the year, the inadequacy of food in rural west Bengal (1.7%) too was found to be much higher than the all India average (0.5%).

Again, with respect to the seasonality of hunger, its extent in West Bengal has been far higher than all over India. The NSSO data on seasonality of hunger is particularly striking: a substantial number of rural households suffering from food inadequacy even in the months of kharif harvest show their exclusion from the so-called success of land reform or other pro-poor programmes.

Chart 1. Per 1,000 households by number of calendar months during which there was not enough food everyday for the households

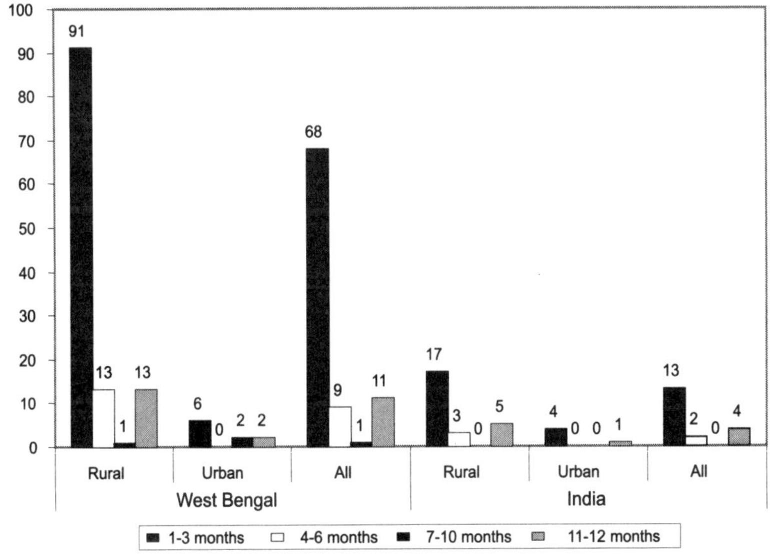

Source: Report No. 512(61/1.0/5) Perceived Adequacy of Food Consumption in Indian Households 2004-2005, NSS 61st Round, July 2004-June 2005

The persistence of hunger coincides with two other facts: one, the rate of decline in rural poverty in West Bengal has been much slower between 1993-94 and 2004-05 than in the previous two decades (1973-74 to 1993-94), which again coincided with much higher agricultural growth rate (the annual exponential growth being 6.4% during 1981-82 to 1990-91), and two, West Bengal taking a reverse trend with respect to real wage. As Chakraborty and Mukherjee point out:

> It is the only state where real wages for both casual agricultural and non-agricultural workers actually declined in the period between

> 1993-94 and 1999-2000 – two NSS rounds . . . Given the evidence that between the last two censuses the percentage of agricultural labourers in total (main + marginal) workers actually increased and the absolute number increased significantly, it seems that the non-farm sector could hardly absorb the growing number of people with very little human capital. In other words a large number of rural inhabitants are stuck with the kind of work that has little prospect of generating adequate income to get out of poverty, given the stagnating average wages in both agriculture and non-agriculture.[16]

Chart 2. Number Per 1,000 households whose members did not have enough food everyday in the months – Rural

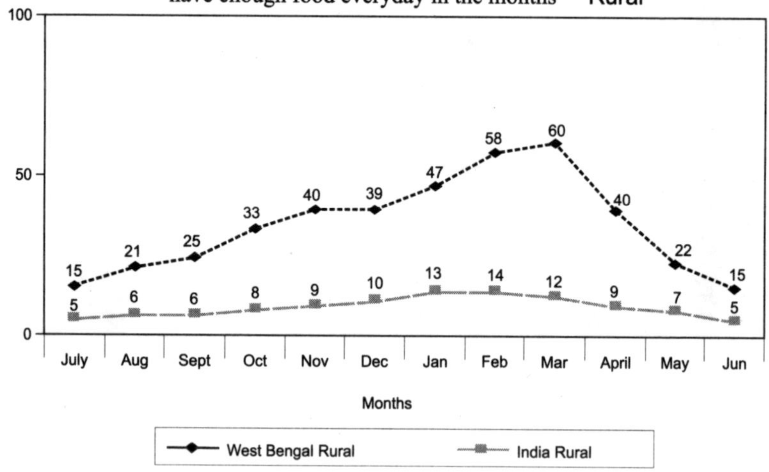

Source: Report No. 512(61/1.0/5) Perceived Adequacy of Food Consumption in Indian Households 2004-2005, NSS 61st Round, July 2004-June 2005

Now who are the poor and hungry? Let us disaggregate the NSSO data further on the line of occupational class and social identity. While in 2004-05, "households not getting enough food everyday for some months of the year" in rural West Bengal constituted 1.3% of the total (Table 1), the figures among the agricultural labourers and other labourers were 1.8% and 3.7% respectively (Table 2). Again, the average proportion of rural "households getting inadequate food for some months of the year" was 10.6% (Table 1), but the figures for the agricultural labourers and other labourers were 23.3% and 8.9% respectively (Table 2).

TABLE 2. Per 1,000 distribution of Households by Food-availability Status by Household Types–Rural

	West Bengal		India	
	Getting inadequate food everyday for some months of year (Rural)	Not getting enough food everyday in any month	Getting inadequate food everyday for some months of year (Rural)	Not getting enough food everyday in any month
Self-employed in non-agricultural ctivities	44	9	12	4
Agricultural labourers	233	18	51	7
Other labourers	89	37	21	9
Self employed in agriculture	34	1	5	1
Other households	35	14	8	5
Not recorded	0	0	7	11
All Class	106	13	20	4

Source: Report No. 512(61/1.0/5) Perceived Adequacy of Food Consumption in Indian Households 2004-2005, NSS 61st Round, July 2004-June 2005

While the proportion of agricultural labourers suffering from hunger in some months of the year was greater than that of the other labourers, it was the other way round in the case of round-the-year hunger. Whatever be the case, the labouring class of West Bengal, in general, had to face much more acute hunger than that of their all India counterparts. To explain this contradiction – the pro-poor image of the Left Front *vis-à-vis* the violation of the right to food of the labourers – we need to go into some more details of the constitution of the labouring class.

According to the 2001 Census, 71% of the agricultural labourers of West Bengal came from the adivasis, dalits and Muslims, though their share in the total population was 54%. Now, if we look at the NSSO reports, we find that the adivasis and dalits are the sections most vulnerable to hunger. In 2004-05, the proportion of adivasis of rural West Bengal

TABLE 3. Per 1000 distribution of households by food availability status by Social Groups

	Getting enough food everyday for some months of the year						Not getting enough food everyday in any month					
	West Bengal			India			West Bengal			India		
	Rural	Urban	All	Rural	Urban	All	Rural	Urban	All	Rural	Urban	All
ST	175	74	168	37	8	35	9	0	9	5	0	4
SC	144	17	119	33	8	27	19	12	17	7	3	6
OBC	66	5	54	10	4	9	2	4	2	2	1	2
Others	80	3	53	19	1	12	11	5	9	6	1	4
All	106	7	78	20	4	16	13	6	11	4	1	4

Source: Report No. 512(61/1.0/5) Perceived Adequacy of Food Consumption in Indian Households 2004-2005, NSS 61st Round, July 2004- June 2005

"getting inadequate food everyday for some months of the year" was 16.8%, which was much higher than "other" categories (5.3%), also compared with the all India average of the adivasis (3.5%). Similar was the condition of the dalits. Dalits in rural West Bengal who got inadequate food everyday for some months of the year formed 11.9% against the all India figure of 3.5% (Table 3).

The NSSO does not provide separate figures for the Muslims; indeed, as the nutrition data provided by the National Family Health Survey (NFHS) indicates (Table 4 and Table 5), if separated from the "others" the inadequacy of food among the Muslims could be much higher than the figure for the "others".

TABLE 4: Status of women's health among different social groups in West Bengal

	Women with BMI ($18.5kg/m^2$) in %		Women (15-49) with any anemia in %	
	NFHS II	NFHS III	NFHS II	NFHS III
SC	49.4	42.5	67.1	66.8
ST	64.2	55.6	80.6	78.0
Muslim	47.6	42.7	59.2	61.3
Others	39.9	36.5	59.1	60.8
All	43.7	39.1	62.7	63.2

Source: National Family Health Survey (NFHS) III, West Bengal 1999-2000 and 2005-06, Intrnational Institute of Population Sciences, Mumbai, 2007

Table 5. Nutritional status of children in West Bengal NFHS II (1998-99)

	Underweight (%)	
	NFHS II	NFHS III
SC	56.1	40.0
ST	57.4	59.7
OBC	36.1	22.7
Muslim	58.0	40.3
Others	45.8	37.0
All	48.7	44.6

Source: National Family Health Survey (NFHS) III, West Bengal 1999-2000 and 2005-06, International Institute of Population Sciences, Mumbai, 2007

It is true that there has been a general decline in the extent of undernourishment among women and children in West Bengal, but still the degree is much higher among the dalits, adivasis and Muslims compared with others. Also, there has been a slight increase in anaemia among Muslim women and under-nutrition among adivasi children.

Failure in Programme Implementation

Clearly, hunger and under-nutrition have persisted in West Bengal society. But, given the composition of the hungry population – socio-economically and geographically marginalised and mostly without access to media – the case of food inadequacy did not find a proper place in the political and academic discourse. Also, the vulnerability of these people never allowed them to rise in protest against the deprivation of the Right to Food.

Why are they still so hungry? As for the villages cited earlier, though landlessness had lessened, the inequality in terms of land ownership is still high. Most of the adivasi households have less than one acre of cultivable land. Moreover, the lands they possess have been mostly single-cropped (as opposed to those of the non-adivasis). Secondly, own harvest, wage employment (which has been around Rs.30 per day) and other income can sustain the hard-pressed adivasi households for only eight to nine months of the year. Thus, most of the households have reduced intake of food to sustain them during the hungry months of Bhadra and Aswin (August-October). As Pitho Marandi told me:

> I have a family of six members – three adults and three children. We require at least 3 kgs of rice every day. Where would we get that? So we eat less in order to save some rice for the hungry days lurking ahead. All of us earn something. Even the children are engaged in plucking green sal leaves to make leaf-plates. They can at least supplement a portion of the food requirement of the household. When would they go school, and how? A hungry stomach does not allow learning.

During that visit, I had been to another five villages and found the situation worse in some of them. Not only the indigenous people, but for the poorer communities like mal, majhi (bagdi) and dom of the area, hunger and

TABLE 6. Per 1000 distribution of households by food availability status by Ration card type

	Getting enough food everyday for some months of the year						Not getting enough food everyday in any month					
	West Bengal			India			West Bengal			India		
	Rural	Urban	All	Rural	Urban	All	Rural	Urban	All	Rural	Urban	All
Antyodaya	299	0	273	58	4	53	19	34	20	4	3	4
BPL	203	47	186	36	15	33	29	24	23	8	3	7
Others	54	3	38	11	3	8	5	3	4	3	1	2
No Ration-card	95	2	51	18	2	12	11	8	10	5	2	4
All	106	7	78	20	4	16	13	6	11	4	1	4

Source: Report No. 512(61/1.0/5) Perceived Adequacy of Food Consumption in Indian Households 2004-2005, NSS 61st Round, July 2004- June 2005

poverty are still synonymous.[17] Many of the parents of these poorer communities said that they could not provide their children with enough food (the Mid-Day Meal was yet to be launched in the schools in the area when this visit was made) and this caused the poor attendance in the school (*Khaite di parini, iskool ki patheiba?*) Many parents said, "*khali pete ki parha hai? Parha nai kari parne master pitla, ar iskoolke gelanni*" – children cannot learn in empty stomach. When they fail to recite the lessons, teachers beat them and children stop going to school.[18]

But then, what about the Public Distribution System (PDS)? As Pitho Mandi said, "Seldom did I get any rice or wheat from the ration shop. When there was the allotment I did not have the money to buy, and when there was money the dealer said that there was no allotment. Tell me what do I do?"

Indeed, a further desegregation of the NSSO data on food inadequacy show that the Antyodaya and Below Poverty Line (BPL) households, which were supposed to be protected by the PDS, had actually suffered most from food inadequacy.

TABLE 7. Monthly consumption per household from PDS of rice

	Average quantity consumed (kg) by Households holding Antyodaya or BPL ration cards from PDS and other sources				Average quantity consumed (kg) by all Households			
	West Bengal		India		West Bengal		India	
	PDS	Other Sources	PDS	Other Sources	PDS	Other Sources	PDS	Other Sources
Rural	3.411	54.74	9.527	25.23	1.248	53.248	4.09	27.03
Urban	3.138	37.956	10.657	19.832	0.551	28.899	2.311	18.241

Source: Report No. 510(61/1.0/3), Public Distribution System and Other Sources of Household Consumption, 2004-05, NSS 61st Round, (July 2004-June 2005), Vol.I.

The Central government's policy on the PDS has been marked by a withdrawal syndrome.[19] The policy of shrinking the PDS has been more consistent than making it universal. This had its impact on the delivery of the PDS in West Bengal. But what is intriguing is the fact that despite shrinking the PDS, the all India picture of buying food from the PDS has been much better than that of West Bengal. While the food consumed by the Antayodaya and BPL households every month in West Bengal from PDS was 3.4 kg in rural areas and 3.1 kg in urban areas, the corresponding all India figures were 9.5 kg and 10.7 kg respectively. Not only was the level of accessing the PDS by the poorer households at all India level higher than that of West Bengal, it was also found to be higher in terms of combined figures (all rural households in West Bengal bought 1.2 kg as against the all India figure of 4 kg).

In fact, the NSSO data show a much poorer reach of the PDS in West Bengal than all over India. While the proportion consumed from PDS in rural West Bengal has been about 13%, the all India figure has been above 24%. The urban figures (consumption from PDS in West Bengal is 5.4% as against 13% all over India) present a greater contrast.

TABLE 8. Number per 1,000 households reporting consumption from PDS and Other Sources

	West Bengal			India		
	PDS	Other Sources	All Sources	PDS	Other Sources	All Sources
Rural	128	985	989	244	853	924
Urban	54	927	937	131	891	922

Source: Report No. 510(61/1.0/3), Public Distribution System and Other Sources of Household Consumption, 2004-05, NSS 61st Round, (July 2004-June 2005), Vol.I

All these show that West Bengal has been maintaining a huge gap between requirements of food among the state population and the state's failure to meet that requirement. The PDS in West Bengal has indeed been impaired and this has a clear connection with the socio-economic fabric of West Bengal where political governance is concentrated in the hands of the urban elite who needed the PDS in 1959 and 1966, but does not need it now and can depend on free market mechanisms and has, therefore, maintained silence on implementation of public policy on hunger.

The Government of West Bengal had complained time and again that Centre has reduced its allocation of grains. There is substance in the argument. The monthly average figures of rice and wheat allotment followed a declining trend since 2002-03 (except for the AAY category). While the total allotment of wheat and rice was 521400 MT in 2002-03, it came down to 351700 MT in 2006-07.[20] Having recognised this, one is struck by the fact that the Government of West Bengal has not even been able to fully lift the allotted grains under different categories. In spite of showing some efficiency in utilising the Central allotment, the performance of the Government of West Bengal is a sharp contrast with some major states. As in the case of allotment under BPL category, the utilisation of allotment has increased from 41.7% in 2001-02 to 73.8% in 2006-07.[21] Nevertheless, the figure was not only lower than some major performing states but also the all India average. The case was similar for AAY.

However, the line followed in the case of Above Poverty Line (APL) category was somewhat different. In this category, West Bengal's figures of lifting over allotment have been higher than some of the smarter states and also the national average. However, the utilisation of allotment under APL category has generally been poor across the country, which is directly linked to the competitive market price of grains during the period. As soon as the market price went up in 2005-06, the demand for grains under APL category also increased, which resulted in an increase in the lifting of the allotment by all states. But, given the very thin line of difference between the APL and BPL in West Bengal,[22] the lifting under APL category needed to be enhanced manifold, which has not been done. There was no reason why the government did not lift the allotted APL category grains when the open market price was clearly on the increase.

LEFT'S SHIFT OF ATTENTION – FROM THE POOR TO THE POWER

The state food security programme failed to manage the food crisis, particularly wheat, due to the increased open market price which played a major role in the ration rage in West Bengal in 2007. It was mainly the people from the APL category who led the revolts against the ration dealers. Nevertheless, given the long persisting anger against the ration dealers, the ration rage garnered immediate support from the masses in general. Although the BPL category people were not to benefit much from the movement, they took part in it to express their fury against the ration dealers who were infamous for their corrupt practices.

Was the corruption among the ration dealers a new phenomenon? No. Let us look into the business of a ration dealer in some details.

A dealer has his ration shop in a village 13 km away from the block headquarter of Gopiballabhpur in Paschim Medinipur district. He is a middle farmer and was given the dealership in 1973. Apart from his own village, his shop serves three other localities in the area. He has 816 BPL cards, 866 APL cards, 138 Antyodaya cards and 2 Annapurna Anna Yojana cards spread over 450 families. With 4 acres of cultivable land, he is self-sufficient in food and other necessities. He can hardly save any money from his agricultural income. However, he has managed to accumulate substantial assets from the dealership. He has a rice-holler, which is run by his elder son, an electrical equipment shop in the market which is 13 km away from his village and run by his younger son, two motorcycles and a number of other things marking his rural affluence. According to the accounts provided by him, he would have to "sell the property" had he run the business with fairness. The incentive he got for BPL wheat was Rs.14 per quintal. However, in effect, the margin is actually negative when one counts the losses in terms of shortages, carriage and others. The policy irrationalities, according to him, justified his "selling a major chunk of the allotment of rice and wheat in the open market, where I make Rs.200-250 of profit per quintal per week. Not only the APL goods", he says, "I also sell out some other allotments". According to him, his monthly income from the business was around Rs.15,000. A major part of his income came from kerosene. He sold more than half of the allotment (about 1,000 litres) in the open market from which he earned about Rs.5,000. Also, he charges about 0.25 paise per litre over the stipulated price.

He managed to keep the dissatisfaction of the people at bay through various means. Firstly, "most of the customers are illiterate and have no information about the allotment/supply". The dealer kept the cards with him. Secondly, he kept a small group obliged. He extended favour to the non-adivasis (*hatua* in local tongue) and some young tribal men who could be potential troublemakers. Thirdly, "all the local political workers and other powerful persons are 'well fed' by the dealers. They collect regular donations and also take various obligations – kerosene, wheat, sugar, etc.". Kinship was also a big factor; in most places, the dealers were the relatives of the local leaders.

While talking with a district-level leader of the CPI(M) in Birbhum, we found that most of the contentions of the ration dealer was not at all unknown to him. He admitted that "in the past one and half decade class collaboration has emerged in rural West Bengal. Ration dealers are only a part of this scenario. For some years government policies were either guided against the poor or the pro-poor policies remained unimplemented . . . whatever be the case there has been a big change in political activism that now favours the neo-rich in the rural areas". As an individual, he felt ashamed to take sides with dealers during the ration rage in 2007, but "unfortunately it was our party's policy to protect them".

The CPI(M) stated that some anti-people forces were engaged in destabilising the PDS system and, thus, it had to stand by the dealers attacked by the mob. But, it did not clearly state why the party that came to power through the Food Movements of 1959 and 1966 never tried to streamline the PDS system in the state. Rather, it maintained the status quo in the system, the connection of which with the poor was, in any case, never strong. After the introduction of the targeted PDS (TPDS), the exclusion of the affluent section from the PDS has actually made the position of the poor even more vulnerable as it was the affluent whose grumbling capabilities had kept the system somewhat functioning. As was seen in 1959 and 1966, the movement for Right to Food was actually led by the middle class while the poor followed it. However, the general dissociation of the middle class from the PDS has made the isolation of the poor from the public discourse over the delivery of services complete.

The affinitive ties between the ration dealer and the local political leaders – symbolic of the class collaboration in rural areas (mentioned by the CPI(M) leader) – exhibit in a miniature way the features of the overall political structure of West Bengal. The availability of food in open market and the conspicuous consumption of the urban and rural middle class on one hand and the post-reform policy of targeted PDS on the other have created a situation where the PDS has become virtually irrelevant. It was only when the market price of wheat plummeted that some rural affluent people suddenly woke up to the malpractices of the ration dealers. But, till the time food was available in the open market, there was no hue and cry against the long-prevailing corruptions of the dealers and the food department. In fact, most of the local political activists belonging to all kinds of political parties received financial patronisation of the dealers.

To be exact, it was not the question of food security, but the strong tendency of the exclusion of the poor from social policies that most of the policies of the ruling partners and, thus, the government were guided by all these years. In the field of education, it is the poor who are excluded from the services due to a lacklustre delivery; while affluent could develop a safety net through private schooling or private tuition, the poor had no option but to remain illiterate.[23] The miserable health delivery system has excluded the poor from the basic health services; while the rich could enjoy the comfort of paid private health care, the poor had to depend on the quacks or traditional healers or suffer without any treatment.[24] (As a zonal level leader of the CPI(M) sarcastically commented, "there were two Ps – Poor and Power – our party's intoxicating clinging to the latter has added another P which has changed the entire notion of left politics: it is now PPP – public private partnership that has become the mantra of the day and the poor have been sent to oblivion".)

The case of the ICDS has been very similar. The delivery of the programme in West Bengal has been miserable, and the quality of food served is horrible. Yet, the vulnerability of the poor forces the children to access this lacklustre service.[25] While the ruling Left Front partners let the state delivery system function in a regrettably poor manner, the opposition parties or the civil society too remained silent for a long time.

What influenced the behaviour of the Left, particularly the CPI(M), towards the poor? What explains the dichotomy of their taking sides with the poor through the intervention in land reform, operation barga and wage movements in the early years of the Left Front and the persisting neglect in the delivery of state services, including food security particularly in the later years? It was perhaps the convergence of the social structure of West Bengal and the composition of the left parties, particularly the CPI(M) that accounted for the policies of the Left Front in its early years, which was in favour of some interventions while continuing to safeguard the agenda of the urban and rural middle classes – the class that the Left political leadership represents. It should not, therefore, be surprising that the Chief Minister of West Bengal initially argued against the launching the Mid-Day Meal Scheme[26] and the School Education Minister's put a note in the government file stating "we are against Mid-Day Meal".[27]

Before the Singur episode, the ruling party was able to subdue protests with the help of cadres and the police force. But, from 2006, the political course of West Bengal has taken a dramatic turn. The CPI(M) started receiving serious challenges one after another. Within a year, the Nandigram episode, the ration rage of 2007 and other demonstrations against the government changed the political scenario. While the ration rage of 2007 did not receive much attention in the beginning, it was soon recognised as a major outburst against the existing rule. The issue of food was vital, but the implicit demand for rights perhaps became most vital. It appeared to the poor as a channel to express their anger against the "authority" imposed on them by the combination of party machinery and bureaucratic machinery, which together had re-established a feudal raj, though in modified manner.

It was this process that resulted in new forms of subjugation; land patta, ration card, NREGA job card and recognition of other rights of the people were soon converted to "benefits" to be accorded, and were used as collateral against the "beneficiaries" receiving these benefits for physical sustenance – bluntly speaking, to ensure two square meals a day. In other words, the "support" that the party garnered among the masses was converted to "loyalty" – those who were not inclined to be loyal were taught lessons mainly through the denials of the basic requirements. The mode was generally sugar-coated and was found to be more convenient than exhibiting physical brutality. However, there were physical punishments too. We know of the instance in Dinhata of Coochbehar district where police firing on 5 February 2008 killed no less than five Forward Block activists who had taken part in a demonstration organised by their party demanding better implementation of the state-sponsored programmes like NREGA.[28] The failure in implementing the public programmes has roots in this political dynamics. While the governmental bureaucracy operates in a feudal manner, the party bureaucracy at the lower level matches it with another sort of feudal rule in the rural areas. Party activism boils down to management of government largesse towards ensuring loyalty.

THE CIRCULAR PATH OF FOOD

By 2006, the changes through land reforms had already been undone by the re-establishment of the rural elites. The rich of yesteryears changed colour but not the content; they accepted the patronage of the ruling party only to reorganise and strengthen their economic base through political manoeuvring of the opportunities offered through diversification and growth-oriented development. As Barbara Harris White notes, "The era of diversification and growth did not affect the agrarian structure much as it provided commercial elites with new opportunities for investment in agro processing and storage [in Bardhaman]".[29] Along with this, emerged many opportunities for the rural elites: government contract works, transport business, shops and other establishments, and so on. On the other hand, opportunities for the poor continued to shrink: reverse tenancy in land,[30] reversal in real wages of the agricultural labourers, appalling performance of the government in implementing programmes like NREGA and the failure to protect people from hunger, particularly in marginalised areas, like North Bengal and Paschimanchal.

Nevertheless, as current events show, while the villagers could hardly come up openly to contest the regime for past several years, recent agitations against the PDS system and at places such as Singur and Nadigram plus their electoral stand in three consecutive elections – Panchayat Elections of 2008, Lok Sabha Elections of 2009, and the Municipality Elections of 2009 – have brought back the question of Right to Food on the public political agenda. The issue of food security and hunger had brought the left parties to power, but 33 years of uninterrupted Left Front rule has failed to resolve – in fact even recognise – the issue of persistent hunger in West Bengal. The issue of food is now as powerful as it was in 1959. And, as it seems, the circle has come close to its full. Food appears to take the revenge of neglect.

NOTES

1. Cited in Das, Suranjan and Kumar Bandyopadhyay, Premanshu, (eds), *Food Movement of 1959: Documenting A Turning Point In The History Of West Bengal,* K P Bagchi, Kolkata, 2004.
2. *Basia latifolia,* the flowers are dried, fermented and distilled to produce a liquor of intoxicating qualities. (The fruits of the same tree are used to produce oil.)
3. See for details, Rana, Santosh, 'Gopiballabhpurer Dhankata Abbhutthan', in his collection of essays, *Samaj Sreni Rajniti,* CAMP, Kolkata, 2006.
4. Das, Suranjan and Kumar Bandyopadhyay, Premanshu, (eds.), *Op. Cit.*
5. Dreze, Jean and Sen, Amartya, *Hunger and Public Action,* OUP, New Delhi, 1999, p.229.
6. The Pratichi Education Report I, with an introduction by Amartya Sen, TLM

Books in association with the Pratichi Trust, Delhi 2001, pp.5-7.
7. Dreze, Jean and Sen Amartya, *Op. Cit.* p.229.
8. *The Indian Express*, 24 June 2004.
9. For the various reports and subsequent Supreme Court orders see, *Supreme Court Orders on the Right to Food: A Tool for Action,* Secretariat of the Right to Food Campaign, New Delhi, 2005. Also available at www.righttofoodindia.org.
10. Supreme Court Order on the Writ Petition (Civil) No. 196 of 2001 by Peoples Union for Civil Liberties Rajasathan on 28 November 2001.
11. Interview with the Officer-in-Charge, Mid-Day Meal, Department of School Education, Government of West Bengal, February 2009.
12. The Pratichi Child Report, with a foreword by Amartya Sen, Pratichi Trust, Delhi, 2009.
13. The Pratichi Education Report I, with an Introduction by Amartya Sen, TLM Books in association with the Pratichi Trust, 2002, p.105.
14. Chakraborty, Achin and Mukherjee, Subrata, MDG-Based Poverty Reduction Strategy for West Bengal; Institute of Development Studies, Kolkata, mineo, 2009.
15. *Ibid.*
16. *Ibid.*
17. In santali, "*rengec*" means hunger. Also it means poor. *Rengec' kana* – feeling hungry. *Rengec' hor kanain*' – I am a poor man. In the local tongue of Gopiballabhpur area, *bhok* denotes hunger and *bhokila* denotes both hungry and poor. However, the relatively affluent non-Adivasis, sometime use the term *garib* (poor) for self-ascription. For example, *Amar garaib nok.* (We are poor people). Such poverty does not relate to hunger, but to the want of wealth or prosperity. On the other hand, they consider the hand to mouth toilers *bhokila* (hungry). *Bhokila nok ga* – the hungry people, or more specifically, *bhokila mulia-kamunga* – the hungry male and female workers.
18. The large prevalence of poverty and hunger has influenced the literacy rate of the area. For example, the literacy rate of Gopiballavpur I Block is, according to 2001 Census, 57%, while the literacy rate of Paschim Medinipur is 69%. The number of female literates in this block is just half the number of the male literates. Again, the workers' profiles show that above 40% of the main workers are agricultural labourers, while the state average is 25%. Such regional variations are caused by different reasons – geographical, climatic, and perhaps very importantly demographic. All the blocks of Jhargram sub-division of Medinipur district, an area with high concentration of adivasis, have much smaller literacy rate than the state and district average. Also, the state-level data with respect to the literacy rate and work profile among the adivasis show a clear correlation between these two. For further discussion, see Rana Kumar: *Khandita Unnayan: Jhargram Mahakumar Ekti Rekhachitra,* Prashnabachi, Kolkata, 2006.

Again, the overall literacy rate among the adivasi communities in West Bengal in 2001 is 43% (the overall literacy for the state is 68%). The main workers among the adivasis are consisted of more than 50% of agricultural labourers, while the figures for the other castes is below 20%. Among the SCs, figures for literacy rate and contribution of the agricultural labourers to main workers are 59% and 38% respectively. Among the Muslims in West Bengal, the literacy rate is 57% and the proportion of agricultural labourer is 31%. Also, Muslims are engaged in many different low-income works. Thus, most of the studies on Mid-Day Meal have found much higher acceptance of the programme from these communities.

19. Pattanayak, Utsa, *The Republic of Hunger*, [Public Lecture on the 50th Birthday of Safdar Hasmi] SAHMAT, New Delhi, 2004, Swaminathan Madhura, *Weakening Welfare: The Public Distribution of Food in India,* Leftword, New Delhi, 2000.
20. indstat.com.
21. *Ibid.* For a fuller discussion see Bhattacharya, Dwaipayan, and Rana, Kumar, *Politics of PDS anger in West Bengal*, Economic & Political Weekly, Vol.43, No.5, 2-8 February 2008.
22. According to a study, the selection of BPL population was blotted by 31% exclusion error, which is the third highest in the country. See, Planning Commission (2005) Performance Evaluation of Targeted Public Distribution System, Programme Evaluation Organisation Planning Commission, New Delhi for the irrationalities in the selection of the BPL, See, Rana, Santosh (2007) *Prakrito Daridryo o BPL Talika : sarkari hisabeyr karchupi*; Santosh Rana: Prasnabachi Prakasana, Kolkata.
23. See The Pratichi Education Report I, with an introduction by Amartya Sen, TLM Books in association with the Pratichi Trust, Delhi 2001, particularly the Introduction.
24. See Pratichi Health Report I, with an Introduction by Amartya Sen, TLM Books, In association with Pratichi Trust, Delhi, 2005.
25. See, *Pratichi Child Report I*, Pratichi Trust, Delhi, 2009.
26. In his address at the open session of the All Bengal Primary Teachers' Association at Siliguri on 26 December 2001.
27. Note given on 16 April 1997 on a proposal (file (P) DO No. 1-1/96-Desk (MDM 10M-25/97) of visit by some officials to make a visit to Tamil Nadu to gather direct experience of Mid-Day Meal.
28. It was another mater, however, that the same Forward Block that demanded proper implementation of the NREGA and other programmes had been heading the crucial department of Food and Supply for the last three decades. The RSP – that shows frequent resentment mainly in the media – has been heading the department of Women and Child and Social Welfare, responsible for running the ICDS programme. The performance of these departments – very crucial for human development – has been more lacklustre than better. It's a different dynamics: the CPI(M) state Secretary Biman Bose wrote, "... the backdrop to evolution of the Bengal Left Front comprised a variegated and rich realistic developments. These included the experience of working in a United Front, the variety and

different forms of functioning of its constituents in different time periods, and the bitter fruit of experience we all had to taste as a result of their taking positions contrary to one another" (Peoples Democracy, Vol.XXXI, No.25, 24 June 2007).

The Front partners, however, sometime dared to "taking positions contrary to one another" – read CPI(M) – but the "variegated and rich realistic developments" taught them not to go beyond a limit lest they tasted the "bitter fruit" of kicked out of the government by the big brother CPI(M).

29. Harris-White, Barbara, *Rural Commercial Capital: Agrarian Markets in West Bengal*, OUP, New Delhi, 2008.
30. See *West Bengal Human Development Report*, Department of Planning, Government of West Bengal, Kolkata, 2004.

CHAPTER 2

Whither Right to Food?

Rights Institutions and Hungry Labour in Tea Plantations of North Bengal

GEETISHA DASGUPTA

INTRODUCTION

It is now well accepted that household food insecurity may blissfully co-exist with adequate availability of food at the national or sub-national level. Thus, while we may be at peace observing India achieving self-sufficiency in foodgrains in the 1970s-80s and being able to sustain it since then, there are millions who go to bed without one square meal a day. In the estimate of Food and Agricultural Organisation (FAO), over 225 million Indians remain chronically undernourished. The National Nutrition Monitoring Bureau said, "In 2000-01 about half of the rural children in India, that are below five years of age, suffered from malnutrition and about 40 per cent of the adults suffered from chronic energy deficiency . . . This is due to the fact that a substantial proportion of the people are too poor to buy enough food . . ." (Radhakrishna, 2005).

Despite West Bengal's remarkable achievements in agriculture, the percentage of people not getting two square meals a day is quite high. In fact, the percentage is the highest among all major states. According to

NSS Reports (415, 466, and 512), West Bengal occupies the highest position, both in case of households reporting, "not getting two square meals a day" in some months of the year, as well as "households not getting the same throughout the year". The reported inadequacy in West Bengal has remained at the topmost position now, almost for a decade. In fact, the percentage has seen an increase over the years.

We require detailed and sustained investigations of hunger and food inadequacy to reveal the truth about the "food question in West Bengal", and to establish in the face of persistent denial that there is indeed something wrong in this land. The trend of increasing food insecurity is alarming. A section of the population is now being condemned to increasing poverty and hunger, though the overall official headcount ratio of poverty appears to be on a decline. The nutritional status of the dalits and indigenous population groups is worse. In 1998-99, over 60% of the dalit children below 5 suffered from malnutrition. Apart from malnutrition, hunger deaths are regularly taking place. Death from lack of food, becoming common also in West Bengal, can be traced to a severe lapse in the Right to Food mechanism; and a deep void in the understanding that access to sufficient amount of quality food is one of the most basic rights to be enjoyed by every citizen of the country. All other rights fall short if the right to survival and, thereby, the Right to Food is infringed.

This paper intends to show what constitutes the mechanics of the legal and the administrative world of food rights in the Dooars area of West Bengal, specifically food rights of the tea plantation labourers. Also, in this context, I would try to show how some of the rights-bearing institutions have negotiated the right to food as being not a standalone right but as something constituted of other rights, such as the right to information, communication, and other rights to services and umbrella guarantees such as the fundamental right to life and freedom from deprivation. The People's Union for Civil Liberties (hereafter PUCL) versus Supreme Court of India case of 2001, pertaining to Right to Food, and the interim orders issued in course of the case from time to time have increasingly strengthened the process of destroying the charity façade of these accesses to the state-promised deliverables and have put them as an order of rights. The rights institutions have, thus, come into focus as well as the question of food itself.

ABOUT THE INTERVIEWS

In this paper, we would treat all the set-ups established by legal-political order to facilitate people's access to the rights (like the Block Development Office, the District Magistrate's Office and their subordinate staff, all the offices created for overseeing the smooth and desirable functioning of the food security schemes, and those that undertake audits of these bodies) as institutions meant to facilitate the enjoyment of rights, in this case food right. For the same reason, it does not leave the Supreme Court, the High Court and all other judicial courts out of its purview. The Supreme Court made it clear that prevention of hunger and starvation is "one of the prime responsibilities of the Government – whether Central or State" (Supreme Court Order, dated 20 August, 2001).[1] In the case of state governments, the Chief Secretary is answerable to the Court on behalf of the government. In some circumstances (such as starvation deaths), the Court has stated that the Chief Secretary himself or herself would be held "responsible" for violations of the order.[2] However, such institutions are not enough for safeguarding the rights and people themselves set up platforms for action when they see that the above fall short of expectations. These are civil society organisations, which lend support from the base to the guarantee of rights. These are all rights-bearing institutions and in their common bid to make the subjects into rights-bearing individuals, interfaces occur between rights institutions.

Civil society organisations have an important role in implementing the Right to Food. First, they have played an advocacy role in according greater recognition to the Right to Food, and in initiating a code of conduct. This code of conduct is designed to overcome some weaknesses in the human rights instruments that recognise the Right to Food, for example, the lack of precision in the description of this right and the state obligations involved in achieving it. Secondly, through their participation in the regular sessions of the Committee on Economic, Social and Cultural Rights, they have also highlighted violations of the Right to Food. At the national level too, they have greater role in exposing its violations and in promoting its justifiability has been significant (Gaiha, 2003).

The following report bases itself substantially on interviews, many of them done at formal and informal gatherings of groups of labourers from the tea gardens. Labourers employed in the tea gardens have been interviewed both at their quarters, at the coolie lines as well as at worksite. Some were interviewed at the researcher's place of stay. Interviews were conducted with the National Rural Employment Guarantee Scheme (NREGS) workers and officials. These interviews were taken both at the worksite as well as away. A handful of interviews were conducted with people having grievances about the functioning of the food/work schemes in operation. These were done outside the District Magistrate's Office in Jalpaiguri. Another group of people interviewed consists of a mixed bag of civil society organisation activists from inside and outside the tea gardens, including women's organisations and women's wings of umbrella bodies, plantation labour union workers, and people working voluntarily for the better access of people to the government schemes. Questions were asked regarding the functioning of the government schemes and what they thought they should do additionally to make it work. Also, personal experiences of the labourers were noted. Trained muster roll verifiers in case of NREGS and trained Integrated Child Development Services (hereafter ICDS) operation verifiers from among the women's organisations were interviewed to get an idea about the kind of hindrances they face. The interviewees were picked at random and on account of availability. Some were located with the help of women's organisations.

WHY THE TEA PLANTATIONS OF NORTH BENGAL?

Starvation deaths do not occur only in villages and only peasants do not die of hunger. Talking of starvation and starvation death cases, deaths of workers have been equally noticeable in West Bengal, especially in the 1980s and 1990s when hundreds of mills and other industrial units were closed down. They were called with black humour "sunset industries". Deaths then started in the tea gardens of North Bengal. Food right violations became most common in these pockets, far removed from the metropolitan bustling pots. The worst affected have been the Dooars and the Terai, the significant areas in Jalpaiguri and Darjeeling districts of West Bengal. Jalpaiguri district has been one of the worst sufferers in this connection. In a span of the last 10 years, starvation deaths have occurred noticeably in the plantation zones of this area. It is estimated that over 500 workers or their family members died of starvation in 2003-04 alone (Bhowmik, 2005). With plummeting financial conditions of the tea estates, several tea gardens stopped functioning and their workers faced starvation. Even the ones which continued to function stopped paying regular wages and rations to the labourers. This affected the household food intake directly.

The protracted crisis entangling the plantation sector in India since the late 1990s has attracted wide attention. The crisis reached its peak in 2003-04, when the tea production process was brought to a halt. The survival strategies adopted by the planters' community were broadly confined to cost-saving and labour-displacing measures such as dilution and even abandonment of prescribed agro-management practices, labour retrenchment, lockouts and resistance to routine tripartite negotiations. One of the options available for reducing the average unit cost of production is slashing the expenditure on major cost components like, for example, an immediate wage slash or freeze, as might be suitable in a particular case (George and Joseph, 2005). Thus, there was a deliberate effort to put the major part of the burden on the plantation labourer. George and Joseph point out that the worst hit have been the plantation labourers in Kerala. Many estates, as in West Bengal, have declared lockouts there. Several others have summarily abandoned routine operations.

The tea plantations actually represent an entire framework of work culture carefully put together in pieces over time. Labour was brought from other areas and moulded to fit the required bill. The first set of workers was brought from Jharkhand and Bihar. Entire families were brought and settled in the plantations as coolies. The first batch of planters began their commercial business almost neck to neck with the time when slavery was uprooted. What they needed was a replication of the same institution. Slaves were needed, in some way or the other. Therefore, a huge thrust was laid upon tea and sugarcane plantation. This, however, generated a labour class that was completely dependent on the plantation or the planter for their sustenance. No alternative was left for them for skill diversification besides their present occupation, should there occur any crisis in the present industry. One might ask, and legitimately, that does skill at all play a significant role in ensuring one's Right to Food? The answer might be that neither in case of a smoothly functioning industry nor in a stagnated state, as in the present situation, does skill ensure any better access to food rights. It is true that when a labourer works in a tea garden which is not yet closed, he/she can earn a regular wage, can buy food and get rations at relatively lower costs. However, all such entitlements fall far short of the required levels of goods to survive when the market crashes, and the tea garden labourers have nowhere to go. In that respect at least, the state-sponsored schemes that promise to rescue the unemployed are expected to raise them to a better position.[3]

There are around 6,000 tea growers and 67 bought leaf factories (BLFs) in West Bengal. Tea production in these small tea gardens is quite significant, being around 21-22 million kilograms per year. The increased supply and unequal price competition have considerably eroded the viability of many tea estates. The estates most affected are primarily those which neglected taking measures in the past for improving the productivity of the gardens. The ability of most of the better managed tea gardens to cope with current situations in the tea industry in the state indicates that with prudent management practices, survival of tea units should not be a problem (*Economic Review*, 2007-08).[4, 5]

In a meeting with "hungry workers" on 25 September 2008, at a 72-hour sit-in organised by his party in Siliguri, Partha Chattopadhyay, Trinamul Congress leader and Leader of Opposition in the West Bengal Legislative Assembly, said that even if the land was not fertile for the growth of the tea bushes, it was the responsibility of the state government to take measures so that the fertility quotient rises. At another meeting with the workers of the closed Raipur tea estate, the newly formed Trinamul union's line of action follows a path where direct party membership is not the main aim. Rather, labourers have been promised all aid if they organise themselves under the banner of the Cha Bagan Pratiraksha Committee, formed much on the line of Krishi Jami Pratiraksha Committee of Singur. In a meeting organised at the Raipur tea estate, Jalpaiguri, he said, ". . . It's high time all tea workers united and launched a massive movement together to save the tea gardens. If you don't do it now, the entire tea industry will die. You need not join Trinamul. You can form a Cha Bagan Pratiraksha Committee yourself and I promise every possible support to you" (*Times of India*, 18 June 2007).

The tea industry has been one of the worst sufferers of this oscillation in performance standards. The tea industry employs the largest number of workers in the organised sector. Tea estates in Jalpaiguri employ around 2,50,000 permanent labourers. Wages have been traditionally low in this sector despite changes in governments. Wage deficiencies easily translate into shortfalls in the buying capacity of most essential goods for the household. Sustained deficits corrode the delivery of very basics like food, clothing, shelter, health care and education. Income shortage and shortage of purchasing power among tea garden labourers have translated to a situation where workers have to starve and cannot do anything about it, unless they receive support from outside. The Dooars region has seen closure of 16 estates employing over 10,000 workers. If their family members are included, then the number of affected population increases four to five times. The running estates cannot absorb these workers as, they say, they are themselves sick (Bhowmik, 2009).

To this, one has to add the fact that West Bengal government has no minimum wage regulation for the tea industry. There has been no statutory declaration of minimum wages for the West Bengal tea industry since 1956-57. While in states such as Tamil Nadu, Kerala, Karnataka and even Assam, minimum wages for tea labourers are in place, it seems that the West Bengal government does not think such a step was necessary for the workers in tea gardens who mostly belong to indigenous population groups (Nandy, 2005). The wages offered here are well below the levels in other major tea-producing states. Despite ration subsidy of Rs.10 per day as part of daily wage, owing to the absence of a benchmark related to minimum wage, tea garden workers' conditions remain grim. This was evident from the wage negotiations that followed the strikes in 2005. Before the new agreement, the daily wage of a worker was Rs.45.90. Each worker also got subsidised ration (2.2 kg of rice/wheat at the rate of 40 paise per kg). Ration supply was denied on a day when it would be a holiday, or a worker would be on leave. Following the strikes, the trade unions bargained with the planters for a minimum daily wage of Rs.88. This was derived from the calculations of the need-based minimum wage declared in the Indian Labour Conference of 1957. The employers' association agreed to an increase of only Rc.1, claiming that the industry was in shambles and wage increase was an impossible proposition (Bhowmik, 2005). Moreover, the workers were denied any arrears whatsoever, on the ground that the agreement did not take effect from the date from which the last agreement lapsed.

MECHANISMS: STATE AND NON-STATE/FACILITATING BODIES AND THEIR INTERFACES WITH RIGHTS

Food crisis shot up so much that, in April 2004, the Supreme Court Right to Food Bench passed certain orders for the closed tea gardens. The Government of West Bengal was instructed to:

- Declare all plantation workers in closed gardens as Below Poverty Line (BPL) with immediate effect.
- Supply the garden labourers with Antyodaya Anna Yojna (AAY) foodgrains at the rate of Rs.3/kg of rice and Rs.2/kg of wheat. The quantity allowed would be 35 kg per family per month.
- Send in a medical team consisting of doctors, nurses, pharmacists with medicines, and at least twice a week to each garden.
- Make sure that each worker at least gets 15 days of work each month under the Sampoorna Grameen Rojgar Yojna (SGRY). In gardens closed for more than a year, the workers would get an unemployment allowance of Rs.500 per month.

Additionally, the West Bengal government came up with certain regulations saying that the Labour and Labour Relations Department of the state have to take up steps for immediate regularisation of the new plantations (belonging to small growers mainly) on an urgent basis, including those plantations that involve vested land. The abandoned gardens were planned to put open to bids from promoters. In order to provide temporary relief to the workers of the abandoned gardens and their families, workers of several tea gardens were planned to be brought under relief measures under various programmes. These included supplementary nutrition programme under the ICDS, mobile health clinics under the State Health Development Project, drinking water under the PHE (Public Health Engineering) Department, rural water supply programme under the zilla parishad, cooked Mid-Day Meal Scheme under the School Education Department etc. (*Economic Review*, 2004-05). Numerous wage employment schemes have been set on a roll.

Keeping in view the above minimum provisions stipulated by the Court the other arrangements set in place by the Court injunctions, we can map the interfaces of the people with the rights institutions. This foregrounds in a way the contradiction inherent in the entire Right to Food issue namely that while the public in these orders appears only as a recipient class (therefore object of a state-sponsored charity), interfaces and encounters of various types and in forms occur with regard to rights acquisition and rights denial, both of which transform the non-derogatory nature of a right as one of intermittent contestation. As Gaiha (2003) points out, the implementation of this right is a major concern and the three areas of the state's responsibility are: (1) the obligation to respect, (2) the obligation to protect, and (3) the obligation to fulfill.[6] For example, with respect to the protracted closure of several tea gardens in the Dooars, the Union minister of state, Mr Jairam Ramesh said on 15 September 2007 (*The Statesman*, Business page, 16 September 2007) that, the government would make use of the Section 16(E) of the Tea Act of 1953 for the first time against six tea gardens of the Dooars to take over the gardens lying closed for more than three months without investigation or finding a new management for the gardens, which failed to reopen and regularise themselves despite repeated talks and promises to the government about the same.

Factors such as public pressure and social audit arise here. Public action, therefore, is not the only state action but consists of various social and political activities that go far beyond the atomic individual or single institutional initiatives. The domain of public action includes an equally significant share of non-state activities.

In order to fight back the crisis evident from the first rush of food shortage reports, the government devised certain policies with focus on household level food security. In April 2001, People's Union for Civil Liberties (PUCL), Rajasthan filed a writ petition in the Supreme Court seeking legal enforcement of the Right to Food. The basic argument was that the Right to Food was an implication of the fundamental "Right to Life" enshrined in Article 21 of the Indian Constitution. Following this, Supreme Court hearings on various aspects of the right to food have been held at regular intervals. This public interest litigation (PIL) is far from being over, and it may take years before the Supreme Court pronounces its final "judgement". But many interim orders have already been passed. (Supreme Court Orders on The Right To Food: A Tool For Action, 2008). For determining that a household gets sufficient food, the per capita/consumer unit food energy intake is taken as a measure of food security. Calorie intakes are compared. The government has decided to implement some new measures or invigorate the old ones. These are institutions like the Public Distribution System (PDS), which distribute items like foodgrains and sugar at administered prices through fair price shops. A range of food-for-work and other wage employment programmes are there, such as the National Rural Employment Guarantee Scheme. In the latter category, people are paid partially or fully in rendering their labour for public works. Moreover, they are able to suggest programmes for public works themselves, like social forestry, making of pavements, road construction and repair, upgrading community sanitation and water supply facilities.

FUNCTIONING OF SOME GOVERNMENT SCHEMES

Some programmes are meant directly for women and children. For example, the mid-day meal and the supplementary nourishment programme are for women and children. Table 1 gives an idea of the schemes in operation and their output over the last few years in eight different closed/abandoned tea gardens of the Dooars. The table corroborates the fact that there are huge discrepancies as far as the results of the food-for-work and cash distribution programmes are concerned. Here, as one would find, there is involvement of direct cash distribution. The dilemma at the administrative level has always been one of whether it is more effective to distribute cash doles or assist the people in kind. The following table shows that in some tea gardens like Kathalguri, Samsing and Chamurchi, there have been more than 6,000 man-days of work created, some like Red Bank, Raipur, Bamandonga and Tondoo have received less than 5,000 man-days of work. Surendranagar has had only 1,458 man-days' of work. Cash distribution for Surendranagar was Rs.15,600 thousand which was also drastically less than Kathalguri, which received Rs.1,17,200 thousand and was the third highest amount of cash dole receivers among the gardens reviewed on the list below. Samsing received the highest amount of cash as well as one of the highest number of mandays of work. While in case of Special Grameen Rojgar, Kathalguri, Surendranagar, Chamurchi, Red Bank or Ramjhora failed to draw any monetary investment, Samsing drew Rs.1,02,300 thousand with Raipur as a distant second at Rs.1,200 thousand.

TABLE 1. Status of Food for Work Programme Sampoorna Grameen Rojgar Yojna (SGRY) and Cash Distribution Programme of the Government of India as on 04.01.2006 (w.e.f. 15.12.2005)

Name of tea garden	Present Status	Food for Work Programme			Special Grameen Rojgar (Cash Distribution)	
		Number of Man-days	Cash Distribution (in thousand Rupees)	Food Grain Disbursed (in Quintals)	Number of Beneficiaries	Amount of spent (in thousand Rupees)
Kathalguri	Closed	8,500	1,17,200	68,920	0	0
Surendranagar	Abandoned	1,458	15,600	12,456	0	0
Chamurchi	Abandoned	6,276	85,020	50,682	0	0
Red Bank	Abandoned	4,375	60,500	35,125	0	0
Raipur	Abandoned	3,543	71,596	24,745	200	1,200
Ramjhora	Closed	5,515	1,76,480	27,575	0	0
Samsing	Closed	6,572	2,31,440	39,432	1,705	1,02,300
Bamandonga and Tondoo	Closed	4,100	82,000	28,700	0	0
Total		40,339	8,39,836	2,87,635	1,905	1,14,300

Source: Economic Review 2007-08, Page 165, Para 5.145, Government of West Bengal

Following the public interest suit by the PUCL, the Supreme Court has laid down a formal structure of accountability, mentioned below. However, as we shall show, tracing the Right to Food along these lines is not easy and may be confusing. Box 1 elaborates the structure of formal accountability.

BOX 1

LINES OF ACCOUNTABILITY: The 8 May 2002 Order of the Supreme Court

On 8 May 2002, the Supreme Court laid down specific lines of accountability and grievance procedures for the implementation of all "interim orders". The key directions issued on 8 May 2002 are as follows:

1. "The Gram Sabhas are entitled to conduct a social audit into all Food/Employment schemes and to report all instances to misuse of funds to the respective implementing authorities, who shall on receipt of such complaints, investigate and taken appropriate action in accordance with law."
2. "On a complaint being made to the . . . CEO/Collector regarding non-compliance of the orders of this Court the Concerned CEO/ Collector shall record the salient features of the complaint in a register maintained for this purpose, acknowledge receipt of the complaint and forthwith secure compliance with this Court's order."
3. "The CEO/Collector of all the Districts in the States and territories shall scrutinise the action taken by all the implementing agencies within their jurisdiction to ensure compliance with this court's orders and report to the Chief Secretary."
4. "The responsibility for implementation of the order of this Court shall be that of the CEO/Collector. The Chief Secretary will ensure compliance with the order of this Court."
5. "Dr N C Saxena, former Planning Secretary, Government of India, and Mr S R Shankaran, former Secretary, Rural

Development, Government of India, shall function as Commissioners of this Court for the purpose of looking into any grievance that my persist after the above-mentioned grievance resolution procedure has been exhausted."

6. "On the Commissioner's recommending a course of action to ensure compliance with this Court's order, the State Government/UT administrations, shall forthwith act upon such recommendation and report compliance."
7. "The Commissioners shall be at liberty to take the assistance of individuals and reliable organisations in the State and Union Territories. All officials are directed to fully cooperate with such persons/organisations, to bring about effective monitoring and implementation of the order of this Court."
8. "The Gram Sabhas are empowered to monitor the implementation of the various schemes and have access to relevant information relating to, inter alia, selection of beneficiaries and the disbursement of benefits. The Gram Sabhas can raise their grievances in the manner set out above and the redressal of the grievances shall be done accordingly."

Source: Supreme Court Orders On the Right to Food: A Tool for Action by Jean Dreze, 2008

Whatever emerges from the idea of relative deprivation, starvation is a sure indication of poverty.[7] As Amartya Sen and Jean Dreze put it, this can be plugged only by concentrating ". . . on the ability of people to command food through the legal means available in the society, including the use of production possibilities, trade opportunities, entitlements vis a vis the state, and other methods of acquiring food. A person starves either because he does not have the ability to command enough food, or because he does not use his ability to avoid starvation" (Sen and Dreze, 1989). But locating the Right to Food as a right, this appears to be a problematic affair, especially when one seeks to see what people conceive the right to be, and accordingly, the contradictions that emerge when a particular perception comes face to face with the existing delivery mechanisms, that is, the state. In fact, a big question mark develops over the issue of whether the state is any more acknowledged as the sole delivery mechanism.

DEMAND FOR SOCIAL AUDIT OF NREGA

Facing the first hindrance at the level of securing the Right to Work (as the means to right to food), a letter dated 16 April 2008 (undersigned by Tapas Modak of Churabhandar Gram Panchayat, on behalf of 102 job applicants from the same panchayat, and received with due stamp by the Block Development Officer, Maynaguri) seeks to remind the state authority that an application for job under the NREGA was made at the BDO's Office (see Annexure 1). But no work opportunity had been forwarded though 15 days have passed after the initial letter. Therefore, the BDO's office should try and arrange for unemployment allowance for the persons applying for job till the latter could be assured. The next letter to the BDO, dated 8 May 2008 (see Annexure 2), draws upon the first letter and says that despite pleading for unemployment allowance on the pretext of not having been given any job under the NREGA, the 102 applicants did not receive any monetary assistance or information pertaining to that even after the passage of a month. Moreover, when they went to seek information, they were told that since they had not applied for the allowance by filling up a certain form number 4, they were not being given the unemployment allowance. But the rules and regulations do not speak anything about the form number 4 mentioned by the BDO's office. Under such conditions, they were now requesting the BDO to intervene and arrange for their allowance or else they would be forced to organise a sit-in demonstration and block the National Highway number 31.

This was, therefore, a dialogic situation where one person was speaking on behalf of 102 others to secure certain benefits promised by the government that the latter had failed to deliver, and in such a case was negotiating the right to organise a demonstration exposing the government's and the local administration's inability to deliver or explain the non-deliverance. The author of the letter, we should note, does not apply for a job himself. He, in a representative manner, writes the letter. This is a visible step towards information acquisition. Therefore, the state ceases to be regarded as the one and only facilitating mechanism, as far as Right to Food is concerned, because while we look forward to the state for the availability of food, at the same time, we advocate community vigilance and social audit mechanisms which stretch to the individual citizen level in its most ambitious form. The state, of course, adopts the path of legal intervention and directives towards implementation consequent upon complaints filed from the ground level. But it is a long route and takes time for the actual policy benefits to reach the bottom through the routine intermediary structures. It is often a very convoluted question: who should be giving the people food, in case they fail to sustain themselves?

If one chooses to ask the question straight away, who should be held "directly responsible" in case there is a breach of the Right to Food, meaning, who should be approached if any of the multifarious schemes the government has designed to ensure equitable distribution of food along the length and breadth of the society fails to deliver; the answers which emerge are fascinating. The "idea of responsibility" varies to a great extent from case to case, but keeping a more or less tangible relation with the issue of information dissemination among the subjects of deliverance. Invariably, there are occasions when we find the state mechanism falling short of communicating the information to the hungry about available ways out of the food crisis. A look at the annual Information and Publicity budget of the West Bengal government corroborates this point. Under the Tenth Five Year Plan, the information expenses in 2003-04 were expected to be only Rs.0.94 crores whereas the ultimate expenditure was Rs.4.29 crores. Only in 2005-06, the budget was Rs.12.84 crores, a onetime information and communication bid in the wake of the introduction of the NREGS in 2005. The figure again went down to Rs.7.76 crores in 2006-07 (*Economic Review*, 2003-04 and 2007-08).

As we know, the basic change NREGA confers on people is guarantee on the right to employment and making the government accountable (Gopal, 2009). Herein, the state's evident inability makes way for the non-state bodies as actors to pitch in. The next letter, dated 29 July 2008 (see Annexure 3), signed by Tapas Modak, is written on the letterhead of an operating civil society organisation, Swadhikar.[8] The letter is titled "Social Audit According to the NREGA". It says that three years have passed after the implementation of the NREGS. Yet, the local administration has not organised any social audit meeting prescribed under the Act. Moreover, even if three consecutive years were added, the people of Churabhandar had not got 100 days of work. The letter further says that the social audit is supposed to prescribe facilities that need to be built for local area development and that, in turn, would generate man-days of work. But none of these were done. The people of Churabhandar, therefore, wanted such a social audit meeting to be held in seven days' time in the presence of the BDO. We can see how, in this way, the rights process assumes the structure of an interlocked system of schemes, failures, facilitating and advocating institutions that would make people more active for their rights and enable them to demand justice from the state. But does food become available through this route? We do not have a confirmed answer.

Hunger Deaths

In such situation, a perfectly logical structure of accountability and service delivery of the state may lose meaning and relevance for the people at the receiving end, who are now reduced to symbols of charity when the former systematically fails to set up communication with the latter. At such points, people rely more on community structures; the state is kept aside. It is the community which stands for guaranteeing the rights of the betrayed. Geeta Chikbarik's parents died of starvation in 2005. She had four siblings to feed, and she herself was only 15 years old at that point of time. It was not long before she herself fell sick, trying to earn a handful. When her neighbours understood that Geeta too faced the threat of death, there was a mass uprising. Geeta's family was being taken care of by the neighbourhood people who were themselves unable to gather a square meal for their own families, but continued to stand by the girl. The District Magistrate and the Block Development Officer were forced to intervene after repeated sit-ins by the tea garden people. They thought she should be taken to the hospital for medical attention and food. However, she was discharged in three days, with diagnosis of severe malnutrition. She died after a few days of her release and her death certificate said it was a case of cardio-respiratory failure. It has been a standard practice of the health service personnel of the plantation sector to underestimate the health crises faced by the underfed and starving patients. Grave cases of malnutrition and starvation deaths have been certified as cardio-respiratory failures – since that is the final cause of death for all – and summarily dismissed from public attention

The death registers show that most of the workers die due to blood dysentery and cardio-respiratory failure. However, the maximum percentage dies of causes "not given" or "others", which — it is not difficult to understand – are hunger deaths given the present condition of these gardens [Sunil Scaria, nd]. Geeta's siblings are now being taken care of by the erstwhile munshi of the Kathalguri garden, Gopal Chikbarik, who is also a distant relation of Geeta. Having been the munshi at one point of time, Chikbarik commands some amount of extra resources than other labourer families in the tea gardens. He affirms that conditions in the gardens have been deteriorating over time, and more rapidly now. The Chikbarik case points out, with some clarity, how the community becomes a critical factor when the state fails to ensure the rights.[9]

The Chikbarik case, among many other things, calls for a review of the health care situation of the tea gardens. This is all the more because Right to Food is one social right which cannot be seen in complete isolation from other rights such as right to education or right to information. Food, education and health must be interlinked to build capacity of the population so that they can become self-sustaining in due course of time. The government has provisions up its sleeve, but implementation is where there is a major gap. As mentioned above, the Government of West Bengal was advised to send trained medical personnel to each closed/abandoned garden twice a week. But the real situation, documented in the figures given by the state government, in Table 2, illustrates a further aggravation of rights violation. Unlike elementary education, health care is yet to be widely accepted as a basic right of all Indian citizens. This ambiguity has facilitated the continuation if not intensification of state abdication in this field in the 1990s. Public expenditure on health has declined as a proportion of GDP, from an abysmally low base (about 1%). And the lack of any major initiative in the field of health care during the last 10 years contrasts with wide-ranging innovations in the field of elementary education. (Dreze, 2004) The West Bengal government's figures follow in Table 2 and show that though in one garden the number of visits had been up to the requirement, all others had been totally deprived of their entitlements. Samsing and Bamandonga-Tondoo had been visited only twice while Surendranaga and Red Bank had three visits.

TABLE 2 : Status of Situation of Health Care in Closed/Abandoned Gardens in terms of Health Care Entitlements like Mobile Medical Van Visit Conducted by the Government of India as on 4 January 2006 (w.e.f 15 December 2005)

Name of garden	No. of days mobile medical van visited the garden	No. of patients treated with medicine
Kathalguri	5	218
Surendranagar	3	27
Chamurchi	5	146
Red Bank	3	121
Raipur	16	384
Ramjhora	5	210
Samsing	2	286
Bamandonga and Tondoo	2	88
Total	41	1,480

Source: *Economic Review*, 2007-08, p.165, para 5.145, Government of West Bengal

POLICY OF EXCLUSION AND THE FUSS OF "JURISDICTION"

The right to non-exclusion, as put forward by Jean Dreze and Amartya Sen, can be discussed in this context. A subsistence food ration provision is something that everyone should have as an inalienable right. This should be accompanied with different types of basic necessities like education, and health care because their absence would only protract the scarcity of the food and would fail to make the Right to Food incontrovertible. Therefore, universal support is the minimum requisite for this right. In fact, one can say that it is public action coupled with social audit of entitlement delivery that would bridge the gap between the promises and the delivery, that is, the schemes formulated and their implementation for the purpose of public good, making the access unhindered. This public action could be collaborative as well as adversarial, depending on the nature of perception that the people receive. Sen and Dreze (1989) point out, "... the public can do a great deal for itself even without governmental assistance . . because the nature of government policy can depend very extensively on the nature of public activism, including articulated demands and criticisms". This point is more relevant in case of the tea workers whose industry is on the verge of closure and who are caught in a storm where, on the one hand, they have their entitlements only as per the Plantations Labour Act, 1953, whereby their entitlements can only be delivered by the tea estates and, on the other hand, the condition is such that they cannot legitimately demand assistance from panchayat as long as they continue to be plantation labourers. In such a case of closure, they have to wait for government doles and relief and cannot demand it from the panchayat as long as they are not juridically recognised as panchayat subjects.

In September 2007, when an evaluation of the supplies for the ICDS and PDS by *Swadhikar* revealed that in as many as 26 ICDS centres, the children were offered only two to three biscuits a day, and that eight ration shops were selling rice and wheat much below the standard supplies, the Child Development Programme Office was approached. The office does not keep a phone. Neither do the officers come to work regularly. Women, who work in the Anganwadis, have been threatened with their jobs for talking to "outsiders". The state government evaluations of the services are as follows:

Table 3 shows the work undertaken by the different kinds of food for work programmes in the eight closed/abandoned tea gardens of the Dooars. Here also, the net output is far below the expected and discrepancies are obvious from the figures. Apart from Raipur, no other garden had had a new tube well sunk, and apart from Bamandonga-Tondoo, no other garden had a pilot project started for pregnant/lactating mothers. The distribution of rice under the Supplementary Nutrition Programme (SNP) has been as low as 109 quintals for Red Bank, 264 quintals for Chamurchi and 364 quintals for Samsing. Only Ramjhora received 1,122 quintals. Apart from Bamandonga-Tondoo, all the others received less than 50% of Ramjhora.

The distribution of foodgrains has been elaborated a little more in Table 4. Issuing BPL cards has always been a big problem and the age-old misconception of one card for a household, even if it has more than one nuclear units living under its roof. The situation is same as Bela Bhatia and Jean Dreze (2006) speak of a regular feature of the denial of separate job cards to nuclear families living together as a joint household. According to the guidelines, each nuclear family is entitled to a separate job card. This point, however, has not been clearly conveyed to the panchayat *sevaks*. The distribution of rice and wheat also fall far below the required levels. While Raipur received only 47.07 quintals of rice and wheat each, Kathalguri received 238.00 quintals of rice and wheat.

TABLE 3: Status of Supplementary Nutrition Programme (SNP): ICDS, Mid-Day Meal, SNP for Pregnant and Lactating Mothers/Sinking of Tube Wells in Closed/Abandoned Tea Gardens, as on 4 January 2006 (w.e.f. 15 December 2005).

Name of the garden	No. of new tube well sinking completed	No. of of children under ICDS, SNP sinking (6 months to 6 years – daily basis) basis)	Normal SNP for pregnant mothers and adolescent girls (rice distribution in Quintals)	Pilot project for nutrition to lactating mothers	Cooked mid-day meal scheme started in no. of schools
Kathalguri	0	3,266	487	No	1
Surendranagar	0	3,893	441	No	1
Chamurchi	0	1867	264	No	2
Red Bank	0	1,400	109	No	1
Raipur	4	4,510	770	No	1
Ramjhora	0	6,270	1,122	No	2
Samsing	0	1,492	364	No	
Bamandonga and Tondoo	0	4,946	585	Yes	3
Total	4	27,644	4,142		19

Source: *Economic Review*, 2007-08, p.165, para 5.145, Government of West Bengal

The norm laid down by the Central Government, of having one Anganwadi Centre per 500 of population is largely ignored. For example, in Chamurchi GP, there are only 6 ICDS centres for a population of 8,000. The facilities available are *kachcha* latrines and no kitchen. The food served is cooked in the open. It is not at all possible for the small number of ICDS there to take care of every child in the block. Pregnant women are denied the services promised to them by the state, like monetary aid of Rs.500 per month till delivery. Jashomati Orao, from Namji line, Betguri tea estate, Malbazar block, says, against a demand of the monthly financial aid, the women responsible for disbursal of the money tells that only Rs.400 would be paid and the rest would go to the office people as cost of services made available. The right guaranteed, therefore, comes at a price payable to the people working for and making up the face of the state machinery. Is this a kind of rent payment to the state for its services to its citizens at each of the delivery points? Persistent agitation by the people with the help of the outsiders and self-help groups (SHG) were mainly responsible for the increase in the number of Anganwadi Centres from 227 to 977 in Malbazar (Seetamani Orao, Mahila Jagriti Sangh, Malbazar).[10]

TABLE 4: Distribution of Foodgrains in Closed/Abandoned Tea Gardens under SPL AAY in November 2005

Name of the garden	No. of families which I Cards were issued	Adult Members	Minor Members	Rice Distribution (in Quintals)	Wheat Distribution (in Quintals)
Kathalguri	6,500	5,616	2,368	238.00	238.00
Surendranagar	1,458	711	205	28.47	28.47
Chamurchi	6,276	3,949	410	145.39	145.39
Red Bank	4,375	2,264	715	91.75	91.75
Raipur	3,543	1,170	350	47.07	47.07
Ramjhora	5,515	3,277	1,217	135.69	135,69
Samsing	6,572	3,505	1,417	170.40	170.40
Bamandonga and Tondoo	1,150	1,393	1,496	115.00	115.00
Total	35,389	21,885	8,178	971.77	971.77

Source: *Economic Review*, 2007-08, p.165, para 5.145, Government of West Bengal

One good example of what we are discussing can be the NREGS. It fell short of people's expectations, notwithstanding the fact that the scheme got the backing of legislation. Against the promised 100 days of work (and, therefore, food) a year, in 2006, only 66 days of work was made available to the people of Maynaguri. In 2007, it further shrunk to 27 days. "After repeated deputations at the BDO's office and express instructions from the latter, there was some formal work distribution, though the work was not given finally," says Tapas Modak, Churabhandar of Maynaguri Block.[11] The administrative offices often take the path of straightaway refusal to receive the work applications people seek to file when NREG work is not found available. When Tapas Modak organised a sit-in at the NBDO office after repeated denial of NREGS work, and there was significant amount of furore raised over the latter, the local political bosses and union goons came with the threat of imprisonment to ensure that there was no media coverage. Swadhikar self-help group from Maynaguri says there are discrepancies also in the muster roll. Moreover, the muster roll is never taken to the field and the administrators tend to work from offices, far away from the field. The daily wage needs to be coaxed out as the money is generally kept away even if work is done. This leaves the unemployed to another paradoxical situation: work with private employers like local landlords would earn them less amount of money as daily wage compared with the state-sponsored programme of NREGS. Yet, they would get their wage on completion of the day's task, enabling them to buy the necessaries. The state scheme, on the other hand, debilitates this smooth process because the money is paid much later and mostly in lot for work for a number of days. Thus, the situation they face and the choice they have to make is: where should they work?

However, the NREGS continues to be one of the most important policy assistances required by the plantation labourers. The tea gardens can offer only four to five months of intensive work, from July to October. During this time, there is maximum leaf yield. The rest of the year, they need work from the NREGS. The NREGS is, therefore, promising – particularly in terms of finding work in the months – which are non-functional with respect to the tea garden work schedule. But the NREGS requires rigorous initial groundwork. In each of the villages, at least 1,000-1,500 job cards are to be procured. Voluntary workers have to go to almost all houses to talk about job cards and why the people need them. There are also deputations to this effect. It is an extremely difficult task to procure job cards. Jasomati Orao says she had to go to every household to create awareness about job card procurement. In an optimistic mood, she says, ". . . it is obvious that I should talk to the young in the garden . . . however, I do not even leave the old men and women . . .".[12]

Even after such mobilisation work at the social level, due to which it could be ensured that at least a sizeable section of the people had job cards under the NREGS, there have been huge challenges to the right to find work. Sibani Orao from Wasibari Tea Garden says, when she went ahead with a work unavailability petition to the Panchayat Samiti, she was told, "... there's no money and therefore no work; ... by the way, who are you to demand work?"[13] The last statement is self-explanatory in pointing out how exactly the people on the other side of the table view the common people who are on this side as far as rights are concerned. One has to remember that this is a population group which is dependent directly on selling its labour power and procuring food out of that. We are not discussing a population group which produces subsistence crop to see them through most of the year, and would require work only when the need to buy their food outside that crop availability would appear. The tea labourer produces cash crop. Therefore, once the garden is closed down, that labourer must find out work to continue to live even for the next day.

Living in a Hunger Regime

Among the places, there are two gardens infamous for starvation deaths. These are the Kathalguri tea estate in Dhupguri administrative block and Bhernoberi tea estate in Kalchini block. Kathalguri saw as many as 20 starvation deaths across 7 families in 2003-04. Bhernoberi, however, is a much more bitter case, where, in addition to a death toll of 106, malnutrition and starvation still persist. These two tea gardens are classic examples where systematic deprivation pushes the workers to extreme points.

In 2006, Phulwanti Kharia lost her husband Bablu to prolonged starvation. Her home collapsed and her present dwelling was constructed with the Rs 10,000 compensation made available to her after her husband's death through a movement by the Bhernoberi workers. Phulwanti has, however, lost her eyesight. She lives with her three children, two boys and a girl, all of whom suffer from diseases that owe their origin to Phulwanti's malnourished pregnancy and lack of proper nutrition after birth. Phulwanti's mother-in-law laments that the widow does not have her name up in the BPL list yet. It is immensely difficult because Phulwanti lives with her children in that part of the coolie line, which is outside the plots of housing offered by the plantation administration. It is worthy to note in this regard that the garden administration does not offer housing to all its labourers. It constructs a stipulated number of coolie residences, which obviously cannot provide a roof for everyone. The rest are somehow or the other managed by the workers. The standard excuse offered by the planters is that most of the latter category belongs to temporary workers, or workers who have been inducted as permanent later and were initially temporary labourers. These households are, therefore, deprived of the standard sanitation facilities of the pucca coolie quarters and cannot expect up-gradations that might be made available to the latter category. Phulwanti's elder son attends the ICDS centre. When asked about its functioning, darker tales come out. The food served is khichri, which often causes digestive problems for children.[14] The standard alternative offered by the block administration is in the form of distributing raw vegetables or lentils, or rice, or wheat supplies to the children, but that also does not serve the purpose because, more often, there is no one at home to take care of the task of cooking. The plantation sector employs female labour; thus, there is no one at home to cook. This reveals another moment of disconnect between the administration and the people. This fact defeats the guideline that administration to be localised, as the present way does not take into account the basic mode of family life in the plantation sector, where women share equal responsibility of wage earning.

One of the most desired functions of the public platforms is that of communicating to the people, the information about what facilities and deliverables they can access to cope with situations that drive them towards starvation, their rights, etc. Sending the information down also needs sending errands especially because the tea gardens are often situated far from each other, and given the labour conditions historically obtaining in the gardens. Public meetings are held and expositions are made on the right to information. In fact, this is one tool, which is utilised both to protest against denial of rights and make efforts for the acquisition of rights. Slogans, posters and plays are produced for the purpose of communication. Public opinion needs to be elicited and also formed. In the background of the system of indentured labour in the past, and its traces continuing today, the right to information is now held up as a means by which the tea garden worker acquires agency or the ability to represent himself/ herself on the issue of denial of rights – in this case food right. Yet, what is evident is that subjection to continuous destitution and gloom results in a situation where the workers are increasingly resigned to the idea that they are rightful or right-endowed human beings. In such a situation, it becomes difficult to reinforce the access to deliverables guaranteed by the state.

POSTERS: SHIFT IN TONE AND STYLE

It is interesting to note, against this background, how the slogans on posters, which have come up from time to time over the last six years during active struggles and periods of relative smooth functioning, undergo transformation in respect of portraying the evolution of the idea of rights. The gradual change in tone corroborates how people have developed through several years of movement and mobilisation the idea that sufficient food is a right. For example, a poster on ICDS says, "*sehat siksha aur poshan, mang raha aaj ka bachpan*" ("Today children need health, education and nutrition"). This talk, in terms of need, a requirement placed in the form of a pleading before an authority responsible for delivery, also doubles up as a consciousness-imparting phrase. It also continues the need-based and rights-based approaches. However, it never crosses the polite undertone it carries. If we juxtapose this with another one on PDS and Right to Food campaign, which says, "*bhookhe pet, bhare godaam, anyay hai, apraadh hai*" ("hungry bellies and filled in godowns this is criminal and unjust"), we get the idea that food is now being conceived as a right and not something someone may want to make available to them out of personal volition. People view the breach of this right as a criminal offence. It marks a moment of break with the earlier ideas of justice in the form of the state aid and assistance. Further, a slogan on non-recruitment of required number of people by the NREG says, "*machine hatao, mazdoor lagao*" or ("shun the machines, employ labourers"). This slogan assumes almost an urgent tone of instruction that clearly goes ahead of the last two slogans. As if it is now telling the public what is good for them and what is not. The worker demands that machines be removed and the same amount of work be given to the people who do not have work at the tea plantations. Therefore, a shift in stance is seen in "*bhookh se mukti, har vyakti ka adhikar*" ("freedom from hunger is the right of every person"). In this way, rights are recommended. A right is a demand, a claim, a proclamation of entitlement that is justiciable. Thus, a shift from "*mang*" or "appeal" to "*adhikar*" or "haq" (right, claim) has occurred in course of a six-year movement. Also, there is shift from politics of pleading to politics of demand, which, if unfulfilled, would either lead to clashes or dragging the aberrant authority to the court. In order to ensure that rights are fulfilled, a continuous momentum is required, which would open up for public scrutiny the gaps between rights guaranteed and their fulfilment, and thereby helping the ensuring of rights.

Perhaps "entitlement" is the concept that lends this required momentum. Entitlement comes as the other side of accountability. In fact, it is the way the state views the issue of compensation in case of death of a person while on duty, portrays in a way that also shows how it sees its accountability. For example, in Kathalguri, a completely closed down tea estate, the compensation for the loss of a family member to death while on work or work-related reasons stood at Rs.8,000. The factory shed was subsequently broken down and the workers complained that the union leaders have sold off its doors, windows and bricks in the recycling market. Acts like this have led to repeated protests inside the gardens against the labour unions, which are seen to have betrayed the plantation workers systematically over the years. It is another paradox that unions work in the tea gardens today, not for the benefit of the workers whom they stand for, but to make merry with the patronage they receive from the planters, in order to keep the workers' issues subdued. One can, therefore, ask who is accountable for this state of affairs – the State, the union or the planters?

Social security against inability to command access to food or against the inability to prevent illegal transfers of deliverables protects a person from perishing. People are enabled to access means available in the society, including the possibilities of production, trade opportunities and other avenues of procuring food. Sitamani Orao, Mahila Jagriti Sangh, Malbazar, says, ". . . infrastructure development can be made in all the Gram Panchayats (GPs) to a large extent. There are social and community infrastructure needs such as planting trees, making embankments, and laying kacha and pucca roads through the coolie lines. If the Block Development Office would take up such projects, it would also result in an increase in the number of man days . . ." In other words, the notion of social security needs to be widened and linked to the concept of right – the food right is contingent on the right to social security.

Owing to the employment guarantee scheme in operation, the worker has a choice of not opting for the low-paying private landlords and go to work at the NREGS sites, if payment is on time. However, this choice unlike now, has to be present at all time. There is palpable pressure from the tea estate owners to stop the NREGS. Rs.75 being the benchmark of minimum wage legalised by the NREGS (at the time of the present research), the landlords have protested often because they also have to pay more than what they used to pay these people initially. This relates to the fact that in the absence of a minimum wage in tea industry in this state, workers work at much less wage on day basis, than what they would get if they had found work under the NREGS. Issuing of job cards was completely stopped following combined pressures of the moneyed sections of society in the Kacha district of Assam. Swadhikar, a civil society organisation and whose name we have referred to earlier in this account, is now engaged in fighting a case in Guwahati High Court on this breach. There are two concrete grounds of suing: 1. Right to Work: The Preamble of NREGS promotes Right to Work as a substantive right, though this was originally a part of the Directive Principles of State Policy and, therefore, was non-justifiable; 2. Discrimination: Under the NREGS, the government guarantees work to the peasants. However, in this case, the tea labourers are being subjected to harmful discrimination by not being given work. This creates a breach with Right to Equality, a fundamental right.

In Itabhata, another completely closed down estate, every household cites at least two deaths from malnutrition and starvation. There have been repeated threats from the existing labour union, not to talk to the "outsiders" indicting the civil society organisations. Conflict with these organisations have become a regular feature after the Ministry of Panchayati Raj made it a rule that any such organisation, having a valid registration number, and working in a particular area, can send a representative to the panchayat of that area. A talk with the Dooars Jagran, one such organisation working in the Dhupguri block, reveals, ". . . It is very difficult to rule out the terror unleashed by the unions. The ration movement was some kind of an eye-opener for the people, when some inroads into union-controlled areas could be made. It happens many a time that while in course of one to one meetings with social campaigners for the right to food, the workers support to proposals formulated by the Dooars Jagran, but in union meetings, they back out . . ." (Partha

Sarathi Bose, Dooars Jagran).[15] There have been 25 deaths from 70 households in Itabhata. In Kathalguri, only two lines, namely the hospital line and the factory line, have been spared from starvation deaths; all others have seen their kith and kin die from being not able to buy food. Itabhata and Kathalguri are gardens where Dooars Jagran works.

A Right to Food, therefore, becomes something that has to be acquired. While observing the rights movements, it is interesting to note the role that women play in it. Traditionally, in the tea gardens, the womenfolk and children would be deployed for plucking tea leaves, and the men would be required to do the husbandry, i.e., cleaning up the undergrowth, maintenance of the garden, building up of roads etc. Wage payment, however, would vary on gender lines though families in the garden are, in most cases, headed by women. Wage discrepancy along gender lines is an acknowledged practice in this sector. While a woman labourer with two children between six and eighteen years of age has a ration entitlement of three (two plus half plus half) units irrespective of the fact that she might be having a husband, other dependants and additional number of children to feed, a male labourer is entitled to four (two plus one plus half plus half) units of ration. This leads to a further marginalisation of women working at the tea gardens. Thus, even overall household food security may not be a guarantee for individual food security (Chaudhary and Parthasarathy, 2007). Notwithstanding the crucial role played by women in tea plantation economy, household food availability does not automatically ensure food and nutrition security for women as individuals. Understandably, there have been agitations by women over the deaths mentioned in this report.

CONCLUDING REMARKS

The longest strike in tea gardens of West Bengal happened in 2005, when, even after so many starvation deaths, the planters refused to revise the daily wage of the labourer. About 3,00,000 tea workers, more than half of whom were women, took part in the strike which spanned over a period of 16 days. There was an estimated daily loss of Rs.15-20 crores. Yet, the workers, on the verge of severe crisis, took the movement forward, with having nothing more to lose. Anyone familiar with the functioning of the tea gardens would confirm that such industry-wide strike in the plantation sector is very rare.

The Third Report of the Commissioner appointed by the Supreme Court for looking into complaints made about the implementation of the food security programmes formulated by the Court during the interim orders issued says, "... there is still a catastrophic failure to protect the fundamental right to life enshrined in Article 21 of the Constitution and an overarching lack of State commitment to the prevention of hunger and starvation in India". It further observes that there have been routine violations of the Court orders by the respondent governments. All Commissioners' reports maintain that employment is the best way to protect the people against hunger. Wage employment guarantee gives a kind of durable protection against vulnerability, which cannot be ensured by other means. Reports say that the BPL lists are unreliable thus putting a question mark on the BPL enumeration mechanism itself.

The Fifth Report puts on record, "... the complete lack of seriousness shown by many state governments to the implementation of schemes under review. On more than one occasion as the report will show, many states have not implemented Supreme Court's directions on one pretext or the other, and repeated orders from the Court have been blatantly ignored with no proper justification" (Fifth Report of the Commissioner, 2004).

However, nothing surpasses the problem of administrative delay in implementing the rights of the people. The same could also be said about the real intention of the people who pitch in to bail the gardens out their crises. Chitta Dey, the convener of the Coordination Committee of Tea Plantation Workers, the apex body of trade unions including the CITU and the INTUC, says: "It is important for the state government to judge the potential and economic background of the willing entrepreneurs. There are instances that new companies and individuals, who had entered into an interim arrangement with old owners, had failed to meet the financial requirements after a few days, leaving the gardens inoperative again ..." (*The Telegraph*, 4 February 2009). The tea gardens have been facing this as another crisis. Many an affluent person would come, take over the estate or a part thereof overnight, and generate new hopes among the workers who would know nothing about the deal that took place perhaps over a drink only to find out the next day that their jobs have been done away with or that the buyer was only worth a day or two to whom the former owner has sold them off. A transparent handover method is yet to be conceived and established.

A tradition of subservient history coupled with the present state of lack of administrative will has kept the people shackled to a non-questioning mode, where asking for food as a right is an anomaly in itself. The Right to Food cuts across an array of all kinds of human rights issues: such as access to health care and education, respect for cultural factors and the right to organise economically and politically. Along with this, one has to add the rights to gainful employment and information. One of the most intractable problems relates to information dissemination. Public awareness creation depends more on non-state bodies much more than on state mechanisms. People are, in many cases, unaware of their entitlements under the food-related schemes. In such a situation, where oraons, kherias, chikbariks and others remain in a condition of basic rightlessness, the entire rights movement falls short of basic requirement: a persistent rights claiming population demanding food and a government that is willing to confer rights on the subjects.

NOTES

1. The Supreme Court in the hearing of the PUCL, Rajasthan, expressed serious concern over the starvation deaths in some states. The Court observed that the Central and State Governments had the primary responsibility to ensure that the foodgrains overflowing the FCI godowns reaches starving people and not wasted. The Court's anxiety was that the poor, destitute and weaker sections of the society should not suffer from hunger and die of starvation. Schemes without implementation have been of no use.
2. Supreme Court Orders On The Right To Food: A Tool for Action; was prepared by Jean Dreze.
3. The tea gardens were set up as isolated settlements, separated from each other and nearby hamlets by forests. Additionally, a policy of systematic exclusion was followed as far as the labourers were concerned in order to radically disenfranchise them from whatever was happening around. The bid to exclude them from the outside world was such that plantation labourers were not allowed to move out of the gardens. There were rules which made it unlawful for any worker to be found outside the garden s/he worked for. Such an offence would translate to a month's of imprisonment and up to 30 lashes (the maximum number permitted outside public judicial discretion) of whip from the manager of the garden. In such circumstances, what followed was the establishment of ties among the labourers themselves, which sustained them at times of dire distress.

In the beginning, northern Indian plantations employed mostly indentured labour. Planters obtained and held their labourers by a harsh system. Severe penal contracts were attached. As for Assam and Darjeeling, local recruitment was to some extent limited. For Darjeeling, labour was derived from voluntary migration from nearby hill peoples of Nepal and Sikkim. Assam was relatively difficult to settle in, as it was uncultivated and consisted of nearly uninhabited jungle. Recruitment was prohibited in certain districts in Assam and the planters obtained their main labour force from the indigenous people of Santhal Parganas and Chotanagpur. The recruiting methods were akin to slavery. At the outset, a labour force must be assembled which is ready to turn its hand to every task that is required. Setting up a plantation was a delicate as well as rigorous process. It required both the planter and the wage labour to be ready for any kind of work that might be needed for the plantation to take shape. With the passage of time, salaried superintendents replaced proprietary planters. At times, several estates were grouped together and placed under a "group" manager. But whatever may have been the ownership/managerial condition, the status of the plantation labourer did not vary much. The first problem with the recruitment of plantation labour was one of recruitment of labour from a distance. Tea plantations came up mostly in places, which had hitherto been forests. Therefore, labour recruitment involved large-scale migration: a problem in itself. Plantation labour migration was of a special category; the workers migrated from one rural existence to another, unlike many factories, the plantation requires the whole labour force of the family. Over time, the plantation becomes their home, thus uprooting them completely from their erstwhile habitat.

4. The Economic Review 2004-05, p.106 para 4.109 says, "The Tea Board should fix norms for replantation cycles for tea bushes and prepare a replanting programme for each garden, fixing the year wise acreage to be replanted. If the garden management does not cooperate with the Tea Boards in implementing the replantation scheme or fails to execute the scheme, Tea Board should levy a fine on the management. The Economic Review 2007-08 in Art 5.29 additionally says, the tea industry was facing a major problem with the tea prices constantly declining over the last few years till 2003. The situation has slightly improved from 2004. The average tea prices at Kolkata and Siliguri auction markets have increased significantly. Consequently the average price of tea in West Bengal has increased from Rupees 65.36 per kg in 2003-04 Rupees 77.84 per Kg in 2006-07".
5. In para. 4.110, it says, "the Tea Board and the Government of West Bengal should take up with the banks the need to provide bank finance to the tea gardens for the implementation of these schemes at reasonable rate of interest of 9%. The Tea Board may formulate a scheme to provide 5% interest subsidy to the gardens for this purpose. Para 4.111 says, the Tea Board should enhance the extent of subsidy for replantation from the current level of 25% to 50%".
6. The first obligation refers to the state's duty not to interfere in the livelihood of its subjects or their abilities to provide for themselves. The second obligation

entails the creation of a regulatory environment conducive to the protection of the right to food (the state, for example, has a responsibility in setting food safety standards and in protecting land tenure system). The third obligation requires positive action by the state in identifying vulnerable groups and in facilitating their access to food-producing resources or income generation [FAO 1998]. States are obliged to take all appropriate steps to achieve progressively the right to adequate food, subject to the maximum of their available resources.

7. This concept is borrowed from Amartya Sen and Jean Dreze in *Hunger and Public Action.*
8. *Swadhikar* is a civil society organisation operating in the Dooars under Registration Number S/IL/10289 of 2002-03. It works in areas of moblilisation of mass opinion by making information available to the people. The tea workers constitute one of the principal people with whom the body works.
9. This is based on an interview with a chikbarik family at the Kathalguri tea garden on 22 September 2008 at the labour quarter habitat of the family. The principal interviewee was Gopal Chikbarik, who was the munshi of the garden at one point of time. His sons could not find suitable jobs at the tea estate and, therefore, had to travel daily to Bhutan and work there as daily wage labourers. The Chikbarik family is a classic example of deprivation in the tea industry.
10. These are excerpts from interviews with women workers associated with Mahila Jagriti Sangh members Jashomati Orao, Betguri tea estate, Malbazar Bloc and Seetamani Orao, Damdim Tea Estate, Malbazar. The interviews were done at a weekly gathering of the self-help group on 21 September 2008 at their office in Malbazar, Jalpaiguri.
11. This is based on an interview with Tapas Modak on 22 September 2008 at Jalpaiguri town.
12. This is on the basis of a one to one interview done with Jashomati Orao mentioned earlier on 23 September 2008 after a meeting of Mahila Jagriti Sangh.
13. This is based on the excerpts from an interview with Sibani Orao, Wasibari tea estate who had come to attend a meeting of the Mahila Jagriti Sangh at the Kalchini Bloc on 21 September 2008.
14. This is based on a one to one interview with Phulwanti Kharia from Bhernoberu tea estate on 24 September 2008.
15. This is based on an interview on 24 September 2008 with Partha Sarathi Bose of Dooars Jagran, a CSO working with the tea labourers in the Dhupguri Block of Jalpaiguri.

REFERENCES

Bhatia, Bela and Dreze, Jean, 22-28 July 2006, Employment Guarantee in Jharkhand: Ground Realities, *Insight*, Vol.41, No.29, July 2006, pp.3198-202

Bhattacharya, Dwaipayan and, Kumar, Rana, 5-8 February 2008, Politics of PDS Anger in West Bengal, *Economic and Political Weekly*, Vol.43, pp.63-69

Bhowmik, Sharit K, 17-23 September 2005, Tea Plantation Workers' Strike, *Economic and Political Weekly*, Vol.40, No.38, pp. 4103-05

Bhowmik, Sharit K, 28 February-6 March 2009, Politics of Tea in the Dooars, *Economic and Political Weekly*, Vol.44, No. 09, pp.21-22

Chaudhary, Neetu and D Parthasarathy, 10-16 February 2007, Gender, Work and Household Food Security, *Economic and Political Weekly*, Vol.42, No.06, pp.523-31

Dreze, Jean, 24-30 April 2004, Democracy and Right to Food, *Economic and Political Weekly* [Special Article], Vol.39, No.17, pp.1723-31

Sen, Amartya and Dreze, Jean, Chapter 13: *Hunger and Public Action* (1989), New Delhi: OUP, p.276

Economic Review 2004-05, Industry, page 106 para 4.109, Government of West Bengal

Economic Review 2004-05, Industry, page 106 para 4.110, Government of West Bengal

Economic Review 2004-05, Industry, page 106 para 4.111, Government of West Bengal

Economic Review 2004-05, Industry, page 106 para 4.113, Government of West Bengal

Economic Review 2004-05, Industry, page 106 para 4.114, Government of West Bengal

Economic Review 2004-05, Industry, page 106 para 4.116, Government of West Bengal

Economic Review 2007-08, Industry, page 122 para 5.26, Government of West Bengal

Economic Review 2007-08, Industry, page 122 para 5.29, Government of West Bengal

FAO (1998): *Implementation of the Right to Food in National Legislation*, FAO Legal Office, Mimeo, Food and Agriculture Organisation of the United Nations, Rome

Gaiha, Raghav. 4-10 October 2003, Does Right to Food Matter? *Economic and Political Weekly*, Vol.38, No.40, pp.4269-76

Gopal, K S, 17 January 2009, NREGA Social Audits: Myths and Reality, *Economic and Political Weekly*, pp.70-71

Jha, Raghavendra, Gaiha, Raghav and Shankar, Shyalashri, 15-21 March 2008, Reviewing the National Rural Employment Guarantee Programme, *Economic and Political Weekly*, Vol.43, No.11, pp.44-48

Nandy, Vaskar, 26 November-2 December 2005, Tea Industry Wage Agreement in West Bengal, *Economic and Political Weekly*, Vol.40, No.48, pp.5129-31

Radhakrishna, R, 30 April-6 May 2005, Food and Nutrition Security of the Poor, *Economic and Political Weekly*, Vol.40, No.18, pp.1817-21

Tharian George, K and Joseph, Joby, 25 June-1 July 2005, Value Addition or Value Acquisition: Travails of the Plantation Sector in the Era of Globalisation, *Economic and Political Weekly*, Vol.40, No.26, pp.2861-67

WEBSITES

Fifth Report of the Commissioners, August 2005; http://www.sccommissioners.org/pdfs/comreports/5threport.pdf, accessed on 1 March 2009

Fourth Report of the Commissioners, August 2003; http://www.sccommissioners.org/pdfs/comreports/4threport.pdf, accessed on 1 March 2009

Sixth Report of the Commissioners, October 2005; http://www.sccommissioners.org/pdfs/comreports/6threport.pdf, accessed on 1 March 2009

Scaria, Sunil; Labour Rights- Tea Garden workers- Abandoned to Death in http://www.combatlaw.org/information.php?article_id=414&issue_id=16s, accessed on 27 February 2009

Supreme Court Orders on the Right to Food: A Tool for Action, August 2008, http://www.righttofoodindia.org/data/scordersprimeratoolforaction.pdf accessed on 15 March 2009

http://timesofindia.indiatimes.com/India/After_Singur_Mamata_reaches_out_to_tea_garden_workers/rssarticleshow/2129915.cms, accessed on 17 January 2009

http://www.telegraphindia.com/1090204/jsp/siliguri/story_10479162.jsp, accessed on 5 February 2009

http://www.indopia.in/India-usa-uk-news/latest-news/23116/National/1/20/1, accessed on 17 January 2009

CHAPTER 3

Outrage against Hunger and Bureaucratic Feudalism

The PDS Agitation in West Bengal

MANISHA BANERJEE

INTRODUCTION

It is generally accepted that public memory is very short-lived. Therefore, it may also be assumed that the public memory of the outrage generated over the Public Distribution System in West Bengal (2007) is perhaps already fading. Notwithstanding this popular image about public memory, the present essay intends to examine in detail some grass roots level cases, in order to find how and to what degree the "local issue" found a larger political manifestation through its opposition to the regime. However, it is has not been argued here that problems in the PDS is an exclusively West Bengal syndrome. People have been suffering as a result of the corrupt PDS for decades all over India, but the public outrage that broke out over it in West Bengal in 2007 had far-reaching consequences. In fact, the much-hyped "change" which is now the key word in whatever is happening in the state got its foothold from this particular movement against the corrupt PDS system. The common complaints were:

1. The shops did not function regularly.
2. The usual plea of the dealer was non-availability of stock.
3. The ration provided was unfit for human consumption.
4. The ration issued fell short of the entitled quota.
5. The rates charged were more than the official rates.
6. Items were siphoned off by making false entries in the records.
7. The dealers piled a stock of false ration cards in their hold to pursue their corrupt practices.

The mass perception was that the dealer tried his best not to let people have their due so that he could sell these foodgrains in the open markets. Also, there was a common belief that as the dealer had the party backing, no one could actually touch him. It was also commonly held that the dealer paid the party in power as well as the inspecting government offices and that the payment made to the party ensured the latter's ensuring the protection of the dealer. Meanwhile, all the dealers complained that it was the government system (less commission, discounted supply, etc.) that forced them to be involved in malpractices; of course the statement bore truth and it was not that the ruling party was unaware of this. But, instead of pursuing for a systemic change the party found it easy to carry on with stopgap arrangements. Why so? Clearly, it had no intention to break the traditional power structure. The ration dealers, inter alia, contractors, school teachers, and other power-holders, as a general case, are rooted deep in the traditional ground of power, where social, economic and political origin converge perfectly with each other. In most cases, the same dealer also served as one of the leaders of the local party committee or, at least, had been a close associate.

A Quick Outline of the PDS Outrage in West Bengal

There are several opinions regarding the epicentre of this agitation. Howver, in reality, it was almost without a centre: it originated in Bankura at some time in August 2007 and spread into neighbouring Birbhum and Bardhaman, and into almost nine districts of South Bengal and one in North Bengal by October.

As the mass fury burst out against the selling of foodgrains (meant for the PDS) in the open market, the "unruly" masses attacked ration dealers physically. Their assets and houses also came under attack and they were compelled to promise monetary compensation for their alleged "theft". The common allegation in the agitation was that ration shop owners were entrenched in a corrupt nexus – mostly affiliated to or patronised by the CPI(M) leadership. Instead of making a weekly quota of wheat and rice available to the ration cardholders, they often sold these in the open market at a higher margin. Since in most cases, the dealers were sheltered by the ruling CPI(M), the mob resentment was against the party as well, which paved the way for their political defeat in the forthcoming Panchayat Elections. The agitation had all the attributes of a grassroots movement, marked by spontaneity, people's participation, unorganised chaos and a very conspicuous absence of the major leaders of the Opposition.

It is ironical that the Left came to power in the state in the late 1960s riding on the social unrest and popular wave of a Food Movement. It has been again, without a break, ruling the state since 1977. Therefore, the PDS agitation seems to be a nemesis of the Left which had launched most severe movements against the corrupt practices of the then Congress government. It has been the worst nightmare for the ruling CPM which, as champion of the poor, has always been vocal for strengthening the PDS. According to the National Sample Survey (hereafter the NSS) published in 2007, West Bengal has the highest percentage (10.6%) of rural households that do not get adequate food for some months of the year. Reports of starvation deaths have come from different parts of the state causing enough embarrassment to the "pro-poor" government.

Following the Supreme Court Directives in August 2006, the state government issued a notification explaining the quota of wheat and rice and their different prices for the APL, BPL, Antyoday and Annapurna categories. According to rules, every ration shop-owner has to put up a list of the products available with the price range in order to keep the cardholders informed. Ration shop-owners seldom do that and the government turns a blind eye. As usual, the government tried to blame the Congress at the Centre for cutting down the state's quota of foodgrain. The Centre had slashed West Bengal's monthly allocation for the APL section from 228,000 tonnes to 7,700 tonnes and state officials say this is mainly responsible for the shortfall.

Of the 8.35 crore ration cardholders in the state, almost 60% belong to the APL category and they were the ones posing the problem. APL cardholders, who usually buy grains from the open market, are coming to the ration shops after the recent price rise. The monthly average allotment of rice and wheat does show a sudden decline in 2006-07 from that of 2002-03, but the counter-argument is that the government itself has procured less than the allotted quota in the last three years. Price hike in the open market is, thus, the only an excuse provided by the regime. At the same time, it must be admitted that the Centre's decision to allow rice exports to Bangladesh had further complicated the matter. Again Tata Economic Consultancy Service's Report (2006) shows that 40% of the rice and 34% of the wheat from the PDS had been diverted in West Bengal through the "wrong path". Another drawback is that, in West Bengal, the fair price shops are mostly under private ownership. The ration dealers are also fairly organised and supported by two strong unions. The movement also revealed an uncanny consensus among all the dealers of the state and a sort of conspiracy in not providing the subscribers with their quota of food items.

The other excuse provided by the ruling party is that a diabolical conspiracy hatched by the Opposition to dismantle the state's smooth running apparatus. But reality proves that neither the Opposition nor the ruling party ever paid any attention to the faulty and corrupt PDS of the state; otherwise, this would not have gone unnoticed for so long. It had become almost an unwritten practice that ration shops are meant for the poor who have no other alternative and to be a ration dealer, one has to be as corrupt as possible. Everyone overlooked the unnatural flourishing of the dealers within rural poor set-ups.

PDS Anger: Revolt against Bureaucratic Feudalism

One may deduce a connection between the mass outrage against corrupt ration dealers, as well as the entire PDS system in 2007 and the change of power in the following Panchayat Elections of 2008. While this relationship made its presence felt across the state, in some districts, the line appeared much conspicuously. Indeed, a simple mapping of the PDS outrage and the debacle of the regime show a clear correlation between the two. That rural Bengal, which for long has been taken for granted to be the red bastion, was changing its colour was not confined only to Panchayat Elections, the slogan of "change" had remained influential even in the Parliamentary Elections of 2009. And, undoubtedly, this wave of political "change" has drawn a lot from the PDS agitation, which was only too clear from the electoral debacle of the ruling Left in the districts such as Birbhum, North and South 24 Parganas and Nadia, where the PDS agitation was very strong. Of course, exceptions like Bankura district can be cited, where despite a strong current of PDS agitation, results of the Panchayat Elections did not turn to be disastrous for the regime. It is, however, a matter of further inquiry, which could not be accommodated within the scope of this article. At present, we would rather concentrate on the districts of Bardhaman and Birbhum, which are considered as the rice granary of the state and traditional strongholds of the CPI(M).

Let us begin with a case from Bardhaman. Amarpur Gram Panchayat of Ausgram block of Bardhaman district has a large number of Muslims and Scheduled Castes. This Panchayat has witnessed an extraordinary tilt in the local political balance of power originating from the movement against corrupt ration dealers. It has generated a long-standing effect on the local village community that has a direct bearing on the politics of food and hunger. During the ongoing PDS agitation in the state, two villages under the Bisnupur (1,736 voters) and Belemath (730 voters) Panchayats were under the dealership of Musha Molla who had allegedly been cheating the villagers for long and had been enjoying the patronage of the ruling CPI(M). Like many other places in the state, here too, villagers were suffering from various malpractices of the ruling party, which included corruption in various welfare projects of the Panchayat, irregularities in the NREGA programme, faulty BPL list and so on.

But, above all, CPI(M) could successfully blend the old feudal authoritarian legacy (based on patron-client relationship) with the modern bureaucratic functioning in such a manner that it earned the party an unquestioned political loyalty of the masses. For about two decades, Bishnupur had not experienced almost any dissent. There was only one exception, when, two decades ago, the young Azim Dafadar, alias Kajal Chatterjee left home and was murdered in Birbhum, while fighting for an anti-land-grabbing movement in the mid-1980s.

The dissent got its voice when the news of PDS agitation in other areas of the state reached here. Villagers approached the ration dealer and enquired about the quota of wheat that the APL cardholders were entitled to. Like other places, it was soon revealed that he had been cheating them for long and the villagers demanded a cash compensation for the loss. When the dealer dealt with them rather harshly (as he was obviously sure of his CPI(M) patronage to back him), the villagers united under this common cause. A sort of on-the-spot organisation was formed, which first moved to make a deputation to the Block Development Officer of Ausgram II, the Inspector for Food and Supply and The Sub-Divisional Controller (Food and Supply), Bardhaman.

The Memorandum, written in Bengali and signed by 500-odd villagers representing almost all the households, would read as follows (in translation):

"Sir,

It is our humble submission that we, the undersigned persons, are residents of Bisnupur and Belemath villages of Amarpur G P under Ausgram block II. Musha Molla is the dealer (Ration Shop No. 26) for these two villages.

The following allegations against this ration dealer need your attention.

1. The APL subscribers have not received their quota of wheat as fixed by the government (weekly 250 gms, per unit) since March 2001. Neither the government nor the ration dealer has made any announcement regarding this.
2. BPL cardholders have not received their quota of rice and wheat from 1996 to 2005. Even now, some are deprived of these.
3. The subscribers do not receive kerosene as per government allotment. Most of the villages are without electricity. Therefore, the education of students are hampered.
4. The shops have no notice board and stocks and price lists are not displayed.
5. The shop remains open only on Fridays and Saturdays from 2 pm to 5 pm. As majority of the people here belong to either lower middle class or are agricultural labourers, many are not able to take their things on time.

> 6. The Ration dealer does not follow the government rules and no cash memo is given to the subscribers.
> 7. He charges more price than that fixed by the government.
>
> As a result of the above allegations, the villagers are extremely discontent with the dealer. Therefore, we urgently request you to look into the above matters as early as possible and take necessary legal steps against the faulty dealer."

The memorandum clearly reflects the grievances of the local people and the gross irregularities that were going on around the PDS system. What is interesting is that even without the presence of any partisan motivator, the people themselves built up an organised protest in which they initially appealed to the different bureaucratic set-ups involved with the PDS mechanism. At the same time, as it is common with any mass movement, they approached the source of corruption, the local dealer and asked for redress. Once the cause is established and the guilt pronounced, the agitated villagers put a strong fine on the corrupt dealer and the movement turned anti-establishment when the dealer was given refuge by the local CPI(M) leaders. The evil nexus between the party in power and the local exploiter, once exposed, motivated the common people to look for a more radical change than mere punishment of the dealer. This story of protection of the ration dealers by the local CPI(M) leaders and the party has been a common feature throughout the state during the movement. In fact, this is what paved the way for the opposition to gain politically, since in the popular perception, corruption became synonymous with the ruling party.

The Right to Food stir ultimately made the people of Ausgram aware of the violation of other rights as well. And the *Ganaandolan Committee* (Committee for People's Movement) formed by the villagers, who spearheaded the agitation, decided to fight in the Panchayat Elections of 2008. They floated three independent candidates, Ashis Molla, Bahadur Shaikh and Debdas Mete, who fought the election with the symbol of 'table fan', were elected as members of Amarpur Gram Panchayat from Bisnupur, Belemath and Moukhira Gram Samsads. While the local CPI(M) leaders found the announcement of election-contest by the independent candidates to be audacious enough, their winning the election simply astonished the party bosses. As the scale of power forced the dealer to succumb to local pressure and ultimately made him pay a fine of Rs.600,000 for his corrupt dealings. The people distributed the money among the 3,000 cardholders and have made a fund with part of the money.

But the story continues in the direction of the means of primary consumption. Within eight months of their coming to power, this local organisation of the people and their representatives to the panchayat have reopened a village market ('closed' for a long time) near Bisnupur Bus stand and a *haat* (open-air weekly market), which was launched 22 years ago by Azim, alias Kajal, mentioned above, but alleged to have closed down later by the ruling party goons. This market is essentially a market for food – fresh vegetables, fish and other items coming directly from the producers. Thus, what started as a movement against the corruption in supply of essential foodstuff, has ultimately taken a constructive step again in the direction of procurement of food for the not-so-privileged villagers.

Jahiruddin Sk, Secretary of the market committee, who also runs a small tea shop, which actually served as the control room of the agitation, remarks: "We will employ all our strength to prevent the red to come back here . . . we have been under this flag all through our life and even sparing our life to keep it swinging high, but ultimately found that it was nothing more than a triviality." One can see, in this statement, the degree of frustration, sense of deprivation and consequent anger and hatred for the ruling party. The same pattern of the movement could be seen in many other areas in Bardhaman, Bankura and Birbhum as it spread like a prairie-fire from one place to another in no time.

VOICES AGAINST THE POLITICS OF DEPRIVATION AND CONTINUED SUBJUGATION

Khiruli of Sattor Panchayat, Bolpur block of Birbhum district is predominantly a Muslim village that has a population of about 1,000. It has got one Gram Samsad seat, which was retained by the CPI(M) in the 2003 Panchayat Elections. The village economy is primarily agricultural and the majority of the main workers are either cultivators or agricultural labourers, or both. The licensed Modified Ration (MR) dealer, Susanta Ghosh lives in Bergram, about one kilometre away from

Khiruli and the MR shop is attached to his residence. Ghosh is a declared CPI(M) supporter.

In spite of discontent among a section of people over his ill treatment there had not been any explicit outrage till July 2007. In June 2007, some of the villagers of Khiruli heard a rumour that the dealer had not distributed the wheat, stipulated for the APL cardholders for the last 11 months. The news spread across the villages under the jurisdiction of the MR shop and a crowd of about 500 went to meet the dealer to seek an explanation. At the first instance, the dealer denied the allegation. But as the conversations went ahead, he admitted the muddling, but did not appear to be apologetic. This made the assembled mob furious but some leading locals managed to keep things under control. Finally, a date (9 July 2007) was fixed for a public meeting where the dealer would announce his guilt and subsequent compensation. He agreed to compensate the undelivered wheat by doubling thenceforth the stipulated quota, about which the crowd had so far no idea. There was absolutely no information on this before the rumour broke out. Indeed, one of the major causes of discontent was the complete concealment of information, a mechanism that has been developed and used by the regime – both the party and the government – to maintain the hegemony over the people.

The villagers gathered on the date at a local high school fixed for the meeting. Among them there were supporters of different political parties including CPI(M). In fact a CPI(M) local committee member was also there. But the dealer did not turn up which increased people's enraged impatience. They wanted to visit him at his residence. Anticipating a disastrous consequence some of the leading participants appealed to the masses to maintain peace and only four representatives visited the dealer's house. But he was not found in his house too and his wife said that he had gone to attend a CPI(M) meeting. The assembly dispersed with anger only to reassemble again within two to three days. The dealer allegedly said that the CPI(M) had told him not to abide by his promises that he made before the gathering on the first day. Whether the allegation was true or not is unknown but that the dealer enjoyed administrative support was more than certain. Again, the hands of the political controllers guiding the administrative actions were not invisible: the presence of the "long hands" could be felt at every walk of life. Officials of Food and Supply

Department, accompanied by police came to rescue the dealer and disburse the angry masses. As it was followed by Ramadan (the month of fasting) the local inhabitants, being Muslims, could not pursue the case any further. But the sprit remained and in the Panchayat Elections of 2008, this seat was won by the opposition candidate of a newly formed Peoples' Democratic Conference of India (PDCI), the name of which was not at all a familiar one.

Let us also make a quick round of another village named Kuitha (under Sahapur panchayat of Dubrajpur block) in Birbhum district. The village has an absolute preponderance of the Muslims. The PDS dissent was transmitted to this village through an incidence of physical assault on a dealer, Mr Rajibul Alam of the neighbouring village, Sahapur. The dealer promised, in presence of the police, to pay Rs.300 per APL cardholder. This news poured enthusiasm upon the villagers of Kuitha who gathered in front of the dealer's house. Two brothers Naresh Sadhu and Santi Sadhu, both very rich and own many other businesses, ran two ration shops from the same place and served 7 villages. It is, however, a common phenomenon in rural scenario: the traditionally rich and power holders continued to dominate over the economy and politics. The Sadhu brothers are no sporadic case. Nevertheless, the dealers' house virtually took shape of a people's court, where a mass of about 700 was gathered. They were asked a series of questions by the villagers. The answers revealed gross irregularity in the dealers' work: they had not only cheated the APL cardholders but also the BPL ones. Following the proceedings, a paper was signed by the dealers, who agreed to give Rs.300 per APL cardholder as 'compensation'. Interestingly, the case of the BPL cardholders was left unresolved at that moment. But the dealers left the house overnight and started staying in a different village. However, after several messages sent to them the dealers came back and appealed that the previous agreement be modified. According to a new agreement the dealer promised to give 15 kg wheat in addition to the due amount at the government specified price (Rs.6.75).

Since the Muslim festival Eid was over, the villagers asked one of the dealers to distribute the wheat among the Hindu customers first. He did it but with some mischief. He gave 15 kg wheat and assured that the rest would be given later. Similarly, he gave the Muslim customers the same amount and assurance. But he did not give anybody the additional wheat that he promised. In the meantime, his licence has been cancelled by the administration. The consequence of the cancellation of the licence has been very negative. Now people have to collect their ration from a shop 6 km away. Villagers have submitted mass petition to the authorities to give the dealership to someone from the village so that they can get their ration easily. But no positive action was taken till the date of this interview. "*Chorer sasti hoyna, chor dharar sasti hoy*" – (the thief is not punished, rather those who detect the thief are penalised), said a villager.

Later, it was found that the licence was still with him and after giving the compensation amount to all the villagers (both Hindus and Muslims) he was reinstated as the dealer. The protection that the CPM gave him exacted a huge price: it suffered a humiliating defeat in the hands of a combined opposition who won 7 out of 11 seats of the Panchayat with a population of 11,000. A very significant feature of the whole episode was that Asnara Begum, the erstwhile CPI(M) Pradhan, who was made to quit for protesting against the malpractices of CPI(M), had fought as an opposition candidate and has won her seat again.

That the anger against this bureaucratic feudalism that reigned supreme in the countryside was more a general pattern, rather being an isolated phenomenon, could be seen more clearly at Abinashpur, of Suri I block. With a population of about 1,500, Abinashpur is a multi-ethnic village. While the Muslims and Scheduled Castes (SCs) are two major groups, the Hindu middle castes like sadgopes also form a substantial portion of the households. The agitation started as a sympathetic reaction to the ongoing agitations across the district. Rumours floated in the air that "people of such and such villages had received the undelivered wheat and also money from the ration dealers". This sort of rumour added incentive to the already furious masses that were extremely unhappy with the dealer's malfunctioning (ill treatment, cheating, irregularity, keeping fake ration cards, keeping the cards in his custody, etc.).

There was no particular party affiliation among the crowd in this case: supporters of all the parties joined it. The crowd met the dealer, Mr Sisir Bhandari at his residence, from where he ran his shop. He admitted his misdoing and made written commitment that he would pay each BPL cardholder a sum of Rs.250 as compensation within 15 days. However, he did not keep his promise that led the people getting assembled again. They had given him prior notice. But he was not present on that date. Angry crowd pelted stone to damage the glass windows. Hearing this, over the phone, he came back soon, which was followed by the sub-divisional food controller and the local police. A meeting was held in presence of the controller and police. The dealer asked for some relaxation in the fine imposed earlier and it was cut down to Rs.150 (or 10 kg of wheat). But the food controller clearly said that fine could not be imposed; instead the dealer would distribute the due wheat. But the mob did not agree. After some negotiations, another agreement signed by dealer where he promised to pay Rs.150 per APL card. But finally he did not implement the agreement. In the meantime the local administration had ceased his licence. But people still believe that he should make the compensation. Here too, the CPI(M) and local administration had opposed imposing fine and took side of the dealer. Gradually the movement faded out. But the strain remained.

Although CPI(M) could retain the panchayat, it lost the Gram Samsad which it had been winning for decades. It was the course of PDS movement that caused to erode the support base of the CPI(M) here. During Panchayat Election 2008 in Abinashpur Panchayat candidates from different political parties were put up as independents against the ruling CPI(M) under the banner of Janaswartho Raksha Sangram Committee (The Committee for Struggle for Protection of Public Interests) and they won three seats including Abinashpur. One significant win is the tribal seat at Kubirpur, which was for a long time a stronghold of CPI(M). Tapan Das, a local youth who was once a member of the panchayat winning the seat as a CPI(M) candidate , now a fervent opposition sums up, "Anyone if he becomes part of the ruling party can't avoid corruption". He also bitterly observes: "*Ora merey khaoar janyoi Panchayatey jai.*" (They go to Panchayat only for the purpose of looting public money).

THE ORGANISATION AND THE UNMAKING OF THE AGITATION

Significantly, Bankura, Burdwan and Birbhum – three districts where the movement gathered momentum – are strong CPI(M) bases. It was found that after initial hesitation party cadres of the lower rung joined the movement out of their own Will. In almost all the places, the agitation started after receiving news from the adjacent villages. "Real" news and rumours blended together spread like wild fire and the pattern was repeated everywhere. The agitators went to the dealer, spoke out their grievances, called for justice, imposed a fine and when refused, ransacked his properties. In many places, with utmost sincerity the common people submitted mass petitions to the local and district level authorities of the PDS. When the ruling party with the help of administration tried to intervene, chaos broke in. There were instances of death by police firing in this agitation. One can recall such deaths at the time of the historic food movement led by today's ruling left and in which the persons who were killed by the police, had been bestowed the status of martyrs later on.

Absence of prominent leadership was another salient feature of the whole agitation. Everywhere the movement was spearheaded by local youths or other socially active elders under the banner of newly formed grassroots committees. Names like Ganandolon Committee, Jana Adhikar Suraksha Mancha (Platform for Protection of People's Rights) were floated. It should be noted that later during Panchayat Elections these committees functioned as political agencies in putting up independent candidates. Even though the Opposition parties quickly realised the potential and sought to reap the fruits of the movement, yet, for the larger part, this remained mainly the domain of people's movement. As this study reveals, there have been instances, where all the Opposition parties are made to put up their candidates as independent candidates after a common consensus of the people and despite severe objections from the higher level leadership, they fought under the banner of these new committees and succeeded. The concept of *alliance* among different Opposition parties, commonly known as "jot", actually was revived at the grassroot level. Thus, in the Panchayat elections of 2008, the concept of "one-against-the-one" (i.e. one common opposition candidate against a ruling party candidate) was successful in gaining popular mandate and the ruling party suffered a great defeat.

A common observation about the movement is that this was initiated by the APL cardholders, people who are in a slightly better financial position within the village population. Some have even described them as the "rural elite". It is just a matter of chance that the steep price hike made them fall back on a hitherto neglected PDS and thus the ongoing corruption got some exposure. BPL cardholders are being deprived through ages, but they could not voice protests for their rights. But As Dwaiyapan Bhattacharya and Kumar Rana have found out "The rise in the price of wheat and corresponding non-availability from the FPS hit the poor people the hardest, especially those who were victims of 'exclusion errors' (more than 30 percent of the APL population fall in this category)". Yet to give full justice to this people's movements, the discrepancies in the faulty BPL list made by the state has to be looked into. Many had been put into the APL even though they fulfilled the criteria of BPL, to limit the number of BPL cardholders in the State. As Madhura Swaminathan (2001) points out, "For a casual labourer whose earnings fluctuate from day to day, a static (one-time) poverty line is an inappropriate indicator of vulnerability. Another important aspect of income targeting in India is that the official poverty line used as a cut-off is set at an absurdly low level, corresponding to the expenditure required to purchase a minimum of calories. It is in no way an indicator of the adequacy of purchasing power to provide for a minimum decent standard of living".

The BPL list still continues to be a major issue, the apple of discord in rural Bengal. After Panchayat Elections, people who have changed the guards, faced another round of disillusionment with the fact that listing of BPL cardholders is not under the jurisdiction of the panchayat. It is still being monitored by bureaucrats whom people have every reason to believe to be sycophants of the ruling party. Thus, ultimately, considerable change can be brought about if the panchayat is empowered to make the BPL list, or if the centre of the state political power is radically changed. As Nasima Bibi of Katiahat village, Police Station Baduria of North 24 Parganas, speaks out, "*Aro Kshamata din, taholeyi badal kara jabey*". (Give us more power; only then change can be initiated.) She interestingly still belongs to the CPI(M) women's wing.

Sanatan Tudu, the Pradhan of the Opposition-led panchayat at Ghurisha village in Illambazar Block of Birbhum district, finds himself in a catch-22 situation, when he fails to deliver justice to the very people, who put him there for change. One of the primary demands is to amend the BPL list. But the officials at the Panchayat inform him again and again that he cannot do anything in this case. This makes a frustrated Tudu to bitterly observe, "*Sab upor thekey hoi, ami chalileyo kichu kortey parina. Sekhaney to anyo daleyr rajattwo*". (Every thing is done from above. I cannot do anything despite my best wishes. That is the domain of the other [ruling] party).

Another significant contributor to the unmaking of this movement is the hijacking of the agitation by the big opposition parties. Once situation started getting out of control in the back drop of the Singur and

Nandigram incidents, the ruling CPI(M) exerted its damage control mechanism, on the other hand, Trinamool Congress (hereafter TMC), the main Opposition party, started building up a controlling agency for the people's struggle. As in many places it was common that the ration dealers paid regular donations to TMC as well. Some hush-ups and dilution of the movement also took place in this way.

An interview with a TMC leader of Kasba Panchayat, Birbhum will further illustrate the case. Kasba is traditionally a CPI(M) stronghold, but the presence of Trinamool congress was also there. No protest against the allegedly tainted dealer was organised. According to Narayan Bhandari, TMC organiser of the village, 'Some of the villagers wanted to organise protest', but, 'he TMC appealed to abstain from such move.'

- Why?
- The CPI(M) is in power and they might unleash attack on the people. No political movement can succeed in CPI(M) raj. Why should then people shed blood?
- Do you know the dealer?
- Yes, I do.
- How does he appear to you?
- Very nice. Basically it is not the dealer, who is the main culprit. It is the government, which is doing all these.
- Have you ever collected donation from the dealer?
- Yes, sometime. All the parties do. In fact, in all social occasions people ask the dealer for contributions.

FOOD AND POLITICAL FREEDOM

A recent follow-up visit of some areas shows considerable improvement in the PDS. The village monitoring committees are functioning properly, the dealers' behaviour has changed towards the cardholders, and supply, though not up to the mark, has improved a lot. A display board shows the current stock of the dealer, which previously never came into practice although it was mandatory. Nevertheless, it may not be a general case. There have been complaints from many areas that the dealers, party and the department have been carrying out the malpractices as before. Also, in some areas the changed political representation in the panchayat has allegedly been succumbed to the systemic anti-people dynamics, where an alliance of the corrupt persons continues disregarding the political nomenclatures and boundaries.

Yet, the changes, that the PDS anger has contributed to, need not be seen from a cynical point of view. Indeed, this unrest could well be identified as a historic turning point in West Bengal politics. It was the PDS anger, inter alia, Singur and Nandigram resistance that gave the people the much required self-confidence and esteem to start speaking against the regime. That the people found after many decades a collective voice through these agitations has also been admitted, in private conversations, by some CPI(M) leaders. As a leader said, "I never thought that I would have to stand by a man known for his notoriety. I never thought it important to go against this looting of public goods. But, when it came to defend him, I felt as though I am raping my own political ideology that was built over years". In fact, the erosion of morality among sections of the workers of the CPI(M) (in this case, the nexus between the party and corrupt dealers) has also added to the party's debacle in some areas. While the agitators stood on high moral ground, the CPI(M) workers continued to murmur the monotonous phrase like – "This is nothing but a conspiracy against the Left Front government" – which caused more harm than good. Again, majority of them continued to be the local oppressors – the *rajas* of their respective areas. The failure to deliver and aggravating the vulnerability of the masses on the one hand and keeping them fully subjugated on the other, has been the central phenomenon in rural Bengal.

The PDS anger was not just an issue. It was a manifestation against many irregularities of diverse nature: corruption, failure in delivery, etc. All these had been ultimately directed against the regime. As to why the public anger was predominantly expressed through the PDS agitation, is a question that needs to be examined in the light of actual food situation in the state and also in the light of the acuteness of hunger vis-à-vis increase in inequality. Crisis of food is a cruel reality in this state, which claims to produce "excess food". And, therefore, no other issue than food could come out to spearhead an anti-regime movement. There is a famous proverb in Bangla: "*bhat debar bhatar noy kil marar gosai.*" (The proverb is about a husband, who does not provide the required [and promised while marrying] food to his wife, but beats her frequently instead). Precisely, a similar perception was gaining ground among the people for a long time, which took form of the PDS anger underlining two specific demands: *food for all* and *prevention of oppression* on the people. The message is not just for CPI(M), but for all involved in the game of political governance.

REFERENCES

Rana, Santosh, *Prakrito Daridryo O BPL Talika: sarkari hisabeyr karchupi,* Prasnabachi Prakasana, Kolkata, 2007

Bhattacharya, Dwaipayan, and Rana, Kumar, Politics of PDS anger in West Bengal, *Economic and Political Weekly*, 2 February 2008

Report submitted to West Bengal Government on 8 December 2007, by Biraj Pattanayak, Chief Adviser to Supreme Court Commission

Virmani Arvind and P V Rajeev, *Excess Food Stocks, PDS and Procurement Policy* (December 2001), PLANNING COMMISSION Working Paper No5/2002-PC May 2002

Public Distribution System: An Overview by PARIVARTAN – Fighting Corruption website

India Corruption Study 2005 To Improve Governance Vol.II (Eleven Public Services), Corruption in Public Distribution System: Study designed & conducted by Centre for Media Studies, Research House, Community Centre, Saket New Delhi-110 017

Madhura Swaminathan, A further attack on the PDS, *Frontline*, Vol.18, Issue 02, 2001

CHAPTER 4

Right to Food in Paschim Medinipur District

Perspective on Nayagram Block

GEETISHA DASGUPTA

INTRODUCTION

I talked to Bimal Bhogta. I asked him about the food scarcity months in the region of Nayagram block of Paschim Medinipur District in the "dry months", which Bimal has described as *khoramash* (dry months). Bimal is a resident of the Singdhui village who sells wood from the forest. An elderly lady who was listening to our conversation quickly retorts from behind, "*baromash i khoramash* . . ." (All the twelve months [of a year] are dry months).[1]

The allegation is not so much about the arid nature of the region or the months of zero productivity of the soil. It is more about the step-motherly attitude of the administrative regime which does not take care to see that the two months of zero productivity and the adjacent months of low productivity, coupled with the arid nature of the soil in the region rendered more dry due to low rainfall, do not push the people into endemic poverty and hunger. The interviewee and the commentator have both been living in the region for a long time and their forefathers have also probably lived here. They are certainly familiar with the rough conditions that often do not favour cultivation. But the expectation over years have been that something would be done to alleviate the condition and facilitate better cultivation, such as increased irrigation facilities, better aid in agriculture and so on, so that crops do not fail in an area where agriculture is done on a subsistence basis. In absence of that, the expectation shifts to receiving adequate poverty alleviation aid like the government-sponsored schemes, which create opportunity for people to at least procure food in exchange for work and several other necessary facilities. The complaint remains.

This paper mainly deals with the reasons for which the complaint is voiced, but does not call into question about the status of the Right to Food in the region or even about the level of knowledge/consciousness about the Right to Food among the local people of the region. For example, we do not ask them questions like: "whether they consider access to adequate and nutritious food as a basic right, if so, then what is the status of that right and who is responsible for guaranteeing it?" etc. We shall rather be looking at the crucial factors that cause the denial of access to food for the people in the region, laying import on occupational pattern (that renders huge section of the working people marginal or nonworking altogether), education and health. We shall, along with that, consider the alternative arrangements made by the government in the form of schemes like the Integrated Child Development Services, Mid-Day Meal Scheme, Public Distribution System and National Rural Employment Guarantee Scheme to ensure that food reaches all and sundry in the country.

WHY PASCHIM MEDINIPUR?

In the course of my study of the Right to Food in West Bengal, West Midnapore or Paschim Medinipur was the second area, which I took up. ". . . the problem of hunger affecting a large section of the rural population of West Bengal – continues to be ignored by all. The West Bengal government admits that around 10 million rural people (around 1.95 million rural families) do not get two square meals a day throughout the year; another two million people (0.55 million families) do not get one square meal a day. The rural poor of Purulia, Paschim Medinipur, Bankura,

Birbhum, Uttar Dinajpur, Dakshin Dinajpur, Maldah, Murshidabad and Jalpaiguri are the worst affected."[2] The Pratichi Education Report of 2002 warned against the hunger prevailing in this belt.[3] Among the 4,612 villages that the Government of West Bengal identified as "backward", most are located in Purulia, Paschim Medinipur, Uttar Dinajpur, Jalpaiguri, Maldah and Dakshin Dinajpur. These are the villages where marginal workers and non-workers together constitute almost 60% of the village population. Additionally, 30% of the population in these villages is from the adivasi communities. On these state-designated backward villages, a survey was conducted in 2007, which showed that at least 20% of the people living in those villages get only one meal per day.[4]

Taking cue from the government's method of identifying the hunger prone and also hearing from news reports regarding the district's several blocks, I decided to see the Nayagram administrative block for the present research. The district of Paschim Medinipur lies on the border of West Bengal and Jharkhand, and this is also true of the block I visited for my research, viz. Nayagram.[5] Hunger in this belt has also been reported in newspapers. The adjacent block of Gopiballabhpur shot to news for hunger-induced malnutrition and death. When there was a death in Amlashole, a remote village in Binpur P S (Gopiballabhpur II), the government rushed with immediate measures and then chose to forget it completely. The greater malady was never addressed. Extremely dry, in terms of rainfall as well as government attention, much of the land is unarable. The Medinipur District Gazetteer noted about the Nayagram Estate – that, it "... is situated in the most jungly part of Medinipur; cultivation is sparse, but there is reported to be ample room for extension". There was, therefore, a natural demand for proper irrigation and shrub-land clearing. A large part is also covered by forests. In fact, commercial lumbering is practised by only a handful as lumbering itself is a capital-intensive trade. The principal section of working population of this area has to depend on agriculture or related jobs as the mainstay for an occupation. This area can roughly be said to have extensions of the characteristics of the adjoining Jungle Mahals covering large parts of Paschim Medinipur and Purulia districts. Actually, Nayagram block itself is not physically a part of the tract. However, there are influences of the adjoining Gopiballabhpur area too, which the District Gazetteer includes in the forest region.

THE NAYAGRAM BLOCK AND ITS POSITION IN PASCHIM mEDINIPUR

Unlike Jalpaiguri, where I did my first bit of research on the Right to Food, Paschim Medinipur, especially Nayagram, is a population of mainly unorganised labour. Therefore, the essential factors to the rights movement characteristic of the tea belt, such as labour unionisation, channelisation of demands, holding an immediate authority responsible for the breach of rights and even the idea of breach of rights as such, are conspicuous by their near absence in this part. Rather, this is largely an agricultural or agro-based people, who face few months of high yield and several months of low to almost zero productivity. Work is, therefore, not available round the year for a farmer or an agricultural labourer working on others' land. For much of the year, the word that does rounds in these households is "bhokila" meaning "extremely poor and wanting" or interchangeably, "hungry".

Hunger, therefore, is part and parcel of daily life, casting a regular spell each year and doing rounds like seasons in a year. The Bengali calendar months of bhadra and ashwin (mid-August to mid-October) are the hardest months in terms of sufficient food acquisition for the families and this trend has been depicted in the earliest details available to this researcher, as well as the recent figures. Rather, earlier, there was much more open access to the adjoining forests and the resources which the forests offered, such as direct food items (animals or birds or vegetables which grow in the wild) or indirect items (like firewood or dried leaves) which would allow the people to earn a living.

The population of Nayagram block is predominantly constituted of Scheduled Tribe (ST) and Scheduled Caste (SC) groups. There is a very high percentage of ST (30% as against a state average of 5.5%) and SC (28% as against a state average of 23%) in the backward villages enumerated by the government. The history of the region depicted in the District Gazetteer as well as the 1961 census shows a severely skewed and a most deprived past of the people. Nayagram is a block which has one of the highest numbers of people belonging to the bagdi (SC) and lodha/santal (ST) communities in Paschim Medinipur district. Traditionally, backward in terms of education as well as economy, the people have not proceeded at all from the picture recorded by the 1961 census of their being chiefly agricultural labourers, severely dependent on land, which would allow them only one principal crop a year. Of the abovementioned 4,612 extremely backward villages enumerated by the Government of West Bengal, 64 belong to Nayagram block. That makes the share 22% of the total of 294 villages in the Nayagram block[6] and approximately 1.39% of the total number of backward villages in the state.

Citing from the 1951 census, the 1961 census also notes the following characteristics about the occupational pattern of Western Medinipur:

1. Western Medinipur is primarily agricultural.
2. The independent producer of crops within a subsistence form of economy is the general feature.
3. The major part of the population does not enter into the relations of exchange economy, though there are distinct signs of departure from subsistence economy in case of *Bhag Chasis* (share-croppers) and landless peasantry and also according to the regional variation of the importance of Commerce and Production other than Cultivation as occupation.
4. Non-agricultural classes are markedly concentrated in the towns.
5. There are distinct regional concentrations of non-agricultural classes in the rural areas, e.g., Belda, Manikpara, Dahijuri, Dantan, etc.[7]

The same census notes the following about the broad picture of the peasant economy of the Western part of the Medinipur district:

The principal economic activities, connected with the production of commodities, may be divided into three groups:

(a) Agriculture,[8]
(b) Other forms of exploitation of resources, e.g. mining, forestry, fisheries, etc., and
(c) Rural handicraft industries.[9]

The same pattern is observed in the district of Paschim Medinipur till date. The same pattern is also exhibited by the Nayagram block. The two villages that were visited for the purpose of research in Nayagram block are Singdhui and Bara Pat. Both are under the Patina Number 1 Gram Panchayat. The first one is a lodha majority village and the second a completely santal[10] village, as would be clear from the table below. The difference between the two is that, Government of West Bengal, according to the 2001 census, thinks that while Singdhui is one among the most deprived 4,612 villages in the state, Bara Pat is not[11] as would be clear from the following Table 1. Singdhui is significant because of its huge adivasi population of 90.97%. The rest of the people mostly come from other backward classes.

Therefore, both the villages covered, are inhabited by the adivasi community. The interviewees were chosen simply on the basis of availability at the place and time of visit. There are certain features which, on the one hand, contrast the region with other adjoining areas or the rest of West Bengal for that matter and, on the other, show some similarities with the other drought-prone adivasi areas of the country. There is much similar when compared with the indigenous population belts of nearby states of Orissa or Jharkhand. The economy is such that an individual has principally his labour power, which can be exchanged only against some amount of necessity acquisition. The block population can be conceived principally in terms of agro-based workers with cultivators and agricultural labourers. There is a considerable section that works in household industries. There is quite a large section of marginal workers as well as non workers. In fact, in Nayagram block, 41.1% of the population belongs to non-worker category and 24.4% are marginal workers.[14]

OCCUPATIONAL PATTERN AND ITS RELATION TO FOOD ACCESS

The agricultural labourers constitute 23.3% while cultivators are 24.3% of the total 72,908 workers. The total workers constitute only 58.9% of the total block population.[15] The distribution is given below in Table 2. Not only that, if one goes through the 1991 census figures, given in Table 3, one finds that there has been an increase to 44% from 14.53% in Jhargram Subdivision in headcount of agricultural labourers, whereas in Nayagram block, the percentage of agricultural labourers has grown to 23.3% from 14.33%. The percentage of cultivators has also grown in both cases.

The percentage of cultivators among the main workers is 33.6% in Nayagram while the percentage value is 25.2% in Singdhui and 39.4% in

TABLE 1: State/District/Subdivision/Block/Village-wise Distribution SC Population & ST Population

Subdivision/ Block/ Village	Total Rural Urban	Population Person	Scheduled Caste Person	Scheduled Caste Percentage	Scheduled Tribe Person	Scheduled Tribe Percentage	Most Deprived Villages
West Bengal	Total	80176197	18440525	23	4409691	5.5	4612
Paschim Medinipur	Total	5193411	936891	18.04	771741	14.86	600+*
Jhargram Subdivision	Total	1008030	185478	18.4	302510	30.01	371
Nayagram Block	Total	123937	22757	18.36	49387	39.85	64
Singdhui[12]	Rural	797	0	0	725	90.97	Yes
Bara Pat[13]	Rural	234	0	0	234	100	No

Source: Census of India 2001; West Medinipur District Statistical Handbook 2005; Data gathered by researcher; *Rana (2006)

Bara Pat.[16] What is more interesting is the fact that the percentage of marginal workers in the whole of Nayagram is 41.4%; it is 35.1% for Singdhui while it is at a relative lower value of 13.9% for Bara Pat. One can definitely raise a question: Is the marginalisation of workers almost double of Bara Pat in Singdhui because of the lodha population? The answer seems to be positive.

The lodhas, since the colonial times, have been traditionally regarded as a criminal tribe, who are supposedly not very much agriculture-reliant. They have been inducted into agriculture, not a long time ago. There is very little incentive for them to be involved in agriculture in a much-sustained manner. This also explains why percentage of cultivators among the working people of Singdhui is lesser than that in Bara Pat. One needs to remember that almost 91% of the population in Singdhui is from lodha background. There is still huge amount of dependence on the forests among this group of people. For instance, Nimai Mallik from Singdhui tells us that in earlier days he used to sell things sourced from the forest.[17] The forest would be a steady source of wood, leaves and many other things, which would either have an exchange value in the market, or would be a food component. Since the area under cultivation is comparatively less in the village, it might be also difficult to find work locally for agricultural labourers. They would then have to move out of the village to get work. But even moving out on a daily basis might not be guarantee for work, as the adjoining areas are also no better in terms of work opportunity creation. So much so, that even 183 days of work a year becomes impossible, and hence the marginalisation.

Marginalisation is comparatively less among the labour force in the Bara Pat village, which, as summarised by Table 1 is a 100% tribal village inhabited by santals. Talking to a group of people in Bara Pat,[18] one gets to know, "... agriculture does not employ labour for the whole year. In fact how many days in a year would agriculture employ a person after all? When the season is on, a male labourer would typically be paid Rupees 40/day while a female labourer would be paid Rupees 35/day. Additionally, they would get to eat the minimum of one meal consisting of rice every day. But in off-season, which extends for better part of the year, they would have to find out extremely low paying stone quarrying jobs".

The percentage of total workers has grown from 42.59% to 58.9% for Nayagram block. The tables show a sharp increase in household

TABLE 2: Percentage Distribution of Population in Jhargram Subdivision and Nayagram Block According to Different Categories of Workers and Non-workers, 2001 (Population in Number)

			Class of Total Workers							
Subdivision/ Block	Total Workers (TW)		Cultivators		Agricultural Labourers		House hold Industries		Other Workers	
	No.	PC	No.	PC to TW	No.	PC to TW	No.	PC to TW	No.	PC to TW
Jhargram Subdivision	475394	47.2	127134	26.7	208981	44.0	46800	9.8	92479	19.5
Nayagram block	72908	58.9	17685	24.3	16984	23.3	24533	33.6	13706	18.8

Source: West Medinipur District Statistical Handbook, Page 36-37

industries (from 7.21% to 33.6%) as well as other workers' category (3.80% to 18.8%) for the Nayagram block. But this is nothing when compared to the all West Bengal figure where the percentage of total workers involved in "other work" is almost 50 and the scope of diversification is much higher.

When contrasted with the figures depicted in the 1961 census of Medinipur district, the neglect of the region by the delivery mechanism becomes more apparent. There must have been the absence of something or else the picture would not have been so stark. This something, as far as the people involved in agriculture are concerned, is government attention for the upgradation of the land so that more hectares could be converted to cultivable land. One notes that in the Nayagram block, only 6,280 hectares of land is covered by irrigation facilities. It has been a long made but never fulfilled promise from the state to bring more acreage of land under irrigation schemes. This anticipation is seen right from the 1961 census till date. There is still a promise by the name of the Subarnarekha Barrage Project which once completed would inundate 99,248 hectares in the kharif and 30,766 hectares in the rabi season in the districts of Paschim and Purba Medinipur. About 49% of the command area lies in Paschim Medinipur where tribal population in 12.3%.[19] Among the total workers in Nayagram Police Station, 64% were cultivators while 30% were agricultural labourers on a rough estimate. Around 3% of the workers were employed in household industries while the category "other workers" did not contain any more than 1.5% of the total working people.[20]

Whereas this is the case of labour allocation, the cultivation of the crop like boro, which has brought about changes in agricultural fortunes for the whole state of West Bengal, has grown from 0.1% in the 1944-45 survey (refer to endnote vi) to only approximately 2.2% going by the 2004-05 figures.[21] Moreover, though the ratio of aman crop to boro crop in case of West Bengal is 75:25, for the district of Paschim Medinipur, the ratio is 92:8.[22] For Nayagram block, the production figure for aman is 436.5 million tonnes while the production of boro is only 10.3 million tonnes.[23] This challenges the thought that what a farmer grows on his field would sustain him throughout the year. Therefore, the failure of one crop generates a whole year of insufficiency in terms of food as well as other necessities. This rather old pattern of agriculture is due to the arid nature

TABLE 3: Percentage Distribution of Population in Jhargram Subdivision and Nayagram Block According to Different Categories of Workers and Non-workers, 1991 (Population in Number)

			Class of Total Workers							
Subdivision/ Block	Total Workers (TW)		Cultivators		Agricultural Labourers		House hold Industries		Other Workers	
	No.	PC	No.	PC to TW	No.	PC to TW	No.	PC to TW	No.	PC to TW
Jhargram Subdivision	345807	39.53	150785	17.24	127064	14.53	17834	2.04	50124	5.73
Nayagram block	45358	42.59	18374	17.25	15256	14.33	7681	7.21	4047	3.80

Source: Medinipur District Statistical Handbook, Page 45-46

of the area, which has not been supplemented with adequate irrigation facilities.

The growth in figures of the increase in population of agricultural labourers too need not be taken too enthusiastically, because the increase in numbers does not suggest employment within the block or the subdivision itself. There is a great deal of outward movement. There exists, for instance, the practice of "namal" by which people from this region disperse and visit areas where they find employment. Working as "namal" happens for quite a considerable period of the year when agricultural employment is possible. In some blocks of the district, the majority of the agricultural labourers work on this sort of employment. It is understandable that this seasonal migration of labour takes place because the area under agriculture in the region fails to offer them employment. If they choose not to move, under the pretext of being locally employed, there would be patches when there would be lack of sufficient water for cultivation, keeping the field empty and the agricultural labourer non-working.

The age-old dependence on the forest resources is fast drying up or is being diminished through voluntary measures taken up by the state in the name of forest or other common property resource access regulations. There is very low literacy rate which plummets further when the the people in question are women. Singdhui is considered to be a "backward" village, which means, female literacy rate is below 30% and non-working and marginal workers together constitute 60% or more of the population of the village. Moreover, there are tribe-specific characteristics which make them more vulnerable when they fail to access the basic deliveries promised by the state apparatus.

ALLIED RIGHTS: NEGOTIATING RIGHT TO FOOD EVERYDAY

The backwardness is manifold, and can be traced to several reasons. Legally speaking, modern rights are linked with modern citizenship. But the idea of citizenship itself can be questioned, especially in this region. One may wonder whether it exists at all. Citizenship, when understood in concrete terms of the rights enjoyed by the people and in terms of those rights guarded and guaranteed by the delivery mechanism called the state, seems to be completely non-existent here. For example, food right is very closely

TABLE 4: Distribution of Workers by Different Categories of Workers and Non-working in Paschim Medinipur

Paschim Medinipur District	Total Main Workers		Marginal		Non Workers Workers		Total Population (Workers + Non-workers)	
	Male	Female	Male	Female	Male	Female	Male	Female
Rural	105541	241246 (28.33%)	245990	398894 (14.09%)	1029367	1605013 (57.58%)	2330498	2245153 (100%)
Urban	148097	22838 (27.67%)	12032	7309 (3.13%)	157421	270063 (69.20%)	317550	300210 (100%)
Singdhui		71	98	24	45			
Bara Pat			0	0				

Source: Paschim Medinipur District Statistical Handbook, Page 45

associated with other rights such as health and education. And, for the people of our concern, the right to use what the forests offer them is important since this right to a great extent enables them in their battle against hunger.

Since the population we are dealing with is almost completely tribal, the rate of education is not a very happy picture just like other parts of the country where the adivasis are the majority population. This is truer when we observe the female literacy rate. Only 14.6% of the literate population in Singdhui village is female. And comparing data, we find that marginalisation too is more among the women labourers. In fact, when one talks to the village residents of both Singdhui and Bara Pat, even if the male members try to appear somewhat less caustic about the non-working condition of the administrative mechanism as far as food and allied deliverables are concerned and, therefore, choose their words with care, the women are very categorical about the deprivation. Bara Pat shows a somewhat better figure with female literacy being 57.6% of all the literate people and that should not be as sad a figure as Singdhui because 73.1% of the total population of Bara Pat is literate.

But, Bara Pat complains about the nature of functioning of the Integrated Child Development Scheme (ICDS) functioning in the village. Kalicharan Sarai[24] of Bara Pat reveals, ". . . the ICDS workers hardly ever come to the centre. Only the helpers would come. Food is cooked for the children, but quality of pulses and rice is very poor. Also no vegetables are added to the food. Half an egg is provided once a month . . ." He then narrates a different part of the story, ". . . the teacher appointed at the ICDS centre is handicapped. Therefore, most of the days, the teacher would be absent. Being physically challenged, the teacher is immune from being sued for his absence. Sometimes the teacher's father would come and do some routine work to keep the son's job alive . . ." There is a strict compartmentalisation of work at the centre. For example, under all circumstances, a teacher would refuse to raise water from the well for the children to wash their hands after having mid day meal. The children principally go to school or the ICDS centre to fetch food, though that food is not enough. When mid-day meal is not there due to absence of amenities, sometimes children go to school, play and return home. In fact, the village people are in complete darkness about when money or amenities arrive at the school or at the ICDS centre. Nor did they ever want to know. There has been scarcely any protein in the mid-day meal over the last one year. Children go without food at home particularly in the months of monsoon *(ashar and shrabon)* that is, June to August, because this is the time for maximum employment for the adults.

In Singdhui, Aditya Nayek,[25] and ICDS employee says, "... there have been two days of cooking in the month of January 2009. There is no chart to record the nutritional status of the children under the ICDS ... as is the norm. We do not get any help from the Panchayat Pradhan as such about the ICDS. Rather, the Pradhan would work on the request of the people, never out of his own accord ..." The teacher further talks about a school meant for lodha children in the village, there are only 20 (lodha) children. Not necessarily all these children come from the Singdhui village. Limiting the admission to 20 children is indeed a luxury, because the school structure at least could allow more children. These 20 children are chosen by the powers in the panchayat and the block. Aditya Nayek says, "... these are the people who run the school ... like the police super, the Block Development Officer etc. ..."

In the absence of food, health suffers. Health is also a concern directly related with these people because this region has seen hunger deaths. Moreover, the poor standard of health among the adivasis has been a constant pricking factor for the Government of India. In the entire Patina panchayat, there is not even a dispensary where the villagers would get access to health facilities. At the Nayagram block, 68.07% of the children suffer from malnutrition. There is destitution among 1,068 families in the block and in Patina panchayat, 8 families belong to the category of destitute.

In Singdhui, the school mid-day meal is often used to feed people who do not get enough to eat. Conversation with Lakhinder Nayek,[26] the Panchayat Pradhan reveals that NREG work is available only for 15-16 days a year. Therefore, the NREGS is not something that could be depended upon for employing or creating sufficient provision for the villages. He says the panchayat tries to help as much as possible and rarely does take any case to the block level. The mitigation of problems is, thus, much more preferable at the village level. On rare occasions, when some matters like quality of ration in the ICDS were taken to the Block Development Officer, the response was that nothing could be done about it. Often, simply on the basis of village-level decision, inferior ICDS ration has to be abandoned and forest potato boiled and fed to the children. Some more interesting ideas strike as one speaks at length to the villagers at Singdhui and Bara Pat . Bimal Bhogta from Singdhui accumulates forest wood and sells in the market for a living. He complains, "... Panchayat work has not been there ... with a family of five members, I get only 15 kg of rice per week from the ration shop at the rate of Rupees three per kilo...I did not even get work under the NREGS. I was denied work I do not know for what reason ..."

This is a population that needs money on an immediate basis after having accomplished the day's job. Here, they face a stumbling block when the NREG work is made available to them since the latter does not pay money on a daily wage pattern. There is a whole range of formality before a person who has worked on NREG gets to see the money. Therefore, often, a wage labourer chooses work outside the NREG even if he could get work on such a project though NREG pays more than double of what one could earn as a private agricultural labourer.

In a conversation with Nimai Mallik, Kenaram Nayek and Budhiya Nayek[27] about the general condition of the Public Distribution System, the food for work programmes and the ICDS or Mid-Day Meal, Budhiya Nayek comments, "... if there is no food in the ICDS or primary school, Sushen Mallik is the person to be held responsible ..." The conversation was about whom they think should be held responsible for the non-availability of food? Sushen Mallik happens to be involved with food control and supplies to the ration shop in the region, located at Chamarbandh, 2 kilometers away from Singdhui. One can ask a question if the idea of accountability is so stunted among these people. But then one gets to know that Sushen Mallik is also the Local Committee member of the ruling party in the region and, therefore, can act as the magician at times. In fact, the idea of accountability is as immediate as it gets because Budhiya sees Sushen physically controlling the sacks full of all the food that could bring his family or even his village out of starvation for a while. Budhiya, however, has no idea as to how much of what article sold at the ration shop, he is entitled to get and at what price. Kenaram Nayek pitches in when I ask what they think they should do when the dry patch is on. He says, "... There is the forest ... it is there all twelve months. Leaves, potato and wood from the forest are there ..." He adds, "... *khete na pele jongol, jongoler alu ...khashir mangsher bodole goshaap ...*"

(When there is no food – there is jungle: the coarse potatoes of jungle and . . . *goshaap* [iguanas] in lieu of mutton). One can indeed engage in a discussion about essential regional or tribal food habits. But then the abovementioned things could be treated as delicacy if and only when the person has a choice of having adequate quantity of rice on the same occasion when he chooses to have forest potato and goshap in exchange. The principle of choice is crucial in this context. They also add that access to ration depends a great deal on the pradhan too. Keeping the pradhan happy is one of the major concerns as the pradhan is the link with the BDO.

Bara Pat follows a similar trajectory when asked about food and its control. Talking to a group of residents, one gets to know that BPL card is not acknowledged at the ration shop at Chamarbandh mentioned earlier. The shop is owned by Baren Jana. The ration disbursement takes place on the basis of familiarity between the buyer and the owner and not on the basis of BPL card entitlement. For example, Baren knows the jars belonging to different individuals and would disburse kerosene oil accordingly.

However, sometimes, there is some positive result in favour of the locals when collective feud takes place. From October 2008 to January 2009, 26 days of NREGS work has taken place in Bara Pat. It employed one person per family. Therefore, the number of man-days created was only 1,170 at Bara Pat. After that, the panchayat office informed that the fund has been used up and no more employment was possible. The Gram Unnayan Committee or the Village Development Committee issues allowance of Rs.100 per family during festive months once or twice a year. However, this is simply a dole and nothing else. The situation is summarised in Malati Murmu's comment, "*. . . dubar panta baromash . . . khette byabostha korte hoy . . . khatuni parle khele, na hole na . . . pet bhore khabar . . . kothay paabo?? . . .*" (Twice a day we have watered-rice . . . we have to work to earn that much . . . if we can toil that much, there is food . . . Eating to the stomach's content? . . . Where does one get that??)

Curiously enough, though the state government flags a distinction between Singdhui and Bara Pat, calling the former a backward village and the latter not so, there is hardly any marked differences between the two, except of course, differences in terms of certain conditions of labour and literacy. The Right to Food gets negotiated each moment for these people. It is only that they do not reckon the fact that the right in question is contingent upon the sanction of the state. It is not difficult to imagine that a population that is on record, practising subsistence agriculture, and has actually reached the stage of having to buy rice for subsistence, is in a critical condition. One might even ask whether the agricultural production by the population was ever enough for subsistence at all. The latter would dispense the state from many a responsibility towards the population concerned. However, it would not be on paper, under the pressure of creating conditions for better productivity like proper irrigation or requisite treatment of the soil and the land. One does find cultivators who are financially entrenched now in the region especially in Gopiballabhpur. This cushioning has happened at own endeavour without any initiative from the state as such. At this juncture, one needs to ask if the state is losing credibility as far as rights are concerned, from which source the people get their rights guaranteed? The Indian state as a whole and the West Bengal, in particular, must face this odd question since they still take pride in their welfare ideology.

NOTES

1. Interview by researcher in Singdhui Village dated 24 January 2009.
2. Roy, Rajat, Endemic Hunger in West Bengal in *Economic and Political Weekly*, 3 May 2008.
3. The Pratichi Trust (2002): "Pratichi Education Report".
4. Government of West Bengal– (2007b): 'Guidelines for Programme on State Action against Hunger and Inequity 2007', Department of Panchayats and Rural Development, Government of West Bengal, Kolkata.
5. Demographic Details of the Nayagram Block, Paschim Medinipur

General Information		Educational Institution
Block Head Quarter	Baligaria	College
Distance from District Quartyer	120 Km.	Higher Secondary School
Distance from Nearest Rly. Stn.		Secondary School
Geographical Area	50,170 ha.	Primary School
Gram Panchayat	12	No. of SSK
Mouza	336	No. of MSK
Gram Sansad	93	No. of Angawadi Centre
ICJCK		Rural Library
No. of Household	20,513	NCLP School
Total Population (2001) Census	123,937	Literate
Male	62,629	Illiterate
Female	61,308	

SC/ST population(2001)	22757/49387	Total Irrigated Area	6,280 ha.
Small farmer	4,892	Irrigation Facilities (in Heet)	
Marginal farmer	8,625	Canal	
BPL families (survey-2002)	15,506(47.5%)	Tank & Pond	
Land use in Heet		RLI	
Net area under cultivation	23,760		
Area under Pasture, Orchard etc.	200	OTHERS	
Cultivable wast land	805	Power Station	
Forest land	15,113	No. of Mouza electrified	
Residual area		No. of Post Office	
Land reforms (in Heet.)		No. of Co-operative Society	
Total land vested	3,680	No. of SGH group	
Vested land distributed	3,276	No. of Mid-Day-Meal running	
No. of vested land beneficiary	22,274	No. of Comercial Bank	
Patta Holder	21,754	No. of Gramin Bank	
Bargadar	2,074		
Health Facilities		Total Road Connection	
Block Animal Health Center		B.T.	
		Kuntcha road	
No. of B.P.H.C.		Morrum Road	
No. of P.H.C.		No. of Bus route	
No. of Sub-Center			
Fertilizer Shop			
Pesticide Shop			
Seed Shop			
Total irrigated area(Kharif)			
Total irrigated area(Robi)			
Main Worker			
Marginal Worker			
Cultivation			
Agri labours			
Household industries			

Source: http://paschimmedinipur.gov.in/profiles/nayagram.html, accessed on 11 September 2009.

6. Rana, Kumar, *Khandito Unnayan: Jhargram Mahakumar Ekti Shankhipto Ruprekha* (Mimeograph), November 2006.
7. *Census 1961: West Bengal: District Census Handbook – Medinipur, Volume I*; published by The Superintendent, Government Printing, West Bengal (1966), p.146.
8. Appendix II of the census 1961 is a chapter about Western Medinipur (pp.133-65). This was also a part of the 1951 census and is a special note written by Satyesh C Chakraborty. It defines agriculture in the area as "... cultivation of crops. According to the 1944-45 survey, 57 per cent of the total area of Western Medinipur was used for agriculture" (this 'survey' was the one mentioned in H S M Ishaque – Agricultural Survey by plot to plot Enumeration – 1944-45 –Vol.III, pp.200-17, Calcutta –1947) "The acreage under principal crops have been described below.

"*(i) Paddy* – Paddy covered 89.2 per cent of the total cropped land. There are two principal harvests, *Bhadoi* and *Haimantic*, *Rabi* being unimportant. *Aus* paddy is sown broadcast on dry land in the months of April, May and June and reaped in November and December. 86.3 per cent of total acreage under paddy was devoted to *Aman*. There are two methods of cultivation, transplantation and broadcast. The latter requires less labour, but the former ensures a higher yield and better quality. Transplantation is the general method of cultivation in Western Medinipur. The seed is first sown in nurseries and afterwards transplanted into fields. The preparation of the fields begins in early March. Several ploughings are necessary. It is cultivated in deep water condition. Low earthen dams, locally known as *ails*, are constructed around each plot of land. These must hold water till the end of October. But after the middle of September, normal rainfall is hardly sufficient to meet the requirements of *Aman* paddy. Even in normal years, therefore, artificial irrigation is necessary to ensure harvest.

"There is yet another harvest of paddy in other parts of lower Bengal. This is *Rabi* or spring harvest and the paddy is known as *Boro*. It is unimportant in Western Medinipur. Only 0.1 per cent is of the total acreage under paddy was devoted to *Boro* . . .

"*Ecology as a constraint* – in sum, there are three principal harvests in Western Medinipur, of which *Haimantic* is the principal one. Paddy is the main crop and vegetables and pulses rank second. In the figure below, the year has been divided into three harvesting seasons.

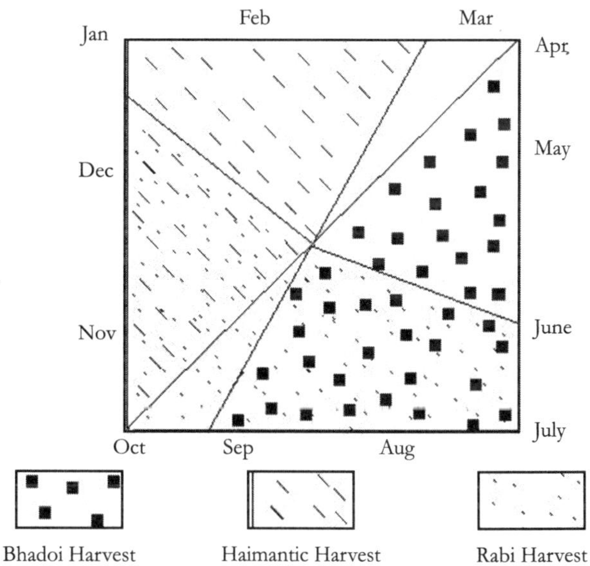

The duration of each season has been calculated by the time required for maturing of their respective principal crops. It indicates that (i) a single plot of land cannot raise two successive harvests of either *Haimantic* and *Bhadoi* or *Haimantic* and *Rabi* as their seasons overlap each other and (ii) *rabi* and *bhadoi* can be theoretically raised from the same plot of land. But, as the rainfall during October and May is very scanty, *rabi* and *bhadoi* can be raised in succession in limited areas only. In other words, in the major part of Western Medinipur, agricultural activities are limited to the cultivation of a single crop, i.e., *aman* paddy. This is a major constraint arriving purely from the ecological requirements of the crops cultivated."

9. Census 1961: West Bengal: District Census Handbook – Medinipur Vol.I, published by The Superintendent, Government Printing, West Bengal (1966), p.147.
10. The Medinipur District Gazetteer (page 59) notes about the Santals that "in some instances they have been known to till their lands with considerable success, and raise good crops of rice and *collie* (kalai), but all that their vigilance can preserve from the ravages of wild beasts, is extorted from them by the rapacity of money-lenders . . .".
11. http://anagrasarkalyan.gov.in/census/Villages-with-Consentration-of-SC,ST(Medinipur).pdf, accessed on 10 August 2009.
12. Demographic details of the Singdhui village, Paschim Medinipur

No of HouseholdS	160		
Total Population	797	Population below 06 yrs	140
Male Population	387	Population below 06 Male	71
Female Population	410	Population below 06 Female	69
TOTAL AGRICULTURE LABOUR	69		
Marginal Agriculture Labour – Male	24	Marginal Agriculture Labour – Female	45
Literate Population	206	Illiterate Population	591
Male Literate	156	Male illiterate population	231
Female Literate	50	Female illiterate population	360
No of Households	160	Working Population	482
MAIN WORKING POPULATION	169		
Main Working Population Male	71	Main Working Population Female	98
Main Casual Working Population	4	Total Casual labour	
Main Casual Working Population			
Male	3	Main Casual Working Population	
Female	1		
NUMBER OF SC	0		
Male SC Population	0	Female SC Population	0
NUMBER OF ST	725		
Male ST Population	352	Female ST Population	373

Source: http://www.indianngos.com/west_Medinipur view_results_detail.asp?ID=4851&mVarTable=[Sheet1], accessed on 11 September 2009.

13. Demographic Details of the Bara Pat Village, Paschim Medinipur

No of Households	45		
Total Population	234	Population below 06 yrs	37
Male Population	127	Population below 06 Male	22
Female Population	107	Population below 06 Female	15
Total Agriculture Labour	0		
Marginal Agriculture Labour – Male	0	Marginal Agriculture Labour – Female	0
Literate Population	144	Illiterate Population	90
Male Literate	91	Male illiterate population	36
Female Literate	53	Female illiterate population	54
No of Households	45	Working Population	115
Main Working Population	16		
Main Working Population Male	5	Main Working Population Female	11
Main Casual Working Population	4	Total Casual labour	
Main Casual Working Population			
Male	2	Main Casual Working Population	
Female	2		
Number of SC	0		
Male SC Population	0	Female SC Population	0
Number of ST	234		
Male ST Population	127	Female ST Population	107

Source:http://www.indianngos.com/west_Medinipur/view_results_detail.asp?ID=4851&mVarTable=[Sheet1], accessed on 11 September 2009.

14. Paschim Medinipur District Statistical Handbook; p.38.
15. *Ibid.*, p.36.
16. Census of India, 2001.
17. Interview by the researcher, dated 24 January 2009.
18. Focused group discussion with 12 residents and some passersby of Bara Pat village, dated 25 January 2009.
19. Paragraph 3.70, West Bengal Economic Review 2007-08.
20. *Census 1961: West Bengal: District Census Handbook – Medinipur Volume I*, published by The Superintendent, Government Printing, West Bengal (1966), p.80.
21. West Medinipur District Statistical Handbook, pp.191, 193
22. Rana, Kumar, *Khandito Unnayan: Jhargram Mahakumar Ekti Shankhipto Ruprekha* (Mimeograph), November 2006, p.7.
23. Paschim Medinipur District Statistical Handbook, pp.191, 193.
24. Interviewed by the researcher on 25 January 2009.
25. Interviewed by researcher on 24 January 2009.
26. Interviewed at Singdhui village by researcher on 24 January 2009.
27. Interviewed at Singdhui village by researcher on 24 January 2009.

CHAPTER 5

Right to Food: Adequate Laws, Inadequate Will and Optimistic Campaigns

RUCHIRA GOSWAMI

There cannot be anything more basic than the entitlement to adequate food to live with human dignity. That we still have to discuss and demand the Right to Food is reprehensible in itself and seems anachronistic and unreal. Yet, nothing can be more real and shocking than people being denied a meaningful and dignified existence because they cannot get enough to eat. Any discussion on the Right to Food is indicative of the tremendous inequalities of the times. All the so-called national and global progress and development of humankind have not translated into guaranteeing the basic entitlements for a healthy and worthy life till date. Famines, populations succumbing to malnourishment, images of hungry and sunken human figures are not historical imageries of yesteryears but quotidian experiences of the world's poor in contemporary times. In spite of scientific progress, technological innovations and setting up of democratic societies – in which power vests with the peoples – universal food security on a national and global scale seems like an unachievable target. The causes are manifold and obstacles many and this discussion does not address these issues. This paper is essentially a discussion on the development of a legal Right to Food in

India. There exists a huge body of extremely well researched literature on the topic – both theoretical and empirical. There are extensive thought-provoking discussions on several areas on the Right to Food – whether there is a legal entitlement to food in India, debates on the justiciability of socio-economic rights, emerging international obligations of states, discussions on food security and food sovereignty, recent developments, achievements and limitations of campaigns of food for all, social policies and schemes for food security. In fact, the list seems to be endless. Like other human rights issues, the Right to Food is a social, economic, political, philosophical and legal question. It interweaves with other several issues – agricultural investment and production, agrarian crisis, debates on development, role of international financial systems, concepts of justice and democracy, budget and prioritisation of funds, political will, social exclusion, role of the law and judicial activism. This paper focuses primarily on the legal entitlement to food in India. While laws have been an important mechanism for guaranteeing rights and initiating concrete changes, the optimistic reliance on the law to transform deeply entrenched inequalities and hierarchies need serious deliberation. Nearly all social movements, campaigns and advocacy strategies in India have relied on the legal system and the judiciary to deliver justice, only to realise that a legal guarantee means little without corresponding social changes. While most claim that law is just one significant instrument of social reform and transformation, engagement with the law seems to be the focal point of all such movements. Trying to cleanse the system of its ills and inadequacies with the help of suitable and pro-people democratic policies, legislations and amendments yielded limited results. While the language rights and especially a legal claim to long-denied resources is extremely empowering, it remains a mere rhetoric if not backed by commensurate structural changes. It is imperative for all human rights practitioners to engage in the struggle to ensure that both the legal and the social are transformed in tandem so that human rights (of food and all other requirements) become meaningful for all.

The first part of the paper discusses the evolution of the right, developed through case laws that expanded on the fundamental right, Right to Life to include Right to Food within its ambit. Elaborating on the international obligations to ensure universal food security, the second part of the paper discusses the persuasive implications of several international documents and conventions that India had ratified. The Right to Food campaign led to the creation of several food-related schemes that has culminated in a Right to Food draft Act. A description, typology and analyses of the efficacy of the schemes and the draft Act constitutes the third part of the discussion of this paper. The effectiveness of the Right to Food campaign and deliberating on the ability of the legal system to address structural inequalities is the subject matter of the fourth part of the paper. Finally, there is a brief description of certain food crisis-related events in West Bengal, which have occurred in the last few years and the challenges that such incidents pose for ensuring food security.

CONSTITUTIONAL GUARANTEES

The Constitution of India does not guarantee an explicit guarantee of the Right to Food. However, over the years, the creative interpretation and expansion of Article 21 that guarantees Right to Life and personal liberty by the Supreme Court (SC) has enabled the protection of many substantive rights and procedural safeguards. In a number of cases discussed later, the Supreme Court has interpreted Right to Life to include basic minimum guarantees that ensures a dignified human existence, going beyond the narrow protection of civil liberties that the provision originally intended to protect.

A more explicit intention on the part of the country to ensure food security to all its peoples is contained in the Directive Principles of State Policy. Article 47 states that it is the duty of the state to raise the level of nutrition and standard of living of its people; the improvement of public health is among its primary duties. Also of relevance is Article 39(a) that states all citizens, irrespective of sex, equally have the right to an adequate means of livelihood. Article 39(e) also intends to protect the health and strength of workers, men and women, and ensure that the tender age of children is not abused and that citizens are not forced by economic necessity to enter vocations unsuited to their strength.[1]

CASE LAWS ON RIGHT TO FOOD[2]

In a number of cases concerned with the protection of socio-economic rights, the Supreme Court of India has engaged in a creative expansion of Article 21 that protects the Right to Life and personal liberty.

In Kesavananda Bharati vs. State of Kerala,[3] a landmark case discussing the basic structure of the Constitution that cannot be amended, the bench observed that the objective of the Constitution was to promote social and economic justice, liberty and equality. It was further observed that freedom from starvation is as important as the Right to Life.

In Francis Coralie Mullin vs. Union Territory of Delhi,[4] the Court interpreted that Right to Life includes the right to live with human dignity and bare necessities of life that includes adequate nutrition, clothing and shelter and civil liberties such as facilities for reading, writing and expressing oneself in diverse forms, freely moving about and mixing with other human beings.

In Shantisar Builders vs. Narayana Khimalal Totame,[5] the SC observed "the right to life would include the right of food, clothing and decent environment and reasonable accommodation to live in that allows the full development of physical, mental and intellectual aspects".

In Olga Tellis vs. Bombay Municipal Corporation,[6] the SC emphasised that term life in Article 21 is not only restricted to mere animal existence of a person. Since the ambit of Article 21 is quite large, it does not merely mean that life cannot be taken away by the state but entails a positive obligation on part of states as well. Hence, the Right to life implies right to livelihoods.

In Bandhua Mukti Morcha vs. Union of India,[7] the purview of Article 21 was expanded once again – to live with human dignity, free from exploitation. It included the protection of health and strength of workers, protection of men, women and children against abuse, creation of opportunities and facilities for children to develop in a healthy manner and in conditions of freedom and dignity, educational facilities and just and human conditions of work, and maternity relief. These are the minimum conditions that exist to enable a person to live with human dignity. No government can take action to deprive a person of the enjoyment of these basic rights.

In Dena Nath vs. National Fertilizers Ltd.,[8] the Court observed that the provision to establish a canteen should be enforced in every establishment under Section 16 to supply food to workers at subsidised rates, as the Right to Food is a basic human right.

In Chameli Singh vs. State of Uttar Pradesh,[9] the SC observed that Right to Life guaranteed in any civilised society implies the right to food, water, decent environment, education, medical care and shelter.

In Kapila Hingorani vs. State of Bihar,[10] hundreds of employees of state-owned corporations, public undertakings or other statutory bodies in the State of Bihar died due to starvation, or committed suicide owing to acute financial crises resulting from the non-payment of remuneration for a long time. When this fact was brought to the notice of the Supreme Court, it held that the state cannot escape its liability when human rights problems of such a magnitude involve starvation deaths. While deciding the case, the Court referred to Article 11 of the International Covenant on Economic, Social and Cultural Rights, 1966, and declared that human beings have a Right to Food and that hunger is violation of human rights.

INTERNATIONAL PROTECTION OF RIGHT TO FOOD

Several international mechanisms recognise the human being's Right to Food

Article 25 of The Universal Declaration of Human Rights proclaims that everyone has the right to a standard of living adequate for the health and well-being of himself and his family, including food, clothing, housing and medical care, necessary social services and right to security.[11]

Right to Food and freedom from hunger is further reiterated and emphasised in The International Covenant on Economic, Social and Cultural Rights (ICESCR).[12] Article 11.1 of the Covenant recognises that everyone has the right to an adequate standard of living, including food, clothing, housing and improvement of living conditions. Article 11.2 explicitly states everyone has the fundamental right to be free from hunger and that state parties – individually and through international cooperation – shall have to take measures and specific programmes for improved production, conservation and distribution of food. It further urges states to ensure equitable distribution of world food supplies by taking into account the problems of food-importing and food-exporting countries.

CEDAW[13] in Article 12 places obligations on state parties to eliminate discrimination against women in health care and to ensure appropriate and free services, if necessary to women in pregnancy, confinement and post-natal periods. It specifically mentions the need for adequate nutrition during pregnancy and lactation.

Article 24 of the Convention on Rights of the Child[14] recognises the right of the child to enjoy highest attainable standard of health and lays obligations on state parties to take appropriate measures to combat disease and malnutrition. This includes the supply of nutritious food and clean drinking water, access to education and basic knowledge of child health, particularly for parents and children.

General Comment 12[15] expanding on Article 11.1 of ICESCR lays down detailed obligations on part of state parties to ensure Right to Food. In spite of reaffirming Right to Food as intrinsic to human dignity in international human rights law, the Committee recognises the glaring gap between the recognition of the right and standards grounded in international law and the ground reality. Article 2 of ICESCR establishes the nature of state parties' obligations for the realisation of socio-economic rights. They are progressively realisable and states are to utilise their maximum available resources for the realisation of social and economic rights. However, General Comment 12 affirms that progressive realisation is not a plea for inaction on part of state parties. There exists a minimum core obligation on part of states for realising social and economic rights. States have a core obligation to take necessary action to mitigate and alleviate hunger even at times of natural or other disasters, and every state is under an obligation to ensure everyone under its jurisdiction has access to the minimum essential food that is sufficient, and adequate and safe in terms of nutrition, to ensure their freedom from hunger.

STATE OBLIGATIONS

The core content of the Right to Food implies adequacy, accessibility and availability[16] of food in sufficient quantity and quality suited to dietary requirements of individuals in a given culture. Detailing each abovementioned term, General Comment 12 further outlines the nature of state obligations and violations of the Right to Food. There exist three obligations on part of states for the progressive realisation of socio-economic rights – obligations to respect, protect and fulfil. In the context of the Right to Food, the obligation to respect means that states will not take any measures that prevent access to food to any part of the population. The obligation to protect means that states will take measures to ensure that non-state parties do not prevent access to food. Obligation to fulfil means that states will facilitate access and utilisation of resources and take proactive measures to strengthen food security. If individuals and groups fail to access food in circumstances beyond their control, such as in situations of crisis that includes conflicts and natural disasters, the state has an obligation to provide for the right directly.

State violations occur when there is any action on the part of the state that impedes the enjoyment of the right or when the state has failed to ensure the basic minimum requirements to be free from hunger. General Comment 12 of ICESCR also distinguishes between inability and unwillingness on the part of the state to ensure the enjoyment of a right. If a state claims insufficiency of resources which prevents the realisation of a right, it has to demonstrate that it has failed in spite of maximum utilisation of resources and, in such circumstances, can seek international cooperation that the international community is under an obligation to provide.

The Limburg Principles on the Implementation of Social and Economic Rights[17] developed by a group of experts at Limburg University, Maastricht, Netherlands, in 1986, interprets and details state obligations for the complete realisation of social and economic rights. Interpreting obligations presented in Part II of the ICESCR, the document categorically asserts that at the national level, state parties shall adopt all appropriate means that includes legislative, judicial, administrative, educational and other social measures for the realisation of the right contained in the Covenant. While some obligations, such as non-discrimination, are immediately realisable, others are progressively realisable. However, this cannot be used for indefinite delay in the realisation of any right. Progressive realisation not only includes increase in resources but also effective utilisation of existing resources. Limburg Principles also outline the nature of international assistance and cooperation that is required for the complete realisation and enjoyment of social and economic rights.

The Maastricht Guidelines on Violations of Economic, Social and Cultural Rights[18] developed in 1997 at the 10th anniversary of Limburg Principles lays down further obligations on states for the realisation of social and economic rights. Reiterating the significance of economic and social rights, the guidelines lay down the obligations to respect, protect and fulfil social and economic rights. It further states that states have both an obligation of conduct and obligation of result. While the former requires action reasonably calculated to realise the enjoyment of a particular right, like the adoption and implementation of a plan of action, the obligation of result requires states to achieve specific targets to satisfy a detailed substantive standard.

With the objective of developing the Right to Food further to ensure its practical application, the FAO World Summit on Food held in Rome in 1996, deliberately reasserted the "fundamental right of each individual to have access to food and to be free from hunger". The High Commission of the United Nations for Human Rights in collaboration with the other specialised agencies of the United Nations – inter-governmental and non-governmental organisations – were invited to better define the Right to Food and formulate non-binding voluntary guidelines to orient states on policies of food security. A Code of Behaviour on the Right to Food was proposed in Venezuela in 1996 and a final version of the Code was presented and accepted by international experts at the International Seminar on the Right to Food in Geneva in 1997. In 1998, FAO dedicated a publication – *'The Right to Food in theory and practice"* – wholly to the right to food and, for the first time, to the Code of Behaviour. In 2000, Jean Siegler was appointed the *Special Rapporteur* on the Right to Food. Responsible for the monitoring the progress of the Right to Food and reporting on the same to the United Nations, his first report mentions the Code of Behaviour as a valid international tool for implementing the Right to Food. Recognising the difficulties in achieving political consensus in relatively short time to develop a convention, the Code was envisaged to create some degree of consensus and interest in food security as voluntary non-binding guidelines for states. There are four objectives of the Code:

(i) Specifying obligations of states at national and international levels as well as other actors in civil society,

(ii) Providing guidelines for developing programmes and policies to guarantee Right to Food,

(iii) Developing guidelines and directions for future course of action, such as formulation of new laws and agreements and international resolutions on Right to Food,

(iv) Generating awareness within civil society for monitoring the Right to Food.[19]

As a country following the common law jurisdiction, India follows a dualist principle. It means that the international obligations stated in international conventions ratified by India do not automatically become a part of domestic law as in monist systems. Such obligations have to legislated by the Parliament to enable international obligations to become binding upon the country. However, as for Constitutional guarantees of socio-economic rights in general, the Right to Food in particular is protected through Fundamental Rights, and Directive Principles of State Policy enshrined in Part III and Part IV respectively of the Constitution. Moreover, as discussed earlier in a number of cases, the Right to Food has been guaranteed through a creative and expansive interpretation of the Right to Life (Article 21). In several among these cases, judicial decisions refer to international obligations under ICESCR and, thus, they have some persuasive value.

The landmark case that propelled the discussion on the Right to Food in the national arena was a Public Interest Litigation (PIL) filed by Peoples' Union of Civil Liberties in 2001 in the wake of several starvation deaths across the country. The PIL drew attention to the piling of food stocks in warehouses that coexisted with massive malnutrition among the masses. A nationwide Right to Food campaign was launched by civil society groups compelling national and state governments to address this bizarre paradoxical situation and take measures to ensure food security.[20] A series of events followed along with campaigns for introducing mid-day meals in schools, to revamp and check corruption in the Public Distribution System, ensuring food for work and financial support for population below the poverty line. In response to the PIL, the Supreme Court issued 44 interim orders till date to the state and national governments for introducing various schemes to address food security. The first major interim order was issued in November 2001, which focused on eight food-related schemes.[21]

1. The Public Distribution System (PDS),
2. Antyodaya Anna Yojana (AAY),
3. Mid-Day Meal Scheme,
4. Integrated Child Development Scheme (ICDS),

5. Annapurna Scheme,
6. National Old Age Pension Scheme,
7. National Maternity Benefit Scheme (NMBS), and
8. National Family Benefit Scheme (NFBS)

A typology of the schemes indicates that all target the most vulnerable sections of the population. The PDS and the AAY are household-based schemes that target poor households. A targeted approach to PDS was adopted in 1997, whereby different ration cards were issued to Above Poverty Line (APL) and Below Poverty Line (BPL) families, which carried different entitlements. While PDS orders also apply to AAY, the latter is specifically meant for destitute households, and states were requested to provide free grain to the households who were too poor to even buy their quota of foodgrains at subsidised rates. In 2003, priority groups, including aged, infirm, destitute men and women, pregnant and lactating women, widows, senior citizens over 60 years with no assured subsistence, households with disabled adults with no assured means of subsistence and "primitive tribes" were identified who would be entitled to AAY cards. The National Family Benefit Scheme provides for a lump sum cash assistance of Rs.10,000 on the death of the primary income earner in a BPL family.

Mid-Day Meal and ICDS target children. The former provides for cooked, hot meals for all children attending a government or government-aided school. The ICDS covers children less than six years of age, with a package of integrated services such as nutrition, health care and pre school education. Since at this age, children's well being is intrinsically linked to their mothers, pregnant and lactating women are also covered by this scheme.

Along with the prioritisation of elderly persons in the AAY scheme, the Annapurna Scheme launched in 2000 is meant to assist those who are eligible for pension but do not receive it. The beneficiaries, after being identified by the Gram Panchayat, are entitled to 10 kgs of grain free of cost through the PDS with the issue of ration cards.

The National Maternity Benefit Scheme provides for lump sum cash assistance of Rs.500 to be provided to pregnant women in the BPL category for upto two live births 8-12 weeks before delivery. This is in addition to the non-cash benefits that women have under the ICDS.

National Grameen Rojgar Yojana became the main focus of the next interim order in 2002 that translated in the National Rural Employment Guarantee Act. These schemes have been converted into legal entitlements since a person with a valid claim under the scheme can approach a court of law if he/she is denied the due share under the scheme.

Umbrella Orders: Essentially to ensure government accountability, several umbrella orders have also been passed. Collectors of states are responsible for ensuring compliance with Court orders in any districts and chief secretaries of states are held responsible for any defaults in compliance. Gram Sabhas have been given powers to conduct social audits of all food-related schemes and report misuse of funds; they have access to all relevant information relating to the selection of beneficiaries and disbursement of funds. Umbrella orders also include public display of the orders for dissemination of information, the prohibition on any discontinuity of any scheme without the approval of the Court and complete utilisation of grain quotas of all state governments.

A study of these schemes reveals that all have not been equally successful. While the success of the mid-day meals is often most discussed and celebrated, the other scheme meant for children, i.e. the ICDS, has limited impact. After an initial period of dormancy, universalisation of ICDS was achieved by virtue of its inclusion in the National Common Minimum Programme. In spite of several recommendations, the ground situation has hardly changed. The scheme is plagued by numerous shortcomings like the shortage of Anganwadis, lack of appropriate allocation of funds, overworked workers with meagre incomes. As a result, there has been little improvement in quality. There is substantial variation in the success of the PDS scheme. While in some states, like Kerala, PDS has relatively been successful, in the poorer states like Jharkhand and Bihar, PDS has not been able to mitigate hunger. As far as AAY is concerned, states are yet to devise a method for the identification and coverage of all households belonging to the "priority groups" as identified by the scheme. The National Family Benefit Scheme has always received negligible attention in the orders and reports and hardly any information is available as to how it works on the ground. The Annapurna Scheme has not really been functional and reports suggest that it has limited coverage and impact. In spite of prohibition of any discontinuation of any schemes, some reports suggest that the scheme has either not been implemented properly in the first place or has been discontinued in some states. Reports suggest that the National Maternity Benefit Scheme is also a failure. Complicated procedures, delayed payments and limited coverage have led the Government to consider discontinuing the scheme. An alternative scheme, Janani Suraksha Yojana (JSY), has been suggested. While the National Maternity Benefit Scheme aimed at providing maternity benefits, the JSY only provides for institutional deliveries and safe motherhood. Whether additional entitlements available under the previous scheme are available under the new JSY is questionable.[22]

Detailed discussion and evaluation of the schemes – made in the Seventh Report of the Commissioners[23] – reveal further inadequacies and dismal performance. Universalisation remains a distant dream, targeted populations and vulnerable groups have not been covered adequately, malnutrition has increased among children in Madhya Pradesh, Bihar, Jharkhand, Chattisgarh compared with NFHS 2 (this report uses NFHS 3 data), state have not undertaken full fund utilisation and expenditure.

The Right to Food campaign[24] has been a lively and powerful movement at the national level. Extensive ground work, elaborate field reports, systematic analysis, monitoring and recommendations by the commissioners, creative advocacy strategies and sustained involvement of civil society groups and individuals has put the human Right to Food on the national radar, compelling political parties to take notice of the situation and increased the level of governmental accountability. The Right to Food case focused on starvation deaths in different parts of India. They were recognised as extreme manifestation of malnutrition and hunger. In 2002, the Court declared that starvation deaths indicated that orders have not been implemented. Umbrella orders have stated that in instances of starvation deaths, widespread hunger, chronic malnutrition, district collectors and chief secretaries of states will be held responsible.[25] Accountability has not adequately been specified in the orders. Does that include suspension or any other punishment of concerned officials? There have been no instances of any authority taking moral responsibility, tendering apologies or resigning in states plagued by chronic hunger. On the contrary, state governments have denied any occurrence of deaths due to starvation and there is side stepping of responsibilities. Governments have continuously shielded officials and have claimed that records of starvation or hunger are false and politically motivated by the opposition parties.[26] The power vested in the Gram Sabhas to conduct social audits is a commendable move to decentralise the entire system. Yet such power is fraught with dangers. Gram Sabhas might not be the most representative and inclusive bodies, and often narrow partisan political motivations can hinder and overshadow the truly democratic and neutral role that Gram Sabhas are expected to perform. All this leads one to question the results of nearly a decade of active campaigning and the proactive role of the Court. The same executive that has been non-functional is now expected to deliver. While it can be argued that one of the major objectives of the campaign and court cases is to act as a wake-up call for governments to rise from its stupor, compel the executive to perform and hold them accountable, whether such enormous efforts have been successful in achieving the objectives remains a significant question. This is not to make a cynical, pessimistic suggestion that nothing will change and all such efforts to address and correct widespread inequalities will yield nothing. It is to interrogate the results of nearly decade-long celebrated court interventions to guarantee Right to Food. Of course, it is a Herculean task for any social movement or campaigns to redress deeply entrenched social hierarchies and structural inequalities and a decade might be too short a time to make a fair evaluation of such efforts. One also needs to question what really qualifies as a social movement, and is the Right to Food campaign a movement for structural social change or a significant and important campaign only to plug the glaring loopholes in the existing order. The campaign has a focused objective – to reform the existing food distribution system and guarantee universal access to food and it is not making any further claims to change the system. While such a focused effort can yield some significant changes, it cannot address issues of widespread structural inequities that are intrinsically connected to the issue it seeks to address.

Another recent development in ensuring a universal Right to Food in India is the drafting of a proposed Right to Food Act.[27] The draft legislation seeks to "ensure dignified economic and social access to adequate food and other requirements of good nutrition for all residents of the country, at all times, in pursuance of their fundamental right to be free from hunger, malnutrition and other deprivations associated with the lack of food". The Act creates legal entitlements and enforces obligations for states to ensure that every person has a dignified access to food necessary for an active and healthy life. By collating several schemes declared by the interim orders in one document, the draft Act provides for the supply of cereals and other nutrition at a very low cost to the poor and vulnerable population. Several developments of the schemes and analyses of various reports suggested the need to identify a broad range of beneficiaries and priority groups other than those living under the poverty line. Therefore, the Act covers all migrant workers, and specific provisions guarantee access to food by the urban poor. The Act also entitles households displaced involuntarily, affected by natural disasters, communal violence or any other natural or man-made emergency or disaster situation to emergency Antyodaya cards valid for one year. These households shall also be entitled to double entitlements under all nutrition-related schemes for a period of one year.

The Act also reiterates the obligation of district collectors and panchayat heads in events of starvation as outlined in the umbrella orders. It mandates an immediate response by district collectors and panchayat heads to any complaint or report of starvation death from any source, by carrying out investigation into conditions of hunger and food denial in the affected family and community and providing immediate and long-term relief based on prima facie evidence of vulnerability and starvation.

As a progressive and inclusive legislation, it tries to ensure enhancing social equity by giving preference to single women and SC/ST women in the appointment of cooks and helpers for the mid-day meal programme and prohibits the use of private contractors under the ICDS. It also mentions special provisions for the inclusion of marginalised children in ICDS, including differently abled children, street children and children from migrant families. Under the PDS entitlements, the Act states that "women shall be considered as the head of the household for the purpose of distribution of BPL Cards and Antyodaya Cards, unless there is no adult woman in the household". As a comprehensive legislation, the draft Act tries to secure maternity entitlements originally guaranteed by the currently abandoned National Maternity Benefit Scheme. It provides for a monthly benefit of Rs.1,000 to pregnant women for pre- and post-natal care. Aiming at gradually universalising the programme from covering women with Antyodaya cards to all pregnant women within five years, it prioritises pregnant women in the BPL category as beneficiaries and mandates unconditional benefits and timely disbursal of funds. It also mandates setting up crèches for children whose mothers are working.

The draft also addresses the needs of the elderly that the Annapurna Scheme and the National Old Age Pension Scheme were supposed to provide for. The Act provides for a pension-based social assistance of Rs.400 per month on an individual basis to widows, elderly and disabled persons in rural areas.

The draft legislation mandates setting up a National Food and Nutrition Commission, an independent monitoring body to ensure compliance with the provisions of the Act and advise the Central Government on matters relating to food. The Commission is similar in its composition, functions and powers to that of other existing commissions in India, such as the National Human Rights Commission, National Commission for Women and the SC/ST Commission. Based on nominations/list of names prepared by the Planning Commission, the chairperson and members will be appointed by a committee comprised of the Prime Minister, the leader of the Opposition and a judge of the Supreme Court nominated by the Chief Justice. The powers and functions of the Commission are (i) evaluation of nutrition-related schemes (ii) preparation of annual report by the Commission and independent reports by members to be placed in Parliament and made public by web posting, (iii) power to conduct enquiries (iv) recommendations to the government on the suitable course of action post enquiry. This includes suggestion of (a) prosecution and other actions in cases of violation of the Right to Food (b) approaching appellate courts for directions of writs (c) recommendations to the government for providing interim relief (d) binding directions to governments to fulfil the objectives of the Act.

The Act is a significant and laudable effort in making entitlement to food a justiciable right. Building on and going beyond the various schemes that entitle the most vulnerable populations to food, the draft legislation transforms social policies into legal rights. Such an effort is indeed praiseworthy. However, the efficacy and ability of the Act to significantly alter the current dismal scenario of food distribution seems to be limited. Rahul Lahoti argues in *The Hindu* that there is an imbalance in the expansive vision and principle of the Act and the narrow means of achieving it, primarily through its focus on calories and ensuring distribution rather than on developing mechanisms for more control and command over the food distributive system as a whole and the policies determining the distribution.[28] Even as a comprehensive legislation sensitive to the needs of the most vulnerable and entrenched within the rights framework distinct from a welfare approach, the Act does not significantly add to and restructure the present PDS or the existing schemes. Whether the legislation is truly rights-based is incumbent on the extent to which one can demand a binding entitlement in a court of law. Ambiguities and discrepancies regarding beneficiaries, clearly delineating those below and above poverty line need to be sorted out first.

It would not be completely erroneous to state that the setting up of the National Food and Nutrition Commission is an exercise in futility. The rationale behind replicating similar kinds of commissions that are only vested with recommending powers – paper tigers with no teeth – seems unclear except that the Act simply chooses to go down the well trodden path. While this is not to deny the limited achievements of the national and state commissions, a critical evaluation of these commissions have brought into sharp focus the contradictions between the tall claims and objectives of the commission when they are set up and their increasing politicisation, limited performance and inability to hold governments accountable once they have been institutionalised. Given this experience, it is surprising that a new Act also suggests a similar body for monitoring of violations of Right to Food.

Right to Food is intrinsically connected to an entire range of other issues – debates on what constitutes development, issues of investment in rural development, stagnation in agricultural development, depleting food security and addressing deeply entrenched hierarchies and fault lines of caste, caste, gender, age, ability and location. The food security schemes take into account these concerns to some extent, but to remedy and transform social and economic inequities through an Act is a tall order. India as well as global social movements and campaigns for change have engaged continuously with the legal system to initiate changes. However, this engagement with legal reforms has yielded limited results. While it is always claimed that the law is just a potent instrument of social change, all energies are driven primarily towards reforming the legal system and engagement with the law becomes an end in itself rather than a means to an end. The Right to Food campaign also seems to fall in the same trap.

While it is a significant step towards increasing government accountability and transparency, public policies and legal enactments for ensuring food security will remain stunted without a social movement initiated and led by the masses themselves.

In this context, a couple of recent incidents in West Bengal demand attention. In Jalangi in Murshidabad district of West Bengal, the changing course of the River Padma has devoured vast tracts of land rendering thousands of people homeless. Denied BPL cards, homeless and unemployed, the poor illiterate people of this area have been victims of government apathy. According to a report published in 2005, 692 people in the worst affected Dayaram village were on the verge of starvation deaths. While many had not received BPL cards, other cardholders entitled to subsidised foodgrains did not receive their quota since rice was not available in the ration shops. Speaking out against corruption meant facing the wrath and violence unleashed by the party cadres of CPI(M). Several other reports by Manabadhikar Suraksha Mancha (MASUM) and news-paper reports in English and vernacular dailies brought into focus the unsympathetic and callous attitude of the state government and district administration and a PIL was filed in 2005.[29] Loss of arable land due to river erosion, loss of livelihoods, shelter and clothing, lack of adequate food, children denied education; the starvation deaths and denial of all socio-economic rights as a result is a classic illustration of what it is to be poor in contemporary India. A similar story of starvation deaths, closure of gardens and denial of compensation was reported in the tea gardens of North Bengal. In 2004, there were reports of starvation deaths in Amlashole in Medinipur district. The initial reaction of the West Bengal government was denial; the government tried to explain that the cause of deaths was malnutrition and chronic illnesses. Later, investigative reports on the deaths of five shabar tribals revealed that that the entire caste was afflicted by severe landlessness, loss of traditional livelihoods and tremendous impoverishment. While these five persons succumbed to hunger, others were on the brink of starvation.[30] In the face of this revelation, Chief Minister Buddhadev Bhattacharjee finally conceded that poverty and starvation existed at Amlasole. At the Assembly, he said openly that his government is aware of the existence of poverty and starvation in the state and is, therefore, taking measures to eliminate poverty.[31]

Again in September 2007, citizens of Bankura, Bardhaman, Paschim Medinipur and Murshidabad districts of West Bengal rose in anger against ration dealers. Violence, arson and a collapse of the law and order situation followed. Citizens were opposing the manipulation of food supplies by ration dealers and later reports revealed the unholy nexus between ration shop dealers and black marketeers. As police fired on the irate mob in Bardhaman, houses and shops of ration dealers were set on fire in Birbhum. As the spontaneous outburst by citizens snowballed into an independent embryonic movement by the affected people themselves, it was quickly transformed into a political game with the Trinamool Congress (the Opposition party) in West Bengal taking up the reins. Shoma Chatterji, however, states that this mafia-dom of panchayat leaders, ration dealers, black marketers, food inspectors, distributing officers, police and party members is not exclusive to West Bengal. Her report gives interesting statistics of food supply diversion in some states. According to a survey conducted by Tata Economic Consultancy Services, diversion of food supplies is a national problem but there exists wide variation across states. While in Andhra Pradesh the diversion for wheat, rice and sugar are 15%, 19% and 16% respectively, the corresponding figures in West Bengal are 40%, 30% and 24%, with the high rates of diversion in Bihar where the corresponding figures are 44%, 64% and 47%.[32] The situation spiralled out of the hands of the common people who started the agitation when ration dealers started a counter-movement led by the party in power in West Bengal. Ration dealers voluntarily surrendered their licences, demanding adequate protection from the looting, burning of the shops and wrath of the people and claimed that unless the government succeeds in providing them adequate security, they would refuse to do their duty. The state government responded by claiming that the licences of 163 errant ration dealers have been cancelled. It further claimed that just because there are some corrupt people among the ration dealers as there is in all professions, the entire lot of ration dealers cannot be branded as corrupt. CPI(M) Politbureau member and West Bengal state secretary Biman Basu in an interview to People's Democracy on 28 October 2007 also stated that part of the problem was the drastic reduction in the Central quota of supplies for West Bengal. Ration dealers, therefore, did not have adequate quantity in their shops, leading to dissatisfaction among the people, he said. He blamed the Opposition party for creating the anarchic situation and derailing the entire PDS in the state. Even the media was blamed for inciting the mob to vandalise shops. Basu says, "It was seen in many places the TV crews were instructing the agitated cardholders to vandalise the shops and set fire to them, all the time promising to show them on TV".[33] Attributing the problem to a bogus and faulty rationing system, representatives of ration dealers' unions called a strike that resulted in closure of about 20,000 ration shops and mass resignation by dealers who refused to be the targets of people's ire. They also demanded that the government should ensure that a dealer can earn at least Rs.10,000-15,000 per month! A district controller of food supplies dubbed mass resignations and refusal to do duty as illegal and claimed that the government can take action against them. There is no information if any action was taken against the corrupt ration dealers (except the claim that their licences have been cancelled) and arm-twisting tactics adopted by them. Instead, the blame game now snowballed at a national level, with Biman Basu sharply attacking the "clear unwillingness of the Congress-run UPA government in Delhi to conform to the more popular aspects of the Common Minimum Programme or CMP". The issue provided an opportunity to the Congress to lash out at the Left that was impeding the nuke deal at that time, and the Congress suggested that the Left first handle the food crisis which hit the common man more directly than the nuke deal. In response, the Left government in West Bengal blamed the Centre for the ration riots that spread across the state. As the mindless political blame game continued, the real issue of food distribution and security of poor people was thrown to the winds.

One wonders what legal recourse is strong enough to destroy this sheer ignorance, negligence, arrogance and armours of impunity of the administration. In spite of PILS and court orders, ground realities both in urban and rural West Bengal in particular and India in general remain nearly unchanged. No number of court orders, social policies and legal enactments can reform this scenario. If this is acknowledged, then it is an imperative to develop other strategies for change instead of an overt reliance on law's transformative potential. This requires a deep introspection among human rights activists, lawyers and all other concerned members of civil society. It is most important to equip the masses to develop their own struggles, shape their ideologies outside the brainwashing of one political party or another and give leadership to the movement. While the middle class need to be shaken out of their stupor, apathy and indifference to such issues and struggles, we have to realise simultaneously that the leadership to such movements cannot only be given by the middle class. This is not to suggest that no positive changes have occurred so far or the impoverished cannot speak for themselves. But such changes have been limited, in pockets and widespread structural change is still distant. It is unnecessary to restate that restructuring society and doing away deep inequities will require much more time and effort. The question is how much longer. Even after 63 years of independence, can we say that time is not ripe for everyone to demand and enjoy equality – not only in matters of accessing food with dignity but also in the right to live like a human being. This paper is just a modest effort to stimulate us to look beyond the successful and not so successful efforts already taken by human rights practitioners and ponder over other mechanisms for change.

NOTES

1. Bakshi P M, *The Constitution Of India*, Universal Law Publishing, 2000, p.1795.
2. For a detailed discussion on the expansive interpretation of Article 21, see Jain M P, *Indian Constitutional Law*, Wadhwa and Company, Nagpur, 2004, pp.1078-91.
3. AIR 1973 4 SCC 225 at 875.
4. AIR 1981 SC 746 at 753: (1981) 1 SCC 608.
5. AIR 1990 SC 630: (1990) 1 SCC 520.
6. AIR 1986 SC 180: (1985) 3 SCC 545.
7. AIR 1984 SC 802: (1984) 3 SCC 161.
8. AIR 1992 1 SCC 695.
9. AIR 1996 SC 1051: (1996) 2 SCC 549.
10. AIR 2003 6 SCC 1.
11. Universal Declaration of Human Rights.
12. International Covenant on Economic, Social and Cultural Rights.
13. Convention on the Elimination of All Forms of Discrimination Against Women
14. Convention on the Rights of the Child.
15. Right to Adequate food 9Art.11), E/C.12/1999/5 (General Comments).
16. Right to Food – Guide on Legislating for the Right to Food, Right to Food Unit, Food and Agriculture Organisation, 2008, pp.66-80.
17. Limburg Principles on the Implementation of the International Covenant of Economic and Social Rights, 1986.
18. Maastricht Guidelines on the Violations of Economic, Social and Cultural Rights, 1997.

19. Towards the realisation of the Right to Food Code of Behaviour.
20. *The Hindu*, 18 January 2003.
21. Food Security and Judicial Activism in India, Human Rights Law Network, 2007
22. *Ibid.*, pp.23-85.
23. Right to Food, Human Rights Law Network, 2008, pp.275-405.
24. http://www.righttofoodindia.org/links/updates.html.
25. Supra 21 at 37.
26. People's Democracy, Vol. XXXI, No.44, 4 November 2007 http://pd.cpim.org/2007/1104/11042007_biman%20intrvw.htm.
27. Right to Food Act 2009 (draft, 24 June 2009).
28. *The Hindu*, 28 July 2009, available online at http://www.hindu.com/2009/07/28/stories/2009072855140900.htm.
29. Murshidabad Starvation Deaths, available online at www.milligazette.com/.../2005/20050902-Murshidabad.htm.
30. Asian Human Rights Commission, Introduction available online at http://www.ahrchk.net/pub/mainfile.php/endangered_humanity/225/?print=yes.
31. http://www.expressindia.com/news/fullstory.php?newsid=33590.
32. Rioters Against Ration Dealers, available online at http://www.indiatogether.org/2007/oct/gov-wbpds.htm.
33. Supra 26 at http://pd.cpim.org/2007/1104/11042007_biman%20intrvw.htm.

CHAPTER 6

Right to Information in a Hunger Regime

SIBAJI PRATIM BASU

I

"Information" – the magic word of the post-cold war-globalised world – is indeed a multi-edged sword. Understood essentially as the domain of the state, it is the key to modern power that shapes and reproduces social order in its most minute and microscopic forms. Understood as "webs" linked by satellites, it makes a host of things – from commerce to "terror" – globally possible. Understood as *entitlement*, it gives citizens the power to access hitherto inaccessible "secret" government documents. If these government documents contain policies, decisions and details of implementations of programmes/schemes concerning peoples' sustainable rights, then Right to Information is, without doubts, a powerful weapon, especially, in the hands of the disadvantaged, whose well-being is a test of democracy from the perspectives of a number of scholars – from Rawls to Sen – who strongly stand for the synthesis of liberty and *justice*. The perceived issue of *food as entitlement*, access to information becomes the first stepping stone towards the claim for healthy and nutritious food for all.

Since the 1990s, India is witnessing a new wave of human rights movements and discourses. The Right to Information (RTI) Act, 2005, came into being as a direct result of tremendous pressure by a number of NGOs and civil liberty organisations. Indirectly though, there was an urge on the part of the state as well as Centre to satisfy the international moneylending institutions to borrow the loans to carry out various humanitarian and developmental projects in the neo-liberal atmosphere of the 1990s. It was a time when rolling back of the public undertakings and various welfare activities run by the government became the mantra of the men d'affaires in New Delhi. The government also became heavily dependent on international funding and trade agencies for survival. This privileged the agencies to demand *transparency* of government policy, activities and accounts.[1] In a way, the demand for Right to Information by the NGOs coincided with the conditionalities laid down by international agencies. The perception of *food as entitlement* also began to gain ground at this time.

However, before the rise of the rights discourse, the issue of food security had been a concern of the newly liberated socialistic Indian government. Since the 1950s, the Public Distribution System (PDS) has been a universal entitlement and among India's largest social assistance programmes. It aims to achieve two key objectives – maintain stability of grain prices by establishing minimum procurement prices and providing subsidised basic foodgrains, sugar and cooking fuel to those in need.

MEASURING TECHNIQUES FOR MEASURING POVERTY

Poverty in India was used to be (officially) measured mainly in terms of calorie consumption. The poverty line was drawn on the basis of monthly per capita expenditure on calorie consumption. For example, in 1973-74, an all-India bottom line was drawn at Rs.49 per month in rural areas and Rs.57 in urban areas. People existing below this expenditure line were considered poor, or as people Below Poverty Line (BPL). In 1999-2000, this corresponded to an average per capita expenditure of Rs.328 for rural areas and Rs.454 for urban areas per month. These expenditures correspond to a total household expenditure estimated as sufficient to provide 2,400 calories on a daily basis in rural areas and 2,100 calories in urban areas, plus some basic non-food items. Thus, adequate methods were needed to go beyond the practice of quantifying poverty in terms of food consumption.

The above estimation and definition of poverty has apparently undergone a sea change in the recently published report (November 2009) 'The Expert Group to Review the Methodology for Estimation of Poverty' headed by the Economist, Suresh Tendulkar.[2] According to the Tendulkar Report, the following are the salient features of the proposed new poverty lines:

1. While acknowledging the multidimensional nature of poverty, the estimates of poverty will continue to be based on private household consumer expenditure of Indian households as collected by the National Sample Survey (NSS) Organisation (NSSO).
2. The expert group has also taken a conscious decision to move away from anchoring the poverty lines to a calorie *intake* norm in view of the fact that calorie consumption calculated by converting the consumed quantities in the last 30 days as collected by NSS has not been found to be well correlated with the *nutritional outcomes* observed from other specialised surveys either over time or across space (i.e. between states or rural and urban areas).
3. The National Sample Surveys of household consumer expenditure surveys carried out by the NSSO provide the basic data for official poverty calculations. For canvassing household expenditure on a recall basis, the NSSO has decided to shift to Mixed Reference Period (MRP) for all its consumption surveys in future, namely 365 days for low-frequency items (clothing, footwear, durables, education and institutional health expenditure) and 30 days for the remaining. This change captures the household consumption expenditure of the poor households on low-frequency items of purchase more satisfactorily than the earlier 30-day recall period. The Expert Group decided to adopt the MRP-based estimates of consumption expenditure as the basis for future poverty lines as against the previous practice of using Uniform reference period estimates of consumption expenditure.
4. Underlying consumption poverty line is the reference of the Poverty Line Basket (PLB) of household goods and services consumed by those households at the borderline of the poor and the non-poor. Given an inescapable element of arbitrariness in specifying the numerical nominal level of PLB, the Expert Group

considered it desirable to situate recommended reference PLB in some generally acceptable aspect of the present practice.

5. Even while moving away from the calorie norms, the proposed poverty lines have been validated by checking the adequacy of actual private expenditure per capita near the poverty lines on food, education and health by comparing them with normative expenditures consistent with nutritional, educational and health outcomes. Actual private expenditures reported by households near the new poverty lines on these items were found to be adequate at the all-India level in both rural and the urban areas and for most states. It may be noted that while the new poverty lines have been arrived at after assessing the adequacy of private household expenditure on education and health, the earlier calorie-anchored poverty lines did not explicitly account for these. The proposed poverty lines are in that sense broader in scope.
6. It may be noted that although those near the poverty line in urban areas continue to afford the original calorie norm of 2,100 per capita per day, their actual observed calorie intake from 61st Round of NSS of is 1,776 calories per capita. This actual intake is very close to the revised calorie intake norm of 1,770 per capita per day currently recommended for India by the Food and Agriculture Organisation (FAO). Actually observed calorie intake of those near the new poverty line in rural areas (1,999 calories per capita) is higher than the FAO norm.
7. The proposed reference PLB is also in the latest available data on the observed consumption patterns from the household consumer expenditure survey of NSS for 2004-05 and takes into account all items of consumption (except transport and conveyance) for constructing price indices.
8. The proposed price indices are based on the household-level unit values (approximated price data) obtained from the 61st round (July 2004 to June 2005) of NSS on household consumer expenditure survey for food, fuel and light, clothing and footwear at the most detailed level of disaggregation and, hence, much closer to the actual prices paid by the consumers in rural and urban areas.

9. The new poverty lines seek to enable rural and urban population of all states to afford the recommended all India urban PLB after taking due account of within state rural urban and inter-state differentials (rural and urban) incorporating observed consumer behaviour both at the all India and state levels.
10. The new poverty lines have been generated for all the states including the north-eastern states. However, in the absence of adequate data, the Expert Group has suggested the use of poverty line of the neighbouring states for union territories.

POVERTY, POLICIES AND RTI

If we accept the Tendulkar Report at its face value, the BPL population would increase by nearly 10 crore from 27.5% to 37.2%, and the government's poverty estimates would be closer to those made by the World Bank which said 42% of Indians lived below poverty line in 2005. The World Bank's poverty line is pegged at US$1.25 a day, or at India's rate Rs.21.6 per day in urban areas and Rs.14.3 per day in rural areas.

And according to the *Report on Conditions of Work and Promotion* (2007) by National Commission for Enterprises in Unorganised Sector, New Delhi (popularly known as Arjun Sengupta Report as he was the Chairman of the Commission), an overwhelming 836 million people in India live on a per capita consumption of less than Rs.20 a day. The report is based on government data for the period between 1993-94 and 2004-05. In this report, one is classified as absolutely poor if the per capita consumption amounts to less than Rs.9 per day. However, if the per capita consumption is Rs.13 per day, then the individual is above the poverty line. Although it claims that the "extremely poor" have also benefited, during the period of survey, since their per capita consumption has gone up from Rs.9 to Rs.12, Sengupta also cautions, "The rich tend to hide their consumption. So if you account for that, they are actually richer than the report reflects. This again reflects the fact that the gap between the rich and poor is even wider". This scenario of consumption, presented by a Commission appointed by the government itself, is enough to understand the persistent presence of hunger among a large population of India.[3]

The question of hunger, therefore, needs to be viewed in a framework of food insecurity which covers the following dimensions: (1) availability of food, to meet demands of growing population and changing dietary needs; (2) access to food, which is a function of purchasing power, sustainable livelihoods and employment opportunities and also entitlement to subsidised schemes; (3) absorption and utilisation of food, which is a function of access to clean drinking water, environmental hygiene and primary health care and nutrition practices; (4) vulnerability, which covers external factors affecting food security, viz., natural and man-made disasters; and (5) sustainability, which involves attention to the conservation and enhancement of natural resources such as land, water, forests and biodiversity.

The following are some of the schemes run by the Government of India to provide food assistance to the poor: Targeted Public Distribution System (TPDS) & Public Distribution System (PDS), Food for work (FFW), Mid-Day Meal (MDM) Programme, Integrated Child Development Scheme (ICDS), Antyodaya Anna Yojana (AAY), etc. According to figures released by the United Nations World Food Programme (WFP) in 2009, more than 70% of the children under five in India are anaemic and 40% of the women have chronic energy deficiency. The WFP report came down heavily on the most extensive poverty alleviation programme in the country, the targeted public distribution system (TPDS), for failing to help the needy because of "imperfect information, inexact measurement of household characteristics, corruption and inefficiency".[4]

In this context, let us mention that to preserve a "human face" of the First UPA government, the National Advisory Council (NAC) was formed, in 2004, headed by the ruling Congress President Sonia Gandhi and with members nominated from varied backgrounds, but especially from the fields of social activism. They included Dr M S Swaminathan, agricultural scientist, Aruna Roy, social activist, Jean Dreze, development economist, Narendra Jadhav, member of the Planning Commission, Harsh Mander, former bureaucrat and activist, among others. Owing mainly to the initiative of NAC, the First UPA Government introduced two important legislations. The first is, the National Rural Employment Guarantee Act (NREGA) to guarantee 100 days' job to the rural unemployed in view of providing employment opportunities that would enable them to combat food insecurity to some extent. The second is the Right to Information Act, which was also passed by Indian Parliament in the same year (2005).

The RTI Act 2005 has often been seen as a Right of Rights, since it enables the right-seeking citizens by providing *information* about government-held papers/documents regarding planning, implementation and expenditure of public policies and day-to-day functioning of government/semi-government departments/agencies. How far, in reality, has the RTI Act been useful to the disadvantaged for the implementation of sustainable rights? How far, during its five year-long journey, has the RTI Act acted as a tool to ensure healthy and nutritious food to the underprivileged at regular intervals? In the following pages, we would try to probe this issue.

II

Proactive disclosure of information is a crucial feature of the RTI Act, 2005. It is especially essential in case of sustainable rights, where the government has a duty to inform people. It allows citizens (at least theoretically) an open access to all records for inspection, and the right to receive certified copies of any documents on demand. These are, without doubts, two essential Right to Information entitlements. Another key feature is the use of the platform for people's participation facilitated by social audit. It gives any citizen the legitimacy, not just to seek information, but also record complaints and suggestions, and demand answers in the public domain. It allows for collective evaluation and the use of the non-written mode, and also mandates demystification of documents and procedures. However, in the same breath, it must be reminded that proactive disclosure policies generally work better in an atmosphere where there are a vigilant citizens, using the Right to Information to seek more detailed information, including regular monitoring of the level and quality of information being disclosed.

RIGHT TO INFORMATION AND NREGA

There has been much kudos to the UPA government from many quarters for implementing the NREGA. It is indeed an act of benevolence on the part of the Central Government, which exercises supreme power in the quasi-federal Indian state in terms of defining poverty, identifying the different categories of poor and then doling out alms to the most disadvantaged. However, it must also be remembered that 100 days of work is not enough to ensure food security throughout the year. Since work is provided in return for wages, NREGA does not address the hunger situation faced by those who cannot work, that is, the old and infirm. Still the implementation of the NREGA poses several challenges. And RTI Act, if properly applied, can put a new dimension in the whole complexion. Here are some examples.

SABARKANTHA

The following case study was conducted by Sabar Ekata Manch (A forum of community-based organisations working on Dalit Rights in Sabarkantha district, Gujarat) and Janpath (A network of voluntary organisation of Gujarat), in February-March 2006.[5] The study was done on the basis of a report that in Balisana village of the Prantij block in Sabarkantha district, workers were being paid as low as Rs.3 to Rs.7 per day for their work on the NREG Scheme. Sabar Ekata Manch and Janpath did the fact-finding survey in different villages of Prantij block, where the similar facts recurred.

After this, Mr Natu Barot of Sabar Ekata Manch contacted the Mahiti Adhikar Gujarat Pahel for guidance on how to acquire the muster roll and payment sheets of the works. Since this kind of information comes under the "pro-active disclosure" category, he was advised to simply file an application asking for the copy of the muster roll and payment sheets under the RTI Act. And his request was complied with immediately.

When the muster rolls were studied thoroughly, it came to light that the amount calculated was based on the quantum of work which was incorrectly written in column 7 of the muster rolls instead of recording it in column 10, which ensured minimum wages to workers. These irregularities and violations were brought to the notice of media through press conference. A small video film was produced with the help of Janpath, which screened it for the media This built due pressure on the government. The payments made afterwards were all done as per minimum wage provision. Thus, the copy of the muster rolls, obtained through the application of the RTI Act, played a key role in effective implementation of NREGA.

DUNGARPUR

Participatory social audit process was conducted at Dungarpur of Rajasthan in 2006 by the Rozhar Evum Suchna Ka Adhikar Abhiyan – a consortium of local NGOs, led by the Mazdoor Kissan Shakti Sangathan (MKSS). The entire process revealed that the NREGA has led to substantial rise in the daily income as well as standard of living. About 50% of the rural household has at least one member employed in NREGA. The social audit, which took place in April 2006, involved around 600 participants from 11 states. The audit participants formed different groups and organised padayatras (processions) to various villages where work under NREGA is going on. The groups created awareness among villagers about different provisions of NREGA, mechanisms to check corruptions and need for public vigilance. They have also verified whether the entitlements promised under the Act reach the bottom level.

The team carried with them checklists on NREGA entitlements and verified the implementation status with officials. Provisions of RTI were used to gather information from officials. The information received from officials was cross-checked with actual beneficiaries of the programme. Broadly speaking, the processes focus on the following goals:

1. Creating awareness of RTI and NREGA,
2. Facilitation of RTI in diverse aspects of people's life, and
3. Conducting training about the exercise of RTI.

During the entire process, the participants found that in almost every village, people were aware of their entitlement to 100 days of work per year although many were not aware of the specific details of the entitlement. The participants were given questionnaires to administer on villagers, panchayat officials and workers at the site. The information collected through this massive interview schedules were discussed and analysed by academics. The panel of academics raised a series of issues reflected in this social audit. While there are some problems in the implementation process, including low wages, the Dungarpur experience shows that there is a significant leap forward in employment, and the local administration is giving the issue highest priority. The social audit further found that all work was organised by the Gram Sabhas, and the sense of legal entitlement shored up by the significant impact of the RTI has led to a culture of transparency and accountability in this district. For example, muster rolls were found at almost all sites without any evidence of them having been tampered with. Another positive outcome is that around 80% of the labourers in this area were women and, therefore, the NREGA is making an impact on the earning capacity of women as well which will positively affect gender equations in the community. From the audit, it was clear that worksite facilities were not being provided properly. Therefore, the workers were able to demand basic facilities when they came to know that the Act entitles not only wages but also certain minimum facilities at worksites.[6]

The experience of Dungarpur social audit helped to rectify some existing problems of implementing NREGA. It has created a strong feeling among officials of other districts in the state that RTI and social audit can make them accountable to the people and can check leakage of funds and corruption. Therefore, the entire experiment created a wave across the state and ultimately led to sharp decrease in false muster rolls and registration. The campaign further proved that NREGA could be implemented effectively if there is a strong commitment and involvement of various stakeholders involved in local governance. It clearly demonstrates that with public monitoring, transparency and administrative functioning and an empowered population, not only is corruption minimised, but development that transforms the lives of the poor also becomes an attainable reality.[7]

JALWAR

Another study from Jalawar district of Rajasthan also reveals similar results. The study was conducted in July 2007 in three talukas. Using RTI provisions, the members of the team demanded muster rolls and job cards for verification. They had detailed discussion with villagers, workers, officials, sarpanch, engineers, programme officers, etc. The social audit team selected muster rolls at random from among those available at the block office and verified them with the labourers concerned. They interviewed about 200 labourers who had worked at these worksites. Surprisingly, the study found that, in each case, the muster roll details matched with the job card details and the labourer concerned. Further, there was no evidence of fake names having been entered in the muster rolls. This reinforces the previous study at Dungarpur suggesting that fudging of muster rolls is very rare in Rajasthan. This remarkable success is closely linked to effective use of transparency safeguards under the RTI.

Public awareness was also high in Jalawar. All the workers were familiar with the muster roll system, job cards and entitlements under NREGA, etc. There are other field experiences, which clearly show the positive impact of NREGA in Rajasthan in terms of exercising RTI provisions. The achievement of Rajasthan in this regard is mainly due to the massive grassroots campaign spearheaded by MKSS and other NSOs. MKSS and Aruna Roy initiated a long campaign in spreading the spirit of right to work and Right to Information. They have played a significant role in information dissemination through manuals, booklets, primers and short films. The technical provisions of the Acts were made in a simple way to understand even an illiterate person living in backward regions of the state. Large public hearings were organised to gather complaints from people on any grievances. The MKSS was instrumental in persuading Gram Sabhas to select the works under NREGA as per the requirement of the region so that the work can be used for creating a permanent rural asset base.[8]

THE WEST BENGAL SCENARIO

However, West Bengal, the fortress of the Indian left and a pioneer in launching a strong wave of food movements in the past, seems to have a different story to tell in terms of NREGA compared with Rajasthan's story of success, according to Jean Dreze and Christian Oldiges.[9] Along with some industrially developed states, West Bengal and another Left-ruled state of Kerala were far behind the national average (17) in creating "person-days" in the NREGS over 2006-07.

Performance of NREGA Across States – 2006-07
State person-days created per rural household (%)

All India	17	Kerala	3
Andhra Pradesh	10	Maharashtra	4
Assam	70	Madhya Pradesh	56
Bihar	8	North-east	45
Chattisgarh	34	Orissa	21
Gujarat	7	Punjab	7
Haryana	9	Rajasthan	77
Himachal Pradesh	20	Tamil Nadu	9
Jammu & Kashmir	13	Uttar Pradesh	11
Jharkhand	14	Uttarkhand	20
Karnataka	17	West Bengal	6

The above dismal performance might have improved on an average (at least officially) but the fact remains that a) despite the recent "improved" picture, a vast terrain of the southern and northern parts of the state continues to live under the shadow of hunger and b) despite this, there have been very few applications of the RTI Act in case of NREGS in West Bengal. In fact, during its five years of existence, the State Information Commission has registered only a handful of cases, which can be associated with people's sustainable rights. The result had been almost the same in case of acquisition of fertile land in Singur in 2006, which had adversely affected the livelihood of a good many farmers and agricultural labours.

SINGUR

Singur, an agriculturally prosperous hamlet in Hooghly District, West Bengal, hit the headlines of the national and international media since the mid-2006 as the state government, despite unwillingness and resistance of a large number of farmers, had acquired nearly 1,000 acres of fertile land and handed it over to Tata Motors for building an automobile manufacturing unit. Farmers, who had an active role in the resistance movement, had faced severe repression by the state government. Women were sexually harassed and several human rights activists and journalists were arrested by the police. To cap it all, a prohibitory Act (Cr P C 144) was imposed to prohibit meetings and restrict outsiders from entering Singur. For two years, the struggle of Singur continued to demand the right to land and livelihood security of the farmers.

However, since late 2006, several petitions under the Right to Information (RTI) Act are pending in Singur before the local authorities demanding transparency in the land deals between the Tata Company and the state government, with special regard to the farm lands in Singur. The government has not responded to a single one – a clear violation of the RTI Act, 2005. Till the time the active resistance against the land acquisition in Singur started, the state government was not willing to give even the people directly affected any information regarding the land acquisition or negotiate rehabilitation proposals. Regarding the required consent of the people for the planned project (according to the 74th Amendment of the Constitution), all meetings held were with party representatives and panchayat members but not with any Gram Sabha or with the project affected. No project details were provided to the Gram Panchayat nor were its consent sought, as reported to a panel for public hearing on 27 October 2006.[10]

PURULIA

However, we have another story from Purulia district of West Bengal, where the application of RTI Act helped, at least in some villages of a block, the poor rural labourers to claim their Right to Food. In this block, owing to the efforts of some students in the US, who trace their origins to West Bengal and a local organisation called the Mandra Lions Club, the people came to know about the RTI. The two groups joined forces in 2006 to educate the people of the three blocks in Purulia – Baghmundi, Jhalda I, Jhalda II – about the importance of using RTI to gain information about the workings of government agencies in matters that directly affect their daily lives.

Inspired by this, poor farmers like Kolebor Kalindi, Basudeb Kumar and others filed RTI applications for information on the amount of ration a BPL cardholder is entitled to, according to the Public Distribution System. The RTI, filed at the village panchayat office, also sought the list of people under the Annapurna and Antyodaya schemes. "We are labourers. After a day's work of making cane baskets, I don't get more than Rs.50 to feed seven mouths. The ration shop would usually give us one or two kg of rice every week," says Kalindi. But after the RTI, he found out that he was entitled to 5 kg of rice every week, at Rs.2 per kg.

What followed was a movement against PDS dealers and, therefore, the families now get more ration than before. "Earlier, they would threaten to beat us up, saying we were demanding more than what we deserved. We hardly ever got sugar. Now, they are compelled to give us our due because we show them the official papers," says Raghu Majhi, another villager. While they were yet to get all that they were rightfully entitled to, the RTI awareness made a significant change in their lives. Immediately, the villagers had filed 100 RTI applications; more than half got responses. Jagabandhu Kumar, 37, of Gobindopur village in Baghmundi block, filed an RTI at the panchayat office demanding information about the provisions under the Integrated Child Development Services (ICDS) scheme.

"My youngest daughter, five-year-old, goes to an ICDS centre. There were times when they were not given midday meals, or when the teachers didn't take classes," said Kumar, a farmer. Armed with the written reply from the panchayat secretary, Kumar took up the issue with the ICDS centre. He claimed mid-day meals have now become regular, with better food quality. Ashish Sinha, another labourer, filed an RTI about the number of days the local ration shop should remain open. "The ration shops only open once a week, when they are supposed to keep them open for five-and-a-half days a week. Armed with the RTI reply, Sinha hauled up the nearest dealer. As the word spread, eight PDS dealers were questioned. The shops are now open four days a week and the dealers have put up boards indicating the stocks they have and the prices," says Tathagata Sengupta, 25, one of the students involved in the movement.[11]

BIRBHUM

But the story of PDS in Birbhum district, especially the state of TPDS seems entirely different. This is one of the southern districts, where public outrage against the corrupt ration dealers rose (2007) to such a height that shook the foundation of the ruling Left during the Panchayat Elections in 2008. Many of the affected persons in the district wrote to their respective food inspectors against less quantity of wheat and kerosene oil distributed by these dealers to both the BPL and APL cardholders. They also complained against the low quality of foodgrains. And, in most cases, they came to know of an unholy nexus between the ration dealers and the ruling party bureaucracy (especially the PDS officials).

Mallarpur is one such village in Mayureswar Block I. Anath Mandal, Kanchan Panda and Ashis Roy run three ration shops in this locality. In this village, the Panchayat Pradhan (Chief) wrote to Anath Mandal asking him to furnish information about the amount of government quota of foodgrains and kerosene oil. It was found that Mandal was distributing only 1 kg wheat per person (which amounted to 5 kgs per family – for a 5-member family) instead of 1.8 kgs per person, according to rules. Therefore, each family was loosing their quota by 4 kgs per week. Besides, the quality of wheat was almost inedible. The quantity of kerosene was also less than the government quota. In 2007, the angry villagers organised a road blockade, especially against the corrupt practices of Anath Mandal. Many lower-rung CPI(M) activists also joined this movement. They also wrote to the local food inspector regarding this.

However, no penal action was taken against Mandal and there was more pain in store for the villagers. Soon, to their utter dismay, they discovered that the food inspector concerned had divulged the names of the people who had lodged complaints to Mandal. This made this ration dealer so furious that he began to misbehave with them when they came to his shop to collect their dues. Gautam Panda, a local (now disillusioned) CPI(M) member and the then member of Mallarpur village panchayat, informed the present author that despite several requests to party bosses, including the former MLA, Sri Braja Mukherjee, to take "political action" against Mandal and others. But nothing was done. The practice of unfair distribution of ration continues in this locality.[11a]

RECENT YEARS

However, according to official statistics, West Bengal has improved remarkably (2009-10) in creating persondays for NREGA compared with its very poor performance in the initial years.

NREGA STATISTICS
STATE : WEST BENGAL

Employment provided to households: persondays [in lakh]:	34.79915 lakhs
Total:	1551.67
SCs:	571.93 [36.86%]
STs:	223.18 [14.38%]
Women:	518.61 [33.42%]
Others:	756.56 [48.76%]
Total fund:	2324.86 crore
Expenditure:	2108.98 crore
Total works taken up:	183500
Works completed:	121858
Works in progress:	61642

[Source: www.nrega.nic.in, accessed on 2 August 2010]

But mere statistics might not always reflect actual realities. Very recently (August 2010) West Bengal's Minister for Development of Animal Husbandry, Sri Narayan Biswas, wrote a letter to Sri Ardhendu Sen, then Chief Secretary of the State Government, complaining about huge corruption and mis-utilisation of the NREGS fund in the northern district of Dinajpur Dakshin (South).[12] According to Biswas, in several villages of Harirampur block of the district, there has been a huge drainage of the NREGS money through "false" job cards and manipulations in muster rolls. It has been claimed by local authorities that 45 persondays have been created in the block. This claim also surprises Biswas very much. "If it were true", he argues, "that would have been reflected in the quality of common men's life in the Block". But there is hardly any noticeable change!

The abovementioned charge of manipulations in job cards and misappropriation of funds of the NREGS is not coming from an opposition party leader, which is highly probable in the party politics-torn West Bengal. Rather a Cabinet Minister – who is also a ruling party member – is making this allegation, and this certainly clouds the tall claims of official statistics on NREGA. But our story of alleged corruption of Harirampur block had a dramatic turn. On 13 August 2010, the police chased the car of Sri Suman Majjhi, the Block Development Officer (BDO) of this block in a situation similar to a bollywood film and ultimately caught him on National Highway 34 in the nearby Maldah district. He was arrested by Maldah Police and then handed over to Dinajpur Dakhsin Police. Apparently, the BDO was fleeing to Kolkata after the District Magistrate had filed a complaint against him at Harirampur Police Station for misappropriation of Rs.1 crore of NREGS fund.

According to the complaint, the allegedly tainted BDO withdrew Rs.1 lakh for the renovation of a local "pond", which, in reality, did not exist. He has spent Rs.3 lakhs as the wage for the "earthwork" job and; Rs.14 lakhs for paving the rural road with bricks, although nothing was done in reality and not a single brick was found![12a] Again, the Paschimbanga Khet Mazoor Samity (West Bengal Land Labours' Committee) had filed a case at the Calcutta High Court against the state government. The Samity complained that the state government has paid only Rs.81 per personday for the NREGS from January to November 2009 in place of the stipulated Rs.87.50. According to Debashis Mukhopadhyay, the Samity's advocate, the Central Government had instructed the Government of West Bengal to enhance the wage, from April 2009, and to make it Rs.100 per personday. But the state government continued to pay Rs81 to the rural labour. Thus, according to Mukhopadhyay, the state government has made a lesser payment of nearly Rs.72 crores in 2009. On 14 August 2010, a Division Bench of Calcutta High Court issued an order to the West Bengal Government to submit a full-length report in this regard within two weeks.[12b] All these remind us of a line of caution, recently expressed by Anu Aga, Member, NAC: "It is important to monitor whether the benefits of such schemes were reaching the needy."[13]

Secondly, even if the NREGS has performed better in some areas, several NGOs and civil society activists have protested over the functioning of the NREGS, TPDS and other food-related schemes in the state. The Jungle Mahal (comprising western districts) and the northern tea garden areas comprise the "state of exception" (in the Agambenian sense), which is also the *state of scarcity*. From drinking water and paved roads to hospitals and, of course, food – everything seems scarce.

And after listing six basic requirements of life (food, drinking water, light, roads, a school and a medical centre) that Amlashole (infamous village for hunger deaths) almost lacks, Ranabir Samaddar pens the story of destitute in these words: "The nearest market is 4 km away and a load of firewood fetches 20 rupees. A starving person can trek that distance only once in four days; weakened by sustained starvation, one can make the journey once a week, then once a fortnight, and then once dies silently, unnoticed . . ." Paradoxically, while some steps are being taken to rush in relief, there is also vehement denial that hunger deaths are taking place. One observer has bitterly commented, "There is a law against everything, none against starving to death". The comment remains partly unclear, for under law you cannot take your own life, but some do takes their lives because of hunger. Article 21 [of Indian constitution] under its hallowed interpretation means that no one can starve you to death. But who will prove that this was a hunger death and force accountability thereupon?"[14]

These are areas, especially of the Jungle Mahal, in which the Maoist politics is on the rise for last few years. The government often talks of "development" in this area, the absence of which, it seems, is the root cause for being the fertile ground of the Maoists. But, in practice, it sends more guns, bullets and vans loaded with police forces instead of rice bags and other amenities for sustainable development. Thus, the main concern of the government seems to be "restoration" of law and order than providing goods/amenities for maintaining sustainable rights. Obviously, the government logic is: restore the order/"normalcy" first and then talk of food and other rights because only the former can ensure the latter. But the fallacy is that even in an earlier situation of so-called "normalcy", the common people were denied, in most cases, these pro-poor rights.

But what looks most distressing is that barring a few exceptions, the RTI has hardly become an instrument in the state in the struggle for sustainable rights. The officers of the State Information Commission (SIC) at Bhavani Bhavan, Kolkata, also do not hide their dissatisfaction over the functioning of RTI in the state. In its published documents, the SIC has pointed out how many important government offices did not care to appoint State Public Information Officers (SPIOs) in their respective offices, for long. Most decisions taken by the SIC during last five years are related to examination, appointment and municipality.[15]

III

At a meeting recently held (14 July 2010), the NAC forwarded to the second UPA government a set of recommendations to be incorporated within the Food Security Bill. They include universalisation of the PDS in one-fourth of the most disadvantaged districts or blocks in the first year, where every household will be entitled to 35 kg of foodgrains per month at Rs.3 per kg. For other districts/blocks, the NAC has recommended differentiated entitlements (in terms of quantity and price), which would be progressively extended to all rural areas over a "reasonable period of time".

Critics, however, say "selective targeting" could lead to corruption and a new type of discrimination. Brinda Karat, Member of CPI(M) Politburo and Indian Parliament, has pointed out in an article in *The Hindu*, that taking up just one-fourth of the most disadvantaged districts/blocks, or 150 of the total 640 districts in the country, would mean that equally poor people would get different treatment from the government on the basis of their geographical location. For example, a poor man in a not-so-disadvantaged district in Kerala will never be able to get foodgrains at a subsidised rate.

Besides, the criteria for those in the urban areas – which are yet to be defined – are too ambiguous, says Brinda Karat. She says that for complete universalisation, too, there is no clarity because the recommendations say "over a reasonable period of time". According to her, this lets the government keep the issue hanging indefinitely with respect to uncovered areas. The NAC "has compromised on the basic issue of universalisation. What it is suggesting is a differently targeted system," she writes.[16]

However, one may counter argue with her stating that, can she, with her principle of "universalisation", meet the minimum needs of the *areas of scarcity* (Jungle Mahal and tea gardens of the north) in West Bengal – the state, which is being ruled by her party for last 33 years? The general situation of PDS, TPDS and other basic amenities is so unequal in these areas that following the Rawlsian principle one needs to give "maximum" to the "minimum advantaged". But it does not, for a moment, mean that giving special assistance to these zones is to ignore/neglect the poor of the not-so-disadvantaged areas. In order to enable the poor to claim their sustainable rights, including food rights, and actually providing them with "primary social goods", the administrators and politicians must refashion their idea of justice with sincere will and imagination, which must be backed by enough initiative and skill.

New Information Regime

While NAC is busy refashioning the food security and distribution schemes, the information regime is also taking a new complexion in recent times, especially with the formation of the Unique Identification Authority of India (UIDAI). The concept of a unique identification was first discussed and worked upon since 2006 when administrative approval for the project "Unique ID for BPL families" was given by the Department of Information Technology, Ministry of Communications and Information Technology on 3 March 2006. The UIDAI was constituted and notified by the Planning Commission on 28 January 2009. On 25 June 2009, the Cabinet also created and approved the position of the Chairperson of the UIDAI, and appointed Mr Nandan Nilekani the first Chairperson. The UIDAI's role is to develop and implement the necessary institutional, technical and legal infrastructure to issue unique identity numbers to Indian residents.

The UIDAI works for collection of demographic and biometric attributes of residents (face, all 10 fingerprints and iris) for the project. It was also decided to include data of the iris for children in the age group of 5 to 15. Thus, within a decade, it plans biological and social mapping of almost the entire population of India and, therefore, creating a new zone of power backed by minutest information – an exercise, which Michel Foucault might have referred to as "biopolitics".[17] The entire array of "primary social goods" is to be delivered to the people, especially the poor, through this new mechanism.

UID and PDS

The official site of the UIDAI pronounces[18] the duties of the state governments in this regard. According to it, the state governments should create a high-quality beneficiary database, preferably commencing from a house-to-house survey. The state government can carry out the enrolment of identified family members by enrolling them into the UID (Unique ID) programme. After digitisation of requisite information, enrolment of the individuals is done as per the UID requirements. The digitised database will contain 10-finger biometrics and photographs of all family members. This enrolled data would be sent to the UIDAI (Unique Identity Authority of India) for de-duplication and issue of a UID, which will be printed on the ration card for each member of the family.

The UIDAI further claims that appropriate action can be taken against families that have a resident who has appeared in another ration card. Appropriate action will be taken in case of family members who are not included. The inclusion of all families in the beneficiary database is important for an effective elimination of shadow and bogus cards. A strategy to issue APL cards by linking it to other forms of benefits, including LPG, needs to be adopted to make the beneficiary database comprehensive. To support enrolment in the UID database, the Centre will mandate that the UID numbers of each family member should be recorded in the ration card and the database should be made available.

The UIDAI also talks of about a "synergic partnership" of the PDS and UID. It lists the benefits of the new system in this way:

- Improved coverage – The ration card is today the most prevalent form of identity in the rural areas. If the UID enrolment is integrated in the process of the creation of a beneficiary database for PDS, the coverage of UID will improve significantly.
- Data updating – Ration cards are a persistent source of citizen transactions with a monthly frequency. If there is a change in the family structure, or the family moves, the ration card is sure to be updated. At this time, the data can also be updated to the UID database.
- Better Identification – Integration with the UID programme will lead to better identification of individuals and families leading to better targeting and increased transparency and, therefore, better functioning of the system and increased public approval.
- Off-take Authentication – The UID database will maintain details of the beneficiary, which can be updated from multiple sources. The PDS system can use this database for authentication of beneficiaries during the off-take recording process. A mechanism for verifying the ID of the person at the time of delivery of grains will help in improving the targeting of the grains.

- Legislative Support – The legislative support in the form of the need for submitting the UID number for several transactions will push residents to acquire a UID. The most convenient mechanism will be for residents to get a ration card and this will create a supporting environment for computerisation of ration cards.
- Technology Support – The UID programme is putting together technology specifications and infrastructure to handle enrolment, storage and identity confirmation of all Indian residents. The PDS system can leverage this and rapidly move ahead with the enrolment process.
- Duplicate and Ghost Detection – The UIDAI will provide duplicate detection infrastructure to the PDS programme. It can also assist in the development of special tools to assist in the assessment of eligibility of applicants.
- Domestic LPG Linkage – The issue of domestic LPG by Oil companies can be made conditional to the production of an APL (non-kerosene) ration card making enrolment a compulsory affair.
- Support for PDS reform – The UID will become an important identifier in banking services and day-to-day needs of the resident. This can support the PDS reform by as an example providing the banking account number for a family to effect direct cash transfer.

Where to Go From Here?

The UID programme of biometric identification for the entire population is facing stern opposition from a number of individuals as well as social and civil liberty organisations for the potential violation of the rights to equality, dignity, privacy, expression and the right not to be discriminated against.[19] This new programme also poses challenges – theoretical as well as practical – to the basic concept of the RTI movement and the Act because the latter presupposes citizens' access to information related to various (albeit limited) government/semi-government documents, the former is a renewed effort towards concentration of classified information relating to almost every aspect of the life of the citizens in the hands of the state. This strengthens the infallible and know-all image of the modern state because after such a detailed collection of individual details, the chance of arbitrary mistakes are minimised. Thus, if it functions properly, it would run like a machine, which would, in turn, minimise the role of human agency towards making claims. Since after such a rigorous process of "individuation" (based on personal physical traits) and "collectivisation" (giving individuals various identity labels in terms of caste, creed, income – APL/BPL, etc.), it would be very difficult for individual citizens to move out of the stereotypes/cells of identities that the state assigns to them.

It is, however, doubly a matter of concern because the way the UID programme seeks to usurp and control a host of "sustainable" rights (including food rights) is really unprecedented. In essence, the Right to Information has been portrayed as the basic right on the basis of which further claims can be made for "sustainable" rights. But the upcoming UID programme will further tilt the already lopsided information regime in India towards the government, allowing its minute surveillance of the lives of citizens and the governance of their "sustainable" rights, even at times of "decline" of sovereign states and in the era of globalisation.

NOTES

1. Zdenek Drabek and Payne, Warren, 'The Impact of Transparency on Foreign Direct Investment' in Staff Working Paper ERAD-99-02, Revised November 2001, World Trade Organisation, Economic Research and Analysis Division, Geneva.
2. http://planningcommission.nic.in/eg_poverty.htm, accessed on 10 July 2010.
3. From *Report on Conditions of Work and Promotion*, National Commission for Enterprises in Unorganised Sector, New Delhi, 2007 http://nceus.gov.in/Condition_of_workers_sep_2007.pdf, accessed on 26 July 2010.
4. *Frontline,* Vol.27, No.17, 14–27 August 2010.
5. http://janpathnetwork.org/annual_report_01.pdf accessed on 13 July 2010.
6. 'Best Practices' www.nrega.nic.in accessed on 13 July 2010.
7. *Ibid.*
8. Drèze, Jean and Lal, Siddhartha, 'Employment guarantee: unfinished agenda', *The Hindu*, Friday, 13 July 2007.
9. Drèze, Jean and Oldiges, Christian, 'Commendable act' in *Frontline*, Vol.24, Issue 14, 14-27 July 2007.
10. *The Right to Adequate Food in India – Parallel Report* by FIAN (Food First Information and Action Network) (Reference: Second to fifth periodic reports of India UN Doc. E/C.12/IND/5 submitted to the CESCR, 40th session) http://www.fian.org, accessed on 9 July 2010.
11. http://www.indianexpress.com/news/a-website-to-log-the-rti-success-stories-of-

purulia-villagers/563923/0, accessed on 3 August 2010.

11a. Interview with Gautam Panda of Mallarpur village of Mayureswar I Block, Birbhum district was conducted on 12 August 2010.

12. *Bartaman* (A Bengali daily), Kolkata, 4 August 2010, http://epaper.bartamanpatrika.com/ accessed on 5 August 2010.

12a. *Ananda Bazar Patrika*, (A Bengali Daily), Kolkata, 14 August 2010.

12b. *Bartaman*, 15 August 2010.

13. *Frontline, Op. Cit.*

14. Samaddar, Ranabir, *The Materiality of Politics: Subject Positions in Politics*, Vol.II, Anthem Press, London, 2007, p.64.

15. http://wbic.gov.in/html/Decisions_July_Aug_10.htm, accessed on 3 August 2010.

16. *Frontline, Op. Cit.*

17. Foucault, Michel *History of Sexuality,* Vol.1, Penguin, UK 1998, p.144.

18. http://uidai.gov.in/documents/UIDandPDS.pdf, accessed on 19 August 2010.

19. http://mizoramexpress.com/index.php/2010/04/citizens-against-uid, accessed on 21 July 2010.

EPILOGUE

THE RIGHT TO FOOD BILL

Hegemonic Practice and Popular Rhetoric

PRADEEP BHARGAVA

In an era when states across the world become more commanding and violent, seemingly benevolent legislations, such as the proposed Right to Food Act are *not* anachronous historical landmarks. The proposed Act bestows powerful instruments to the state for (i) dividing, categorising and controlling population (ii) defining population's basic needs and, (iii) thereby, controlling processes used by population for meeting the basic needs. A question arises as to how constraining could democracy be on the governmentality of the state, which aspires to command population? An election promise has to be fulfilled. So an Act has to be in place for providing the smallest possible quantity of foodgrains at Rs.2 per kg to as small a number of the poor to be defined and identified by the state. The civil society manifesting itself mainly in the Right to Food campaign advocates in right earnest on behalf of the millions who go hungry, generally, to universalise the public distribution system and ensure 35-50 kg per household per month. The empowered group of ministers proposes 20 kg. On the number of food-deficient or the population below the poverty line, the estimates of the state and civil society vary. There is also considerable debate on the criteria for identifying the poor. Therefore, the state and the civil society together construct an identity of the BPL and of a duty bound centralised welfare state. They contest on the number of poor and amounts of grain, but in essence are thinking in tandem. In this aligning contestation, governmentality is established further.

One hundred and ten years ago there was no such contestation. During the drought of Samvat in 1956 and thereafter, famine relief workers built an air-conditioned fort on the top of a hillock in Jodhpur, Rajasthan. The fort came to be known as Chittar Palace or Umed Bhawan. A hall in the palace is devoted to a museum of pencil drawings of the construction workers building the fort. The museum is also air conditioned, using seemingly heritage equipment. The fort is now a star hotel usually occupied by foreign tourists. One part of the palace is occupied by the ex-Maharaja. The fort is a living testimony to the duty fulfilled by the Maharaja who stood up at the time of need to ensure the supply of foodgrains to workers building the fort. This grain was collected by the Maharaja as usurious land revenue from the farmers in the years of good harvest, which now worked for famine relief. Obviously, farmers and agricultural labourers in the 19th century did not have control over what they produced. In the 21st century it is much the same, the process of extraction and giving back the grain to them are albeit different.

Traditions of providing food security, at least, during periods of distress continued during the colonial period. This period was known, among other things, for codifying population and societies and giving the famine codes that exist to this day. In a pragmatic stand, the postcolonial state is afoot towards a Right to Food Bill, that according to the preamble circulated would ensure provision of adequate food to all people at all times and in practice some food to some people for some time (for the time they are poor). This paper attempts to find why the current discourses on rights and duties centres on the centralised state which is seen as the bearer of all duties. All other forms and levels of governance are either ignored or seen as subsidiary to the Centre. The agency of the panchayat is ignored. If it were recognised, the Right to Food could have been realised differently, and it is argued more efficiently.

ON STATISTICS

For the last five decades, the government has continued to collect huge amounts of grains from farmers, transport it to big godowns and, then, with extreme inefficiency take these back to hungry farmers and agricultural labourers who produced the grain and other destitutes. The Public Distribution Systems, the system of defining poverty and generating statistical estimates of the poor (using consumption expenditure data collected by the National Sample Survey Organisation) and some formula for identifying the poor are already in place. The Right to Food Act is perhaps to reaffirm the existing policies and ensure that food becomes a right and no government can possibly take it back. At the core of drafting an act and/or its implementation are the statistics.

Statistics is very old and very interesting. Statisticians estimating poverty lines debate on the choice of food basket, age, gender, occupation and region-specific nutritional requirements, and price indices to deflate the current prices of a poverty line based on a pre-determined food basket that provides 2,400 calories to an individual in rural areas. Over a period of time, the deflators for poverty line were such that the real value of poverty line remained constant but it provided lesser calories at the margin. The same data set is used by statisticians to make different estimates of poverty. The latest is the Tendulkar Committee Report, now accepted by the Government, which conforms to a calorie norm of over 25% below the 2,400 calorie norm. And for a large country with a population of 100 crore, such standardised procedures and norms are established for statistics to be significant across the diverse cross-section of populations, and used for economic projections and designing policies. Just as the state collects data on the number of crimes, murders, or perhaps murderers, or human beings who are educated or employed, similarly they collect data on what people consume and how much. The data helps in designing policies and, at times, to be fair to the deprived, as in the present case, to ensure basic entitlements. But statistics is also politics. In older times, statistics was a branch of political science, dealing with collection classification and discussion of facts bearing on conditions of a state or community.

The post colonial state classifies population into Above Poverty Line (APL) or Below Poverty Line (BPL) carrying forward the legacy of the colonial state to categorise, divide and create animosities among population.

Boundaries between poor and non-poor, howsoever defined, are fuzzy at the margin. It is difficult to be discreet. Besides, poverty or hunger is also transient for some, seasonal or varying even on a daily basis; or when the male member is out of the village working elsewhere, the other members of the family may go hungry. For many, the situation is chronic. The stated preamble of the draft emphasises food for all at all times; how can a centralised state work out the seasonal deficit for each person? Moreover, a centralised state cannot have a formula for identifying which families need ration at all times. The panchayat knows. It does not need a formula. But state officials or the panchayats are asked to, if at all, to assign populations to predetermined universal categories, which could be irrelevant to identify the poor and hungry in their area. Besides, it becomes difficult for the panchayats to assign people to these categories as each one aspires to be in the category to avail subsidies. Adding categories of the most vulnerable could help, but to what extent? Enumerating a Hindu and a Muslim could be a simple exercise but identifying a poor and non-poor is as much difficult as the former is simple. Doing statistics in the traditional sense is exercising power. The civil society wants the Central government to exercise this power, which the latter accepts with great vigour as it helps the state in reaching commanding heights. The draft of the Right to Food Bill in circulation shows that rationality and, thereby, power is located in the impersonal Weberian centralised state: the power to reach the last man and the power to use an iron hand to separate the poor from the non-poor lies with a central authority and that there shall be a single objective measure of poverty and no other.

And the centralised and impersonalised state apparatus and the judiciary would be content with one single measure – easy to administer and easy to adjudicate. The power of doing statistics will finally rest with a small group of intellectuals who shall define the statistic and with local official who shall collect the statistics. The past experience shows complete lack of empathy in the process, the unending struggle to make the statistics public, debate in the Gram Sabha and set the scores right. The power to set the score right is with an even higher official, usually inaccessible to the last man of the Mahatma.

II

It is important to discover the "hidden transcripts" of power – a term used by James Scott – in and around any of the government programmes such as the Public Distribution System or the Mahatma Gandhi National Rural Employment Programme. The programme is decentralised; the money is received directly by the Panchayat Pradhan but is to be spent only by the order of the block officer. Such an order is possible if and only if a "cut" is made available. This is common knowledge in the village. So how are people to contest for their rights against the Panchayat Pradhan? Under such circumstances, social audit has little meaning. People do not resist the Pradhan, knowing fully well the Pradhan's situation. There is no power relation between the Pradhan and the people as there is little resistance at the level of the latter. After all, power not resisted is no power at all. The case is the same with the Public Distribution System where the District Supply Officer has to collect revenue for the politicians in most places.

The benevolent and duty-bound government in the process of ensuring entitlements and identifying the poor potentially creates a divide between the poor and the non-poor, and also between the poor who have been identified and the poor who have not been identified. The BPL then looks at the state for benefits. They generally require a mediator to get benefits from the state, and build – though weak – vertical relationships which include village official, pradhan and block-level officials. Not being aware of or being able to exercise their rights, they constantly look forward to benevolence of this hierarchy and as, is well known, exploited by this hierarchy. The lateral relations of the BPL with APL and other poor not selected as BPL become contentious. The population gets defined directly by the Central government, which is too distant to be contested. Categorisation as BPL disempowers as it creates dependence in the name of realising rights. The labels become permanent.

Ensuring food with dignity is a slogan of the Right to Food campaign. The Civil Society Draft of Food Entitlement Act 2009 states the following before its preamble: "An Act to ensure dignified economic and social access to adequate food . . ." And this dignity is to be assured by providing subsidised food. How can accepting alms be called dignified social access? Or buying grain at Rs.2 or 3 per kg called dignified economic access?

The inherent argument is that the incomes of people are low and are, therefore, not sufficient to purchase food at market prices. Thus, a subsidy is required. An alternative, therefore, could be to increase their incomes to a level, so as to enable them to purchase food at market prices. While this is a difficult proposition, a very near or proximate solution is possible. If procurement price or economic cost (procurement price + handling cost) is say Rs.15 per kg, a household would need Rs.750 per month or Rs.9,000 per annum to ensure the very basic food security of 50 kg of grain per household per month. This amount of money/grain, a worker could get from 90 days of *additional* labour from the Mahatma Gandhi National Rural Labour Employment Act, or 50 days of labour if grain is priced at Rs.10 per kg. The wage could also be fixed, say at 10 kg per day's work. This would be food accessed with dignity. Most of this labour can be provided in the lean period of May and June. This is also the time when most work such as digging ponds and digging pits for forest plantation can be carried out. Several advantages of this are the following:

(i) The dead weight loss of food subsidy is converted to productive work and assets.

(ii) There is self-selection of households who wish to work for assured food.

(iii) Poverty listing processes are done away with.

Such large scale operations can be undertaken neither by the Centre nor the state. Only the panchayats are capable of doing this. Let them do it.

Of course, there are destitutes in villages who cannot work and need alms or food rations. Their identification is best left to the Gram Sabha/ panchayats and their numbers would seldom exceed 2% in a village.

The essential part of my alternative is ensuring an agency of the panchayats, i.e. the panchayats should exercise their choice and action and not act only on the rules and games laid down by the centralised state.

Each panchayat needs a godown where it could store grains, procured from farmers in the panchayats. M S Swaminathan once suggested these. The stocks to hold would be the total amount needed for those registered for food-for-work, the mid-day meal and Anganwadi and Annapoorna households. The stocks could also be held for those willing to purchase at the economic costs. An advantage is that the small farmers unable to reach the procurement agencies directly could sell the same to the panchayats.

Another advantage is that the transport costs to FCI godowns and back is reduced to zero. Leakages from PDS are also reduced.

The cost of constructing godowns can come from the NREGA, and the RBI credit line extended to Central government purchase can be extended to the panchayats. Only those panchayats deficit in food may procure from a central quota. Such deficit panchayats, incidentally, may not be many. The onus of providing work and grain to all those registered with the panchayats is with the panchayats. If the panchayats fail to provide work, they provide grain. Why is it not possible for the panchayats to keep grains and distribute it? Panchayats can also levy on sending grain out of the village panchayat. However, it can work only if the controls are with the panchayat. People can check with a village pradhan and not the colonial hierarchy of officers.

When panchayats exercise their agency without imposing the criteria of the centralised apparatus, people's agency would also be activated. People would ask for accounts as they know that all powers are with the panchayats. When panchayats are solely responsible for holding and accounting for grain, free riders would be put to shame. People are more likely to check with the village Pradhan than a galaxy of colonial officers maintained by the centralised state.

COMPARATIVE SYSTEMS FOR GRAIN PROCUREMENT AND DISTRIBUTION

Centralised system	Decentralised system
Single criterion for identifying poor at all times	Multiple criteria for identifying the poor
High cost of food collection, storage and transportation	Low cost of food collection, storage and transportation
Centralised delivery system with proper rules	Decentralised system of delivery, rules to suit the regional needs
Leakages benefiting an entire hierarchy of government	Leakages could be easily identified and challenged at the local level
Limited quantities irrespective of the needs of the region	Required amounts would reach consumers
Political advantage to the Centre, and panchayats only extension agents	Panchayats exercise their agency: increased contestation at the local level
Who delivers justice: the Bonaparte leader	The justice is sought at the level of the panchayats

The alternative suggested is extremely unlikely to be acceptable for the following reasons:

(i) There is little faith of the Central government in the agency of the panchayats; strong panchayats are a threat to the governments.
(ii) Leakages from a Central government scheme has a large number of stakeholders both big and small.
(iii) The popular rhetoric of the UPA government providing grain at Rs.2 per kg will have little meaning; there is no political gain.
(iv) The government can think only in terms of large parastatals which are easy to administer than a large number of godowns in the panchayats.
(v) The ministries of food and civil supplies and the ministry of rural development hardly communicate with one another.
(vi) Panchayats would be self-administering, a risk which the Central government would not take: the naxalites are self-administering;

The Maharaja needed to build forts not only for their use value but also exhibition value that established his authority. Mayawati has statues. C P Joshi plans for Rajiv Gandhi Panchayat Bhawans. For a democracy or an autocracy to sustain, we need structures with both use and exhibition value. Rural godowns would have more use value. These could also be named Rajiv Gandhi godowns. If panchayats were to *own* the godowns, they could be named after the unsung subaltern heroes, not covered in our textbooks. Alas, none of this could happen: the civil society has faith in a centralised system to deliver; and is satisfied partaking in the governmentality of the centralised state. Gram Swaraj is but for celebration; and panchayats have to be told what to do and not to think and act on their own.

On the other hand, the population has two options: One to get defined by the state as BPL and accept the largesse as its right; and two attempt a *gram swaraj* or own governance or own control over agricultural produce and get defined as a 'naxalite'. The polity is for a strong centralised duty-bound state to feed the hungry and hunt down the naxalites. With both, the state does not have a dialogue.

Annexure

So far, 44 "Interim Orders" have been issued by the Supreme Court in the "Right to Food case" (PUCL vs. Union of India and others, Writ Petition [Civil] 196 of 2001). Many of these orders are of no consequence, e.g. adjournments or listings of dates for further hearings. In the following, we refer to some of the very important orders that have strengthened and redefined various pro-poor government-run schemes. (Source: http://www.righttofoodindia.org/data/scordersprimer.doc)

1. ORDER OF 28 NOVEMBER 2001
    - PUBLIC DISTRIBUTION SYSTEM
        - It is the case of the Union of India that there has been full compliance with regard to the allotment of food-grain in relation to the TPDS. However, if any of the States gives a specific instance of non-compliance, the Union of India will do the needful within the framework of the Scheme.
        - The States are directed to complete the identification of BPL families, issuing of cards and commencement of distribution of 25 kg grain per family per month.
        - The Delhi Government will ensure that TPDS application forms are freely available and are given and received free of charge and there is an effective mechanism in place to ensure speedy and effective redressal of grievances.
    - ANTYODAYA ANNA YOJANA
        - It is the case of the Union of India that there has been full compliance with regard to the allotment of food-grain in relation to Antyodaya Anna Yojana. However, if any of the States gives a specific instance of non-compliance, the Union of India will do the needful within the framework of the Scheme.
        - We direct the States and the Union Territories to complete identification of beneficiaries, issuing of cards and distribution of grain under this Scheme latest by 1 January 2002.

- ❖ It appears that some Antyodaya beneficiaries may be unable to lift grain because of penury. In such cases, the Centre, the States and the Union Territories are requested to consider giving the quota free after satisfying itself in this behalf.

- MID-DAY MEAL SCHEME
  - ❖ It is the case of the Union of India that there has been full compliance with regard to the Mid-Day Meal Scheme (MDMS). However, if any of the States gives a specific instance of non-compliance, the Union of India will do the needful within the framework of the Scheme.
  - ❖ We direct the State Governments/Union Territories to implement the Mid-Day Meal Scheme by providing every child in every Government and Government-assisted Primary Schools with a prepared mid-day meal with a minimum content of 300 calories and 8-12 grams of protein each day of school for a minimum of 200 days. Those Governments providing dry rations instead of cooked meals must within three months [28 February 2002] start providing cooked meals in all Govt. and Govt.-aided Primary Schools in all half the Districts of the State (in order of poverty) and must within a further period of three months [28 May 2002] extend the provision of cooked meals to the remaining parts of the State.
  - ❖ We direct the Union of India and the FCI to ensure provision of fair average quality grain for the Scheme on time.
  - ❖ The States/ Union Territories and the FCI are directed to do joint inspection of foodgrains. If the foodgrain is found, on joint inspection, not to be of fair average quality, it will be replaced by the FCI prior to lifting.

- NATIONAL OLD AGE PENSION SCHEME
  - ❖ It is the case of the Union of India that there has been full compliance with regard to the National Old Age Pension Scheme. However, if any of the States gives a specific instance of non-compliance, the Union of India will do the needful within the framework of the Scheme.
  - ❖ The States are directed to identify the beneficiaries and to start making payments latest by 1 January 2002.
  - ❖ We direct the State Govts./Union Territories to make payments promptly by the 7th of each month.

- ANNAPURNA ANNA YOJANA
  - ❖ The States/Union Territories are directed to identify the beneficiaries and distribute the grain latest by 1 January 2002.

- INTEGRATED CHILD DEVELOPMENT SERVICES
    - ❖ We direct the State Govts./Union Territories to implement the Integrated Child Development Scheme (ICDS) in full and to ensure that every ICDS disbursing centre in the country shall provide as under: Each child up to 6 years of age to get 300 calories and 8-10 grams of protein; each adolescent girl to get 500 calories and 20-25 grams of protein; each pregnant woman and each nursing mother to get 500 calories and 20-25 grams of protein; Each malnourished child to get 600 calories and 16-20 grams of protein.
    - ❖ Have a disbursement centre in every settlement.

- NATIONAL MATERNITY BENEFIT SCHEME
    - ❖ We direct the State Govts./Union Territories to implement the National Maternity Benefit Scheme (NMBS) by paying all BPL pregnant women Rs.500/- through the Sarpanch 8-12 weeks prior to delivery for each of the first two births.

- NATIONAL FAMILY BENEFIT SCHEME
    - ❖ We direct the State Govts./Union Territories to implement the National Family Benefit Scheme and pay a BPL family Rs.10,000/- within four weeks through a local Sarpanch, whenever the primary bread winner of the family dies.

- OTHER DIRECTIONS
    - ❖ We direct that a copy of this order be translated in regional languages and in English by the respective States/Union Territories and prominently displayed in all Gram Panchayats, Government School Buildings and Fair Price Shops.
    - ❖ In order to ensure transparency in selection of beneficiaries and their access to these Schemes, the Gram Panchayats will also display a list of all beneficiaries under the various Schemes.

2. ORDER OF 8 MAY 2002
    - The Gram Panchayats shall frame employment generation proposals in accordance with the SGRY guidelines. These proposals shall be approved and sanctioned by the Gram Panchayats and the work started expeditiously.
    - The respondents shall focus the SGRY programme towards agricultural wage earners, non-agricultural unskilled wage earners, marginal farmers and in particular, SC and ST persons whose wage income constitutes a reasonable proportion of their household income and to give priority to them in employment, and within this section shall give priority to women.

- GoI shall release money entitlements under the different employment generation schemes to each State on schedule, provided that utilisation certificates have been provided by the states certifying that the funds have been used for the specified purpose.
- The Gram Sabhas are entitled to conduct Social Audits into all Food/ Employment schemes.
- Gram Sabhas are entitled to monitor the implementation of the various schemes and have access to relevant information.
- In view of the grievance that the identification of BPL families is not being done properly, the central and the state governments are directed to clarify the issue and work out a policy for amicable settlement.
- The respondents shall ensure that rations shops remain open throughout the months during fixed hours the details of which will be displayed on the notice board.
- Dr N C Saxena and Mr S R Sankaran are appointed as commissioners of the Court to redress complaints that have not been resolved by the Collectors and the Chief Secretary. They can take the help of NGOs and individuals to help them monitor the implementation of the court's orders.

3. ORDER OF 20 APRIL 2004

- MID-DAY MEALS: The court directed that all states have to start implementing the mid-day meal scheme latest by 1 September 2004. Centre was directed to make financial provisions for mid-day meal infrastructure, and also reply to Abhijit Sen Committee's suggestion that centre share a part of conversion costs. GoI [Government of India] should also state when it is planning to implement the Prime Minister's announcement to extend mid-day meals up to class 10.

  Dalits to be given preference in the appointment of cooks and helpers and mid-day meals shall be provided in summer in drought affected states.
- EMPLOYMENT: Allocation for SGRY to stand doubled. All documents pertaining to employment programmes shall be available for public scrutiny, and the price of these documents shall be no greater than cost of providing copies. Minimum wages should be paid in the works and use of labour-displacing machinery to be stopped.

  In case of financial difficulty, the states can approach the Centre for permission to pay 100% wages in grain.
- ANTYODAYA: BPL criterion should not be used in selection of Antyodaya beneficiaries. States have been directed to issue AAY cards to all primitive tribes immediately.

Bibliography

Bakshi P M, 2002, *The Constitution of India*, New Delhi: Universal Law Publishing

Bhatia, Bela and Dreze, Jean, 22-28 July 2006, Employment Guarantee in Jharkhand, *Ground Realities*, Vol.41, No.29

Bhattacharya, Dwaipayan, and Rana, Kumar, 2-8 February 2008, Politics of PDS anger in West Bengal, *Economic and Political Weekly*, Vol.43, No.5

Bhowmik, Sharit K, 17-23 September 2005, Tea Plantation Workers' Strike, *Economic and Political Weekly*, Vol.40, No.38

Bhowmik, Sharit K, 28 February-6 March 2009, Politics of Tea in the Dooars, *Economic and Political Weekly*, Vol.44, No.09

Chakraborty, Achin and Mukherjee, Subrata, 2009, *MDG-Based Poverty Reduction Strategy for West Bengal*, Kolkata: Institute of Development Studies, mimeo

Chaudhary, Neetu and Parthasarathy, D, 10-16 February 2007, Gender, Work and Household Food Security, *Economic and Political Weekly*, Vol.42, No.06

Convention on the Elimination of All Forms of Discrimination Against Women

Convention on the Rights of the Child

Drabek, Zdenek and Payne, Warren, *The Impact of Transparency on Foreign Direct Investment*, Staff Working Paper ERAD-99-02, revised November 2001 Geneva: World Trade Organisation, Economic Research and Analysis Division

Dreze, Jean, 24-30 April 2004, Democracy and Right to Food, *Economic and Political Weekly*, Vol.39, No.17

Das, Suranjan and Bandyopadhyay, Premansu Kumar (eds.), 2004, *Food Movement of 1959: Documenting A Turning Point In The History Of West Bengal*, Kolkata: K P Bagchi

Dreze, Jean and Sen, Amartya, 1993, *Hunger and Public Action,* New Delhi: OUP

Foucault, Michel, 1998, *History of Sexuality,* Vol.1, United Kingdom: Penguin

Gaiha, Raghav, 4-10 October 2003, Does Right to Food Matter? *Economic and Political Weekly*, Vol.38, No.40

Gopal, K S, 10-16 January 2009, NREGA Social Audits: Myths and Reality, *Economic and Political Weekly*, Vol.44, No.2

Harris-White, Barbara, 2008, *Rural Commercial Capital: Agrarian Markets in West Bengal,* New Delhi: OUP

International Covenant on Economic, Social and Cultural Rights

Jain, M P, 2004, *Indian Constitutional Law*, Nagpur: Wadhwa and Company

Jha, Raghavendra, Gaiha, Raghav and Shankar, Shyalashri, 15-21 March 2008, Reviewing the National Rural Employment Guarantee Programme, *Economic and Political Weekly*, Vol.43, No.11

Limburg Principles on the Implementation of the International Covenant of Economic and Social Rights, 1986

Maastricht Guidelines on the Violations of Economic, Social and Cultural Rights, 1997

Nandy, Vaskar, 26 November-2 December 2005, Tea Industry Wage Agreement in West Bengal, *Economic and Political Weekly*, Vol.40, No.48

Pattanayak, Utsa, 2004, *The Republic of Hunger*, [Public Lecture on the 50th Birthday of Safdar Hasmi], New Delhi: SAHMAT

Swaminathan, Madhura, 2000, *Weakening Welfare: The Public Distribution of Food in India*, New Delhi: Leftword

Radhakrishna, R, 30 April-6 May 2005, Food and Nutrition Security of the Poor, *Economic and Political Weekly*, Vol.40, No.18

Rana, Kumar, 2006, *Khandita Unnayan: Jhargram Mahakumar Ekti Rekhachitra*, Kolkata: Prashnabachi

Rana, Santosh, 2006, *Gopiballabhpurer Dhankata Abbhutthan Samaj Sreni Rajniti* (collection of essays), Kolkata: CAMP

—— 2007, *Prakrito Daridryo O BPL Talika: Sarkari hisabeyr karchupi*, Kolkata: Prasnabachi

Right to Food-Guide on Legislating for the Right to Food, Right to Food Unit, Food and Agriculture Organisation, 2008

Roy, Rajat, 3-9 May 2008, Endemic Hunger in West Bengal, *Economic and Political Weekly*, Vol.43, No.18

Samaddar, Ranabir, 2007, *The Materiality of Politics: Subject Positions in Politics*, Vol.II, London: Anthem Press

Sen, Amartya and Dreze, Jean, 1999, Chapter 13: Hunger and Public Action, *The Amartya Sen & Jean Dreze Omnibus*, New Delhi: OUP

Tharian George, K and Joby, Joseph, 25 June-1 July 2005, Value Addition or Value Acquisition: Travails of the Plantation Sector in the Era of Globalisation, *Economic and Political Weekly*, Vol.40, No.26

Virmani, Arvind and P V Rajeev, *Excess Food Stocks, PDS and Procurement Policy*, December 2001, Planning Commission Working Paper No.5/2002-PC, May 2002

REPORTS

Census 1961: West Bengal: District Census Handbook – Midnapore Volume I, The Superintendent, Government Printing, West Bengal (1966)

Economic Review 2004-05, Industry, Government of West Bengal

—— *2007-08*, Industry, Government of West Bengal

FAO (1998): *Implementation of the Right to Food in National Legislation*, FAO Legal Office, Mimeo, Food and Agriculture Organisation of the United Nations, Rome

Food Security and Judicial Activism in India, 8 December 2007, Human Rights Law Network, 2007 Report submitted to West Bengal Government by Biraj Pattanayak, Chief Adviser to Supreme Court Commission

Right to Food, Human Rights Law Network, 2008

The Pratichi Child Report, with a foreword by Amartya Sen, Pratichi Trust, Delhi, 2009

The Pratichi Education Report I, with an introduction by Amartya Sen, TLM Books, (in association with the Pratichi Trust), Delhi, 2001

The Pratichi Health Report I, with an Introduction by Amartya Sen, TLM Books (in association with Pratichi Trust), Delhi, 2005

People's Democracy, Vol.XXXI, No.44, 4 November 2007

West Bengal Human Development Report, Department of Planning, Government of West Bengal, Kolkata, 2004

Corruption in Public Distribution System in India, Corruption Study 2005 to Improve Governance, Vol. II (Eleven Public Services): Study designed and conducted by the Centre for Media Studies, Research House, Community Centre, Saket New Delhi 110 017

Guidelines for Programme on State Action against Hunger and Inequity 2007, Department of Panchayats and Rural Development, Government of West Bengal, Kolkata

Report on Conditions of Work and Promotion, National Commission for Enterprises in Unorganised Sector, New Delhi, 2007

NEWS PAPER, POPULAR MAGAZINE ARTICLES/ ARTICLES FROM WEB

Drèze, Jean and Lal, Siddhartha, 3 July 2007, Employment guarantee: unfinished agenda, *The Hindu*

Drèze, Jean and Oldiges, Christian, 14-27 July 2007, Commendable act, *Frontline*, Vol.24, Issue 14

Swaminathan, Madhura, 20 January-2 February 2001, A further attack on the PDS, *Frontline*, Vol.18, Issue 02

The Hindu, 28 July 2009 available online at http://www.hindu.com/2009/07/28/stories/2009072855140900.htm, accessed on 21 July 2009

Murshidabad Starvation Deaths, available online at www.milligazette.com/ . . . /2005/20050902-Murshidabad.htm, accessed on 19 July 2009

Bartaman (A Bengali daily), Kolkata, 4 August 2010, http://epaper.bartamanpatrika.com/, accessed on 5 August 2010
http://wbic.gov.in/html/Decisions_July_Aug_10.htm, accessed on 3 August 2010

The Right to Adequate Food in India – Parallel Report by FIAN (Food First Information and Action Network) (Reference: Second to fifth periodic reports of India UN Doc. E/C.12/IND/5 submitted to the CESCR, 40 session) http://www.fian.org, accessed on 9 July 2010

Asian Human Rights Commission, Introduction, available online at http://www.ahrchk.net/pub/mainfile.php/endangered_humanity/225/?print=yes, accessed on 10 July 2009

The Indian Express, 8 July 82004; Poverty, "Starvation Exist in Bengal: Buddha" available at http://www.expressindia.com/news/fullstory.php?newsid=33590, accessed on 20 September 2008

Rioters Against Ration Dealers, available online at http://www.indiatogether.org/2007/oct/gov-wbpds.htm, accessed on 22 December 2009

PDS To Be Further Strengthened In Bengal: Biman Basu, available at http://pd.cpim.org/2007/1104/11042007_biman%20intrvw.htm, accessed on 22 December 2009

The Hindu, 18 January 2003

Demographic Details of the Nayagram Block, West Midnapore, Source: http://paschimmedinipur.gov.in/profiles/nayagram.html, accessed on 11 September 2009

Fourth Report of the Commissioners, August 2003; http://www.sccommissioners.org/pdfs/comreports/4threport.pdf, accessed on 1 March 2009

Fifth Report of the Commissioners, August 2005; http://www.sccommissioners.org/pdfs/comreports/5threport.pdf, accessed on 1 March 2009

Sixth Report of the Commissioners, October 2005; http://www.sccommissioners.org/pdfs/comreports/6threport.pdf, accessed on 1 March 2009

Scaria, Sunil, "Labour Rights: Tea Garden workers – Abandoned to Death", http://www.combatlaw.org/information.php?article_id=414&issue_id=16s, accessed on 27 February 2009

Supreme Court Orders on the Right to Food: A Tool for Action, August 2008 http://www.righttofoodindia.org/data/scordersprimeratoolforaction.pdf, accessed on 15 March 2009

http://timesofindia.indiatimes.com/India/After_Singur_Mamata_reaches_out_to_tea_garden_workers/rssarticleshow/2129915.cms, accessed on 17 January 2009

http://www.telegraphindia.com/1090204/jsp/siliguri/story_10479162.jsp, accessed on 5 May 2009

http://www.indopia.in/India-usa-uk-news/latest-news/23116/National/1/20/1, accessed on 17 January 2009

http://planningcommission.nic.in/eg_poverty.htm

http://nceus.gov.in/Condition_of_workers_sep_2007.pdf – accessed on 26 July 2010

Frontline, Vol.27, No.17, 14-17 August 2010

http://janpathnetwork.org/annual_report_01.pdf

Best Practices' www.nrega.nic.in

http://www.indianexpress.com/news/a-website-to-log-the-rti-success-stories-of-purulia-villagers/563923/0, accessed on 3 August 2010

http://uidai.gov.in/documents/UIDandPDS.pdf

http://mizoramexpress.com/index.php/2010/04/citizens-against-uid, accessed on 21 July 2010